Practical Tests for the FCC General Radiotelephone Operator's License Exam

Practical Tests for the FCC General Radiotelephone Operator's License Exam

Victor F. C. Veley

TAB Books
Division of McGraw-Hill, Inc.
Blue Ridge Summit, PA 17294-0850

FIRST EDITION
FIRST PRINTING

Library of Congress Cataloging-in-Publication Data

Veley, Victor F. C.
Practice tests for the FCC general radiotelephone operator's license examination / by Victor F.C. Veley.
p. cm.
ISBN 0-8306-2579-8 ISBN 0-8306-2578-X (pbk.)
1. Radiotelephone—United States—Study guides. 2. Radio operators—licenses—United States. I. Title.
TK6554.5.V436 1993
621.3845'076—dc20 92-30651
CIP

Acquisitions Editor: Roland S. Phelps
Editor: Andrew Yoder
Executive Editor: Bob Ostrander
Designer: Jaclyn J. Boone
Associate Designer: Brian K. Allison EL1
Paperbound Cover Design and Illustration: Graphics Plus, Hanover, Pa. 4054

To my beautiful wife, Joyce, who has been my inspiration and strength for over 40 years, and to those I hold dear: Jackie, Gill, Phil, Ray, James, Nicola, Lisa, Kate, Peter, Paul, and Paula. Also in memory of Charles H. and Margaret A. Veley.

Contents

Introduction

Communications technicians and students have always recognized the need for a practical workbook that will help them to obtain their FCC Commercial General Radiotelephone Operator's License (GROL). The holder of this license is entitled to operate, maintain, and repair communications equipment in the Marine, Aviation, and International Fixed Services. The possession of this license is also regarded as an entry-level qualification for the electronic communications industry and as an asset for subsequent promotion.

To obtain your GROL, you must pass the FCC Element 3 examination, which contains 100 multiple-choice questions (each with five choices). Generally speaking, about 20 of these questions are related to the FCC Rules and Regulations, and the remainder require a knowledge of electronics and communications. The passing score is 75 or more correct and the grade is not recorded on your license. For a practice workbook to be effective, it must contain sample questions that are similar to those that have appeared in recent FCC examinations. This book fulfills this requirement by including nine Element 3 tests for a total of 900 questions; these reflect the extensive Element 3 revisions that occurred in 1986 and also as recently as August 1990.

For each question there is an answer that is found at the back of the book; when required, a complete solution is provided for all questions that involve mathematical equations. As some technicians and students progress through the tests, they might experience little difficulty in answering the questions. However, others might find that they need considerable help. For this reason, each question has a page reference and each answer a section or chapter reference to an accompanying text entitled *Basic Electronic Communications for the FCC General Radiotelephone Operator's License Exam*, #4055, also written by Victor F. C. Veley and published by TAB Books. This extensive text contains more than 950 FCC-type questions and answers.

In order to install, service, and maintain certain marine radar equipment, you must obtain a Ship Radar Endorsement to your General Radiotelephone License. To acquire this endorsement, you need to pass the FCC Element 8 examination, which contains 50 multiple-choice questions with a passing score of 38 or more correct. This workbook contains two sample Element 8 tests for a total of 100 questions.

Before attempting any of the tests you should read the introductory material on "How to Apply for the Commercial General Radio Operator's License," and "How to Pass the FCC Exam(s)."

Finally, I acknowledge a considerable debt to my wife, Joyce, for typing the manuscript. Without her help and support, this workbook would not have been possible.

How to Apply for the Commercial General Radio Operator's License

Prior to 1993, an applicant was required to complete FCC form 756 and pay a fee of $35.00 for taking the General Radiotelephone Examination. The application and payment were then forwarded to an FCC location in Pittsburgh. Subsequently, the applicant received an appointment letter indicating where and when he/she should appear for the examination to be administered. The examinations were held during the first full weeks of February and August.

In January 1993, the FCC decided to privatize the administration of all exams for the various commercial radio operator licenses; this decision was based on budgetary constraints. The February examination was cancelled, but in April and May the applicants were allowed to take the examination by using a one-time interim procedure. This involved the completion of the examination in the presence of a qualified licensee.

For years there have been a number of private organizations that have conducted their own examinations for the certification of technicians and engineers in the field of electronics and communications. At the time of publishing this book, the FCC is in the process of selecting those organizations who will set up a network of testing centers throughout the USA. Each of the centers will be controlled by an examination manager, who will be responsible for administering the various FCC examinations. This network is expected to be in operation by June/July 1993, and the first examinations should be given in August/September. It is anticipated that the content of the FCC exams will not be changed in the immediate future and that the exams themselves might be held more frequently than twice a year.

To apply to take the General Radiotelephone examination, you should:

1. Contact your local FCC office (a list of these offices with their addresses and telephone numbers begins on page xv). Ask for the name, address, and telephone number of the private organization who is conducting the examinations in your area.
2. Call the private organization and request an application form with its instructions. Make a note of the name of the person that you contact. Enquire when the next examination is to be held and ask about any deadline date for filing the application.

3. Complete and return the application form together with the payment of the required fee. As a precaution, you should use certified mail.

If you do not receive an acknowledgment from the private organization, determine whether your fee payment has been processed and then call the person that you originally contacted.

One last point. The FCC has normally allowed an applicant to take the General Radiotelephone Exam (Element 3) and the Ship Radar Endorsement (Element 8) on the same day without the payment of an additional fee. However, the candidate must first pass the Element 3 exam before being allowed to take Element 8. Remember that the Element 3 exam contains 100 multiple-choice questions with a passing score of 75 or more correct. By contrast, the Element 8 exam only has 50 questions with a passing score of 38 or more correct.

How to pass the FCC examination(s)

On the day before your appointment, avoid any last-minute cramming and go to bed early so that you can have a full night's sleep. Leave yourself plenty of time to get to the testing center so as to minimize any stress caused by traffic problems. Make sure that your nonprogrammable scientific calculator is in good shape and wear comfortable clothes because the examination will probably last more than three hours. This also means that you should visit the restroom before presenting yourself for the examination. Smoking is not allowed during the exam, so you might like to consider chewing gum as an alternative.

Before being allowed to take the examination, you are required to identify yourself so that you will need your driver's license or a similar document that shows your photograph. You are not allowed to bring any textbooks or notes into the examination room; however, some scratch paper will be provided. You will need some #2 pencils for the mark-sign answer sheet as well as a ballpoint pen (black ink) to fill out forms related to personal and background information.

When you have received your examination paper and have been told to start, do *not* begin with Question #1 and struggle through to Question #100. Read through the entire exam and answer all easy questions (primarily those concerning FCC rules and regulations, circuit recognition, units, and so on). Probably about 30 to 40 questions should fall into this category and successful answers to these questions will certainly boost your morale.

Repeat the process and gradually fill in the gaps. Unless you are quite certain of the solutions, it is probably wise to leave all math problems until the end. Here is one point to remember. A particular solution might require the transposition of a basic formula. If you find difficulty with the transposition, you can substitute each one of the choices in the basic formula and see which one works—one advantage of taking a multiple-choice exam.

After completing the exam, you must review the entire answer sheet and make certain that:

1. the answer to each question corresponds to the choice you have selected. For example, you might have marked choice A on the answer sheet, but you intended choice B. Choice A must therefore be erased and choice B must be marked instead.

2. no answer has been accidently marked with two or more choices. Such an answer will automatically be graded as incorrect.
3. every question has been answered; there is no penalty for an incorrect choice. It follows that a blind guess is better than nothing because you have a 20% chance of being right. However, there are two ways to find the correct answer to a multiple-choice question. Either you know the answer straight off or you can find the right answer by eliminating all of the false choices (decoys). Moreover, if you are only able to eliminate three decoys, there are only two choices left, so you have raised your odds of finding the right choice from 20% to 50%.

Finally, the moment of truth! You present your paper to the examiner who will use a grading mask to obtain your score. He/she then informs you of the result (pass or fail) and will probably indicate your actual score. Remember that the pass mark is only 75% and your grade is not recorded on your license.

If you are successful, you will be immediately issued with a temporary authorization permit; your permanent license (valid for life) will then be forwarded to you within three months.

It only remains to wish you good luck in the examination and a successful career in the field of electronic communications.

FCC Office Addresses

ALASKA, Anchorage Office
Federal Communications Commission
6721 West Raspberry Road
Anchorage, Alaska 99502
Phone: (907) 243–2153

*ARIZONA, Douglas Office
Federal Communications Commission
P.O. Box 6
Douglas, Arizona 85608
Phone: (602) 364–8414

CALIFORNIA, San Diego Office
Federal Communications Commission
4542 Ruffner Street
Room 370
San Diego, California 92111-2216
Phone: (619) 557–5478

*CALIFORNIA, Livermore Office
Federal Communications Commission
P.O. Box 311
Livermore, California 94551-0311
Phone: (415) 447–3614

CALIFORNIA, Los Angeles Office
Federal Communications Commission
Cerritos Corporate Tower
18000 Studebaker Road, Room 660
Cerritos, California 90701
Phone: (213) 809-2096

CALIFORNIA, San Francisco Office
Federal Communications Commission
424 Customhouse
555 Battery Street
San Francisco, California 94111
Phone: (415) 705–1101

COLORADO, Denver Office
Federal Communications Commission
165 South Union Blvd., Suite 860
Lakewood, Colorado 80228
Phone: (303) 969–6497

*FLORIDA, Vero Beach Office
Federal Communications Commission
P.O. Box 1730
Vero Beach, Florida 32961-1730
Phone: (407) 778–3755

FLORIDA, Miami Office
Federal Communications Commission
Rochester Building, Room 310
8390 N.W. 53rd Street
Miami, Florida 33166
Phone: (305) 526-7420

FLORIDA, Tampa Office
Federal Communications Commission
Room 1215
2203 N. Lois Avenue
Tampa, Florida 33607-2356
Phone: (813) 228-2872

GEORGIA, Atlanta Office
Federal Communications Commission
Massell Building, Room 440
1365 Peachtree Street, N.E.
Atlanta, Georgia 30309
Phone: (404) 347-2631

*GEORGIA, Powder Springs Office
Federal Communications Commission
P.O. Box 85
Powder Springs, Georgia 30073
Phone: (404) 943-5420

HAWAII, Honolulu Office
Federal Communications Commission
P.O. Box 1030
Waipahu, Hawaii 96797
Phone: (808) 677-3318

ILLINOIS, Chicago Office
Federal Communications Commission
Park Ridge Office Center, Rm. 306
1550 Northwest Highway
Park Ridge, Illinois 60068
Phone: (312) 353-0195

LOUISIANA, New Orleans Office
Federal Communications Commission
800 West Commerce Rd., Room 505
New Orleans, Louisiana 70123
Phone: (504) 589-2095

*MAINE, Belfast Office
Federal Communications Commission
P.O. Box 470
Belfast, Maine 04915
Phone: (207) 338-4088

MARYLAND, Baltimore Office
Federal Communications Commission
1017 Federal Building
31 Hopkins Plaza
Baltimore, Maryland 21201
Phone: (301) 962-2729

*MARYLAND, Laurel Office
Federal Communications Commission
P.O. Box 250
Columbia, Maryland 21045
Phone: (301) 725-3474

MASSACHUSETTS, Boston Office
Federal Communications Commission
NFPA Building
1 Batterymarch Park
Quincy, Massachusetts 02169
Phone: (617) 770-4023

*MICHIGAN, Allegan Office
Federal Communications Commission
P.O. Box 89
Allegan, Michigan 49010
Phone: (616) 673-2063

MICHIGAN, Detroit Office
Federal Communications Commission
24897 Hathaway Street
Farmington Hills, Michigan 48335-1552
Phone: (313) 226-6078

MINNESOTA, St. Paul Office
Federal Communications Commission
693 Federal Building & U.S. Courthouse
316 North Robert Street
St. Paul, Minnesota 55101
Phone: (612) 290-3819

MISSOURI, Kansas City Office
Federal Communications Commission
Brywood Office Tower, Room 320
8800 East 63rd Street
Kansas City, Missouri 64133
Phone: (816) 926-5111

*NEBRASKA, Grand Island Office
Federal Communications Commission
P.O. Box 1588
Grand Island, Nebraska 68802
Phone: (308) 382-4296

NEW YORK, Buffalo Office
Federal Communications Commission
1307 Federal Building
111 W. Huron Street
Buffalo, New York 14202
Phone: (716) 846-4511

NEW YORK, New York Office
Federal Communications Commission
201 Varick Street
New York, New York 10014-4870
Phone: (212) 620-3437

OREGON, Portland Office
Federal Communications Commission
1782 Federal Office Building
1220 S.W. 3rd Avenue
Portland, Oregon 97204
Phone: (503) 326-4114

PENNSYLVANIA, Philadelphia Office
Federal Communications Commission
One Oxford Valley Office Building
2300 East Lincoln Highway
Room 404
Langhorne, Pennsylvania 19047
Phone: (215) 752-1324

PUERTO RICO, San Juan Office
Federal Communications Commission
747 Federal Building
Hato Rey, Puerto Rico 00918-2251
Phone: (809) 766-5567

TEXAS, Dallas Office
Federal Communications Commission
9330 LBJ Expressway, Room 1170
Dallas, Texas 75243
Phone: (214) 767-4827

TEXAS, Houston Office
Federal Communications Commission
1225 North Loop West, Room 900
Houston, Texas 77008
Phone: (713) 229-2748

*TEXAS, Kingsville Office
Federal Communications Commission
P.O. Box 632
Kingsville, Texas 78363-0632
Phone: (512) 592-2531

VIRGINIA, Norfolk Office
Federal Communications Commission
1200 Communications Circle
Virginia Beach, Virginia 23455-3725
Phone: (804) 441-6472

*WASHINGTON, Ferndale Office
Federal Communications Commission
1330 Loomis Trail Rd.
Custer, Washington 98240
Phone: (206) 354-4892

WASHINGTON, Seattle Office
Federal Communications Commission
One Newport, Room 414
3605 132nd Avenue, S.E.
Bellevue, Washington 98006
Phone: (206) 764-3324

*Licenses not available at these locations.

Part 1

General Radiotelephone License Practice Tests

General Radiotelephone License Practice FCC Tests Element 3 Test 1

Q1-001 The action of a JFET can be compared with that of a:

A. diode
B. triode
C. tetrode
D. pentode
E. hexode

Page(s) 253 to 256

Q1-002 The IF stages of an FM receiver have been aligned. The next stage to align is the:

A. RF amplifier
B. limiter stage
C. local oscillator
D. mixer stage
E. antenna coupling circuit

Page(s) 389, 390

Q1-003 Who of the following submits an application for the inspection of a compulsory ship station?

A. vessel owner
B. vessel's operating agency
C. ship station's licensee
D. Master of the vessel
E. any of the above choices may submit the application

Page(s) 549

Q1-004 In FIG. 1-1, what is the highest voltage that can be applied across the series combination without exceeding the power rating of either resistor?

A. 316 V
B. 31.6 V
C. 424 V
D. 379 V
E. 63 V

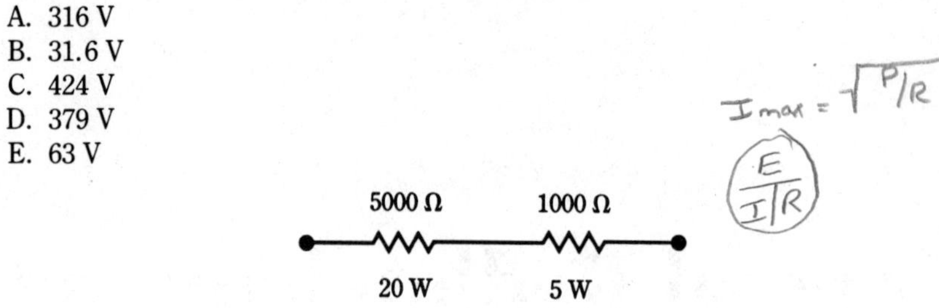

1-1 Circuit for Questions 1-004 and 1-005.

Page(s) 29, 30

Q1-005 In QUE. 1-004, what is the voltage drop across the 5000-Ω resistor when the maximum voltage is applied across the combination?

A. 316 V
B. 31.6 V
C. 424 V
D. 379 V
E. 63 V

Page(s) 30

Q1-006 Which electrode of a indirectly heated triode tube can be compared with the emitter region of a bipolar transistor?

A. heater
B. screen grid
C. control grid
D. plate
E. cathode

Page(s) 225, 226

Q1-007 A transmission line introduces a loss of 7 dB and is used to feed an antenna array whose power gain is 3 dB. If the input RF power to the transmission line is 1000 W, the effective radiated power is:

A. 800 W
B. 2000 W
C. 200 W
D. 300 W
E. 400 W

Page(s) 419

Q1-008 In the circuit of FIG. 1–2, calculate the value of the voltage at point F, with respect to ground:

A. +5.35 V
B. +2.5 V
C. +6.5 V
D. −5.35 V
E. −7.9 V

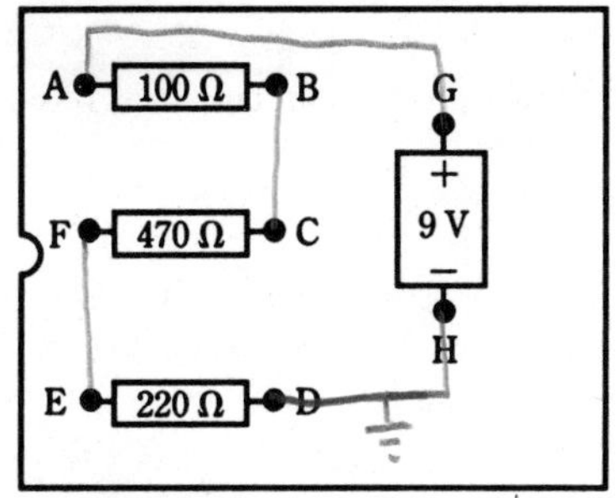

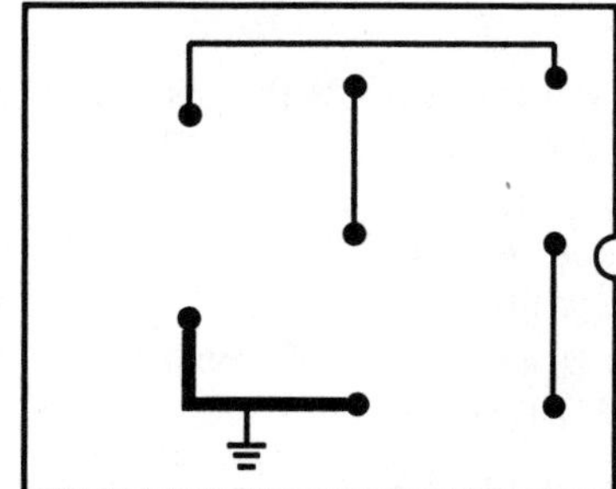

1-2 Circuit for Question 1-008.

Page(s) 623, 624

Q1-009 The sensitivity of an AM receiver can be expressed in terms of:

A. 10 microvolts for a standard audio power level of 50 mW with a minimum signal-to-noise ratio of 20 dB
B. 60 decibels of attenuation at a frequency of 20 kHz above the incoming signal
C. 8 microvolts for an audio power level of 20 dBm
D. the ratio expressed in decibels of the audio output power to the RF input power
E. the overall receiver's voltage gain, expressed in decibels

Page(s) 358, 359

Q1-010 In a direct FM transmitter, a 5-MHz oscillator is modulated by a 300-Hz test tone, which produces a swing of ±1 kHz. If the intermediate amplifiers contains two triplers and a doubler stage, what is the value of the frequency deviation at the output stage?

A. 1 kHz
B. 3 kHz
C. 6 kHz
D. 9 kHz
E. 18 kHz

Page(s) 367

Q1-011 A transmitter is assigned a carrier frequency of 156.8 MHz. If the operating frequency deviates from the assigned frequency by 1 ppm, the amount of the frequency deviation is:

A. 1.568 kHz
B. 15.68 kHz
C. 15.68 Hz
D. 156.8 Hz
E. 1.568 Hz

Page(s) 297

Q1-012 What is the authorized bandwidth of a marine R3E emission?

A. 4 kHz
B. 3 kHz
C. 6 kHz
D. 8 kHz
E. 2.8 kHz

Page(s) 334

Q1-013 A 1-mW signal is the input to an amplifier that provides an output of 100 mW. The amplifier's gain is:

A. +10 dB
B. −10 dB
C. +20 dB
D. −20 dB
E. +100 dB

Page(s) 145 to 147

Q1-014 A marine radiotelephone station has been called three times at intervals of two minutes, but there is no reply. The calling must not be renewed until after:

A. 3 minutes
B. 5 minutes
C. 10 minutes
D. 15 minutes
E. 30 minutes

Page(s) 557

Q1-015 The input power to a loss-free coaxial cable is 5 W. If the reflected power is 7 dB down on the incident power, the output power to the load is:

A. 4 W
B. 1 W
C. 5 W
D. 3 W
E. 2 W

Page(s) 408

Q1-016 The term *residual magnetism* refers to:

A. the flux density, which exists in the iron core when the magnetic field intensity is at its maximum value
B. the flux density, which exists in the iron core when the magnetic field intensity is reduced to zero
C. the external magnetic field when the current is flowing through the exciting coil
C. the flux density, which exists in a nonmagnetic core when the magnetic field intensity is at its maximum value
E. the flux density when the magnetic core is saturated

Page(s) 59

Q1-017 The oscillator of an FM transmitter is operating on a frequency of 8 MHz. If there are two doubler stages and one tripler stage between the oscillator and the RF final stage, the frequency of the transmitter's output carrier is:

A. 32 MHz

B. 48 MHz
C. 16 MHz
D. 96 MHz
E. 64 MHz

2×2×3×8 mHz

Page(s) 367

Q1-018 A continuous watch on Channel 13 must be maintained:

A. by the Master of the vessel
B. by the person in charge of navigation
C. when the vessel is within 100 miles of U.S. shores
D. by the vessel's radio operator
E. Choices A, B, and C are true

Page(s) 555

Q1-019 Which of the following stages has high voltage and current gains, high input and output impedances, as well as input and output signals that are 180° out of phase?

A. common emitter amplifier
B. common collector stage
C. common base amplifier
D. emitter follower
E. none of the above choices is true

Page(s) 239, 240

Q1-020 The IF amplifier of a communications receiver is operated under the conditions of:

A. class A
B. class AB
C. class B
D. class C
E. class D

Page(s) 350

Q1-021 An FM receiver whose intermediate frequency is 10.7 MHz, is experiencing image channel interference from a station transmitting on 121.1 MHz. If the local oscillator is tracking above, the receiver is tuned to:

A. 131.8 MHz
B. 142.5 MHz
C. 110.4 MHz
D. 21.4 MHz
E. 99.7 MHz

121.1 − (2×10.7) =

Page(s) 382, 383

Q1-022 An isolator is a:

A. ferrite device which operates on the principle of the Faraday rotation
B. four-port circulator with one port blocked
C. device which operates on the principle of ferro-magnetic resonance
D. duplexer which connects two transmitters to a single antenna
E. diplexer which connects a transmitter and a receiver to a single antenna

Page(s) 470

Q1-023 The true power in an ac circuit is determined by:

A. multiplying the effective value of the source voltage by the effective value of the source current
B. multiplying the square of the effective source current by the value of the impedance
C. multiplying the square of the effective source current by the resistance
D. dividing the square of the effective source voltage by the impedance
E. multiplying the square of the effective source current by the reactance

Page(s) 124

Q1-024 When transmitted by radiotelephony, the distress signal is indicated by the word:

A. SOS
B. mayday
C. distress
D. security
E. pan

Page(s) 568

Q1-025 The frequency tolerance of a marine transmitter operating within the band of 216–220 MHz, is:

A. ± 10 ppm
B. ± 10 Hz
C. ± 20 Hz
D. ± 20 ppm
E. ± 5 ppm

Page(s) 335

Q1-026 The frequency bandwidth where, below its lower and above its upper frequency limits, the mean power radiated is equal to 0.5% of the total mean power radiated by a given emission, is called the:

A. bandwidth of emission
B. occupied bandwidth
C. authorized bandwidth
D. operating bandwidth
E. choices A and B are true

Page(s) 553, 554

Q1-027 During the desoldering of a microchip, the necessary heat shunt should be clipped:

A. to the pin of the microchip
B. to the underside of the printed circuit board on which the microchip is mounted
C. to the tip of the soldering iron
D. between the tip of the soldering iron and the terminal of the microchip
E. to all the pins on one side of the microchip

Page(s) 102

Q1-028 Five cycles of a sine wave occur in a time interval of 1/50 s. The frequency of the sine wave is:

A. 50 Hz
B. 500 Hz
C. 125 Hz
D. 250 Hz
E. 1000 Hz

Page(s) 105

Q1-029 The signal generator of the auto alarm signal produces:

A. a continuous 1000-Hz tone
B. a continuous 2182-Hz tone
C. two audio tones of frequencies 2300 Hz and 1200 Hz, transmitted alternately
D. two audio tones, each with a duration of 250 ms, with the combination transmitted continuously for at least 20 seconds, but not more than one minute
E. choices C and D are true

Page(s) 551

Q1-030 An FM signal is 60% modulated by a single 200 Hz test tone and the resultant frequency deviation is 3 kHz. If the frequency of the test tone is increased to 300 Hz, what is the new value of the frequency deviation (neglecting any effect of pre-emphasis)?:

A. 3 kHz
B. 5 kHz
C. 4.5 kHz
D. 3.3 kHz
E. 3.1 kHz

Page(s) 362

Q1-031 A varistor can be used:

A. as a voltage regulating device
B. to keep a load voltage practically constant as the load current varies
C. to keep a load voltage practically constant as the unregulated supply voltage fluctuates
D. protect semiconductor components from voltage surges.
E. all of the above choices are true

Page(s) 218

Q1-032 One of the main advantages of a push-pull audio amplifier over a stage used a single stage transistor, is the elimination:

A. of odd and even harmonic distortion
B. of odd harmonic distortion only
C. of even harmonic distortion only
D. of the fundamental component and even harmonic distortion
E. of the fundamental component and odd harmonic distortion

Page(s) 247, 248

Q1-033 The RF power input to a transmission line is 100 W. If the length of the transmission line is 200 feet and its attenuation is 6 dB/100 ft, calculate the line's output power:

A. 6.25 W
B. 25 W

C. 3.125 W
D. 12.5 W
E. 50 W

Page(s) 400 to 403

Q1-034 A compulsory ship is assigned working frequencies in the 1605 to 3500 kHz band and is also equipped with VHF communications equipment. On which of the following frequencies shall a continuous watch be maintained?

A. 2128 kHz
B. 2182 MHz
C. 156.65 MHz
D. 156.8 MHz
E. 121.5 MHz

Page(s) 583, 584

Q1-035 Neutralization of an RF amplifier stage can be necessary in order to:

A. increase the amplifier's gain
B. reduce the amplifier's gain
C. prevent the generation of spurious oscillation
D. reduce the level of the output harmonics
E. prevent the generation of parasitic oscillations

Page(s) 300, 301

Q1-036 For which of the following services does a operator require a General Radiotelephone Operator's License?

A. police two-way radio
B. ambulance two-way radio
C. railroad two-way radio
D. citizen's band radio
E. none of the above choices are true

Page(s) 580, 581

Q1-037 In the circuit of FIG. 1-3, the true power can be calculated from:

A. *(reading of V) × (reading of A) × power factor*
B. *(reading of V) × (reading of A)*

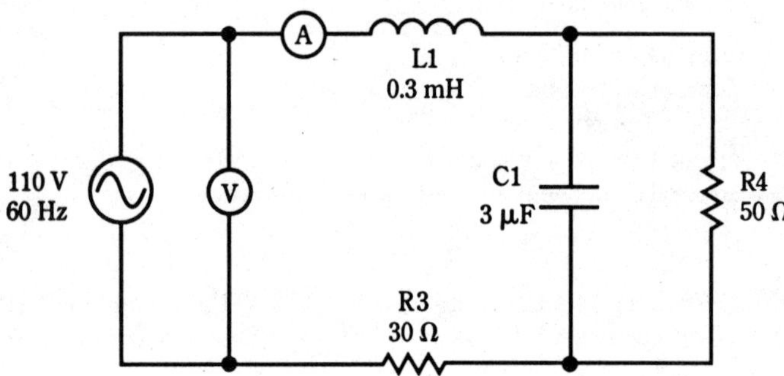

1-3 Circuit for Question 1-037.

C. (*reading of A*)^2 × (R_3 + R_4)
D. (*reading of V*)^2 ÷ (R_3 + R_4)
E. (*reading of A*)^2 × R_3

Page(s) 143

Q1-038 A charged capacitor is connected across a resistor. The time constant of this circuit is:

A. the half-life of the capacitor when shunted by the resistor
B. equal to the natural period of the circuit's oscillation
C. equal to the value of the capacitance divided by the resistance
D. the time required for the capacitor to discharge to a certain percentage of its initial voltage
E. the time required for the capacitor to discharge completely

Page(s) 80

Q1-039 A marine transmitter is operating on a frequency of 2182 kHz with J3E emission. The frequency tolerance of this transmitter is:

A. 20 ppm
B. 20 Hz
C. 30 Hz
D. 30 ppm
E. 50 Hz

Page(s) 579

Q1-040 Convert the octal number, 673_8, into its equivalent binary number

A. 101111101_2
B. 110101011_2
C. 110111011_2
D. 110110101_2
E. 110111111_2

Page(s) 520, 521

Q1-041 Which of the following classes has the highest efficiency?:

A. A
B. AB_1
C. B
D. C
E. AB_2

Page(s) 249, 250

Q1-042 Without the coordination of the U.S. Coast Guard, the Class-B Emergency Position Indicating Radio Beacon (E.P.I.R.B) may be tested:

A. in complete radio silence
B. with G3E emission
C. on the frequency of 156.8 MHz
D. with an output power of less than 1 mW
E. during the first five minutes of each hour for a period not to exceed one second or three audio sweeps

Page(s) 573, 574

Q1-043 A driven array of stacked antennas is connected to a transmitter. The reason for this array is to:

A. provide a decrease in the antenna's power gain
B. provide a more unidirectional radiation pattern in the forward direction
C. increase the amount of radiation in the backward direction
D. raise the resonant frequency of the antenna system
E. reduce the antenna's bandwidth

Page(s) 422 to 424

Q1-044 The battery of the Emergency Position Indicating Radio Beacon (E.P.I.R.B) must be changed:

A. when 60% of its useful life remains
B. after its use in an emergency situation
C. before the expiration date established by the manufacturer
D. after its tenth test has been carried out
E. choices B and C are true

Page(s) 573

Q1-045 At high frequencies in the UHF band the value of a fixed composition resistor appears to:

A. be a short circuit
B. be an open circuit
C. decrease in value
D. increase in value
E. possess a high value of inductance

Page(s) 164

Q1-046 Which of the following emission designators has the greatest necessary bandwidth?

A. 160HJ3N
B. 280HJ2B
C. 300HF1B
D. 160HA1A
E. 1K40H2B

Page(s) 334

Q1-047 The circuitry of a marine transmitter is modified so that its operating power is changed. The correct procedure is to:

A. immediately inform the regional office of the FCC
B. measure the new value of the operating power and enter the result in the station log
C. apply for a new callsign
D. submit a station modification request on FCC Form 506
E. there is no correct procedure because the operating frequency must never be changed

Page(s) 549

Q1-048 Which of the following logic gates corresponds to the truth table of FIG. 1-4?

P	*Q*	*R*
False	False	False
False	True	True
True	False	True
True	True	True

1-4 Truth table for Question 1-048.

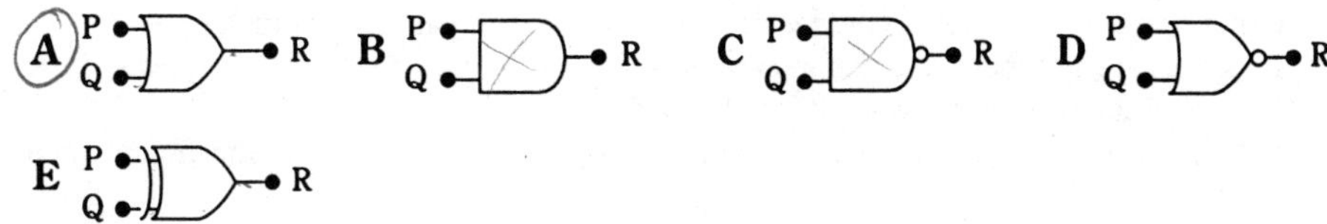

Page(s) 527 to 529

Q1-049 Which of the following frequencies is used for the distress carrier in the 100- to 137-MHz band?

A. 121.5 MHz
B. 124.5 MHz
C. 111.5 MHz
D. 123.5 MHz
E. 112.5 MHz

Page(s) 570

Q1-050 In the amplifier circuit of FIG. 1-5:

A. the batteries must be reversed
B. the emitter-base battery voltage is too high
C. the collector-base battery voltage is too high
D. there is no voltage gain from emitter to collector
E. the output signal is in phase with the input signal

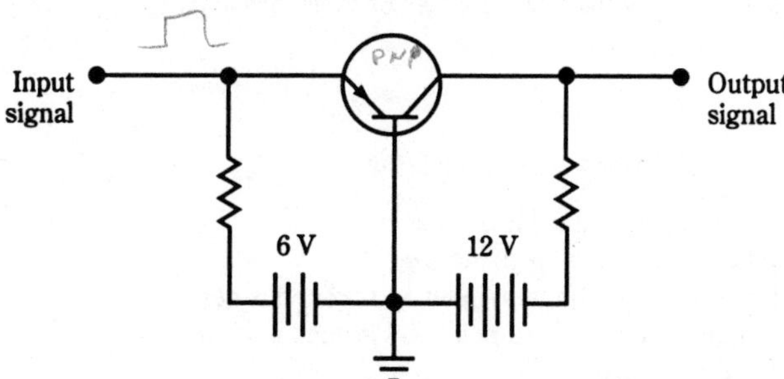

1-5 Circuit for Questions 1-050 and 1-051.

Page(s) 236 to 238

Q1-051 In the amplifier circuit of FIG. 1-5, a positive pulse is applied to the input terminal. As a result:

A. the transistor is destroyed
B. there is virtually no effect on the collector current
C. the emitter current decreases
D. the base current decreases
E. the collector current increases

Page(s) 236 to 238

Q1-052 In order to prevent interference in the marine mobile service, a radio operator must:

A. not transmit a general call or signals not addressed to a particular station
B. not engage in superfluous communications
C. turn off the transmitter when it is not in use
D. before initiating a transmission, make sure that another station is not transmitting on the same frequency
E. all of the above choices are true

Page(s) 592, 609

Q1-053 At an ac source, the readings are: voltmeter 220 V, milliammeter 300 mA, power factor 0.6, leading. The true power is:

A. 66 W
B. 60 W
C. 39.6 W
D. 25.5 W
E. 45.4 W

Page(s) 189

Q1-054 Which of the following vessels are required to install compulsory radiotelephone communications equipment?

A. cargo ships of 300 gross tons and upward but less than 1600 tons on international voyages
B. all passenger ships of 100 gross tons and upwards
C. all voluntary ships
D. small passenger boats that transport six or more passengers
E. choices A and D are true

Page(s) 562

Q1-055 When a vertical antenna is shunt-fed, the:

A. the impedance at the feed point is capacitive
B. impedance at the feed-point is inductive
C. RF impedance between the feed-point and ground is zero
D. dc resistance between the feed-point and ground is zero
E. Choices B and D are true

Page(s) 429, 430

Q1-056 Who of the following is eligible to apply for a General Radiotelephone License?

A. a United States citizen who cannot speak English
B. an alien who is eligible for employment in the United States
C. a mute person
D. a deaf person
E. a nonresident alien who is under age

Page(s) 571

Q1-057 Neutralization is not required in:

A. audio amplifiers
B. frequency multiplier stages
C. CB amplifiers when the base is grounded
D. push-push stages
E. all of the above choices are true

Page(s) 300, 301

Q1-058 During the testing period for a marine radiotelephone station, the operator must first listen to make sure that the channel is not being used. Then, the operator's voice announcement consists of:

A. the official callsign (normally given three times) followed by the word "test"
B. the word "test" (normally given three times) followed by the name of the vessel
C. the official callsign (normally given three times) followed by the test signal whose duration is not to exceed 10 minutes
D. the name of the vessel (normally given three times) followed by the word "test"
E. the official callsign (normally given three times) followed by the reasons for carrying out the test

Page(s) 610

Q1-059 The conductance of the circuit in FIG. 1-6 is:

A. 30 Ω
B. 0.05 S
C. 0.1 S
D. 0.033 S
E. 20 S

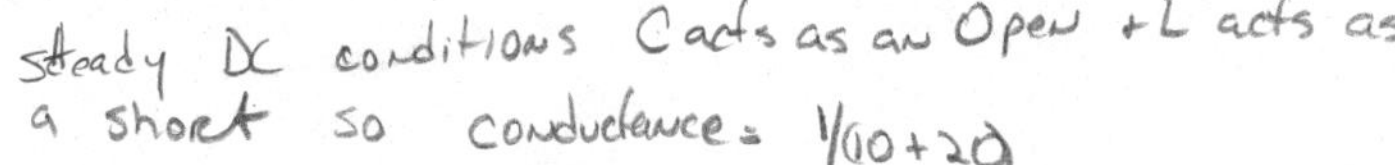

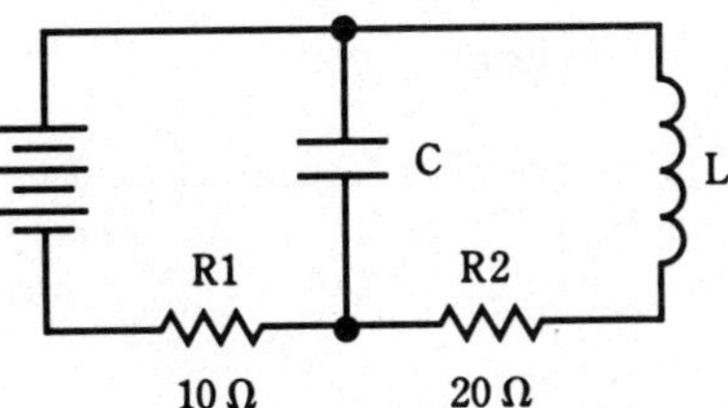

1-6 Circuit for Question 1-059.

Page(s) 81

Q1-060 A compulsory ship is assigned working frequencies of 2550 kHz and 7350 kHz. On which frequency must an efficient listening watch be maintained?

A. 2550 kHz
B. 3750 kHz
C. 2530 kHz
D. 7370 kHz
E. 2182 kHz

Page(s) 583

Q1-061 Which of the following logic gates corresponds to the waveforms of FIG. 1-7?

A. OR gate
B. AND gate
C. NAND gate
D. NOR gate
E. EX-NOR gate

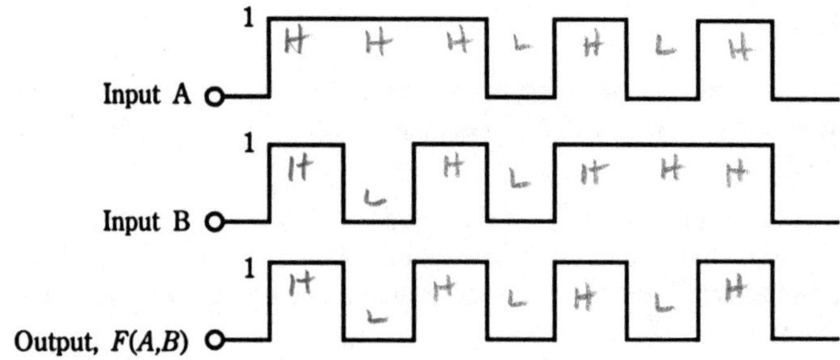

1-7 Waveforms for Question 1-061.

Page(s) 529 to 531

Q1-062 The color-coding of a resistor is Brown, Black, Black, Gold. What is the value of its upper resistance limit?

A. 150 Ω
B. 15 Ω
C. 10.5 Ω
D. 105 Ω
E. 1.5 Ω

Page(s) 23, 24

Q1-063 The output audio stage of a receiver requires a load of 4000 Ω, which must be matched to the loudspeaker impedance of 10 Ω. The required turns ratio of the audio transformer is:

A. 400:1
B. 20:1
C. 1:25
D. 25:1
E. 40:1

Page(s) 168

Q1-064 For a ship station using G3D or G3E emission in the 216–220 MHz band, the frequency deviation corresponding to 100% modulation is:

A. 5 kHz
B. 10 kHz
C. 20 kHz
D. 25 kHz
E. 75 kHz

Page(s) 577

Q1-065 When no signal is being received, the loudspeaker is not entirely silent as a result of the presence of:

A. parasitic oscillations in some of the receiver stages
B. interference from the video signals of TV transmitters
C. negative feedback in each stage
D. spurious frequencies as a result of improper neutralization
E. internal receiver noise

Page(s) 342

Q1-066 In the circuit of FIG. 1-8, determine the value of the output voltage, V_o

A. 4.5 V
B. 3.8 V
C. 3.1 V
D. 5 V
E. 3.5 V

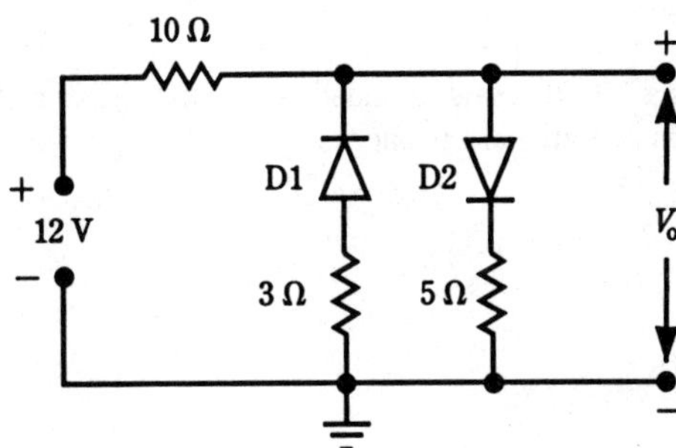

1-8 Circuit for Question 1-066.

Page(s) 198 to 200

Q1-067 A radiotelephone operator may signify "Your last message received, understood and will be complied with" by the use of the word:

A. wilco
B. confirmed
C. roger
D. clear
E. out

Page(s) 591

Q1-068 A two-way communications system in which the stations operate on different frequencies, is called:

A. biplex
B. diplex
C. duplex
D. simplex
E. polyplex

Page(s) 326, 327

Q1-069 An on-board mobile unit is used to communicate with:

A. all on-board units of another ship with which the mothership is already communicating
B. all ships that are assisting in the docking of the mother ship
C. the emergency equipment of any survival craft
D. on-board units of all other ships that are within 5 miles of the mother ship
E. none of the above choices is true

Page(s) 596

Q1-070 An inductor and a resistor are connected in series. Their time constant is obtained by:

A. multiplying the inductance value by the resistance value
B. dividing the resistance value by the inductance value
C. dividing the inductance value by the conductance value
D. dividing the inductance value by the resistance value
E. none of the above choices is true

Page(s) 69, 70

Q1-071 In FIG. 1-9, Z_f is a 150-kΩ resistor and Z_i is a 10-kΩ resistor. Assuming that the value of A is large, the gain of this operational amplifier is:

A. +15
B. −15
C. +16
D. −16
E. +15.5

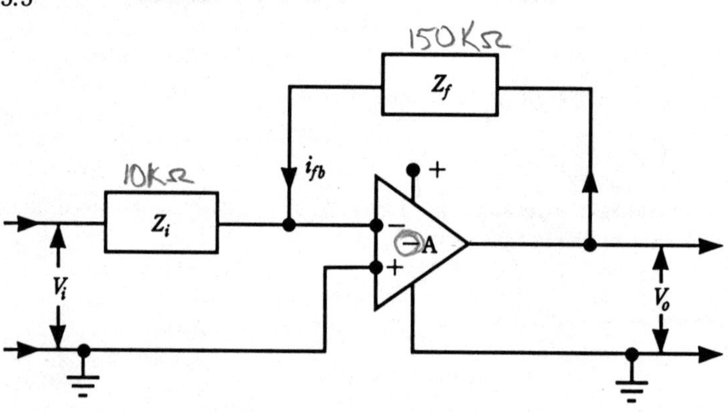

1-9 Circuit for Question 1-071.

Page(s):

Q1-072 On which of the following frequencies are hand-held portable transmitters authorized to transmit?

A. 156.8 MHz
B. 2182 kHz
C. 156.65 MHz
D. one appropriate intership frequency
E. choices A and D are true

Page(s) 596

Q1-073 If an operator's license is lost, the operator:

A. must immediately notify the Commission
B. can obtain a duplicate until the time of renewal
C. may apply for a duplicate to the FCC office that issued the original license
D. must, within 15 days, notify the FCC office in Washington, DC, of the loss
E. choices A and C are true

Page(s) 587

Q1-074 A marine radar set has a microwave antenna system whose azimuth is:

A. the angle of elevation measured in degrees
B. the angle of bearing in the horizontal plane and is measured in degrees
C. measured in degrees from true North
D. the angle that the diameter of the paraboloid subtends at the focus
E. choices B and C are true

Page(s) 436

Q1-075 Hand-held portable ship transmitters must not:

A. communicate with other ships not associated with their own ship
B. communicate from shore
C. transmit with an operating power greater than one watt
D. transmit on Channel 13
E. all of the above choices are true

Page(s) 596

Q1-076 An AM signal can be amplified by a:

A. frequency multiplier stage
B. class-C push-pull amplifier
C. class-C intermediate RF amplifier
D. class-C RF final stage
E. class-B linear RF amplifier

Page(s) 326

Q1-077 If a radio operator services a number of marine transmitters at different locations, where is the operator's license held?

A. in the Master's safe
B. on the operator's person
C. the license is posted at the control point of the primary transmitter

D. the license is deposited with the ship's license
E. none of the above choices are true

Page(s) 598

Q1-078 What happens to a shunt-fed JFET Hartley oscillator if there is a short circuit across the RF choke connected to the drain?

A. there is no change in either the amplitude or the frequency of the oscillation
B. the amplitude of the oscillation increases
C. the circuit ceases to oscillate
D. the output frequency increases
E. the output frequency falls

Page(s) 271, 272

Q1-079 A compulsory ship of 300 gross tons and upward, but less than 1000 gross tons, has a radiotelephone transmitter that must be capable of a daytime minimum range of:

A. 25 nautical miles
B. 50 nautical miles
C. 100 nautical miles
D. 150 nautical miles
E. 200 nautical miles

Page(s) 616

Q1-080 Waveguides are manufactured:

A. to exclude moisture as much as possible
B. with no long horizontal runs
C. from copper or brass
D. with internal silver plating to reduce the loss from skin effect
E. all of the above choices are true

Page(s) 452 to 455

Q1-081 A radiotelephone transmission which is preceded by the word "Pan," is:

A. sent by a ship or aircraft that is threatened by serious or imminent danger
B. concerned with the safety of navigation
C. concerned with important meteorological warnings
D. concerned with the safety of some person on board a ship or aircraft
E. none of the above choices are true

Page(s) 600

Q1-082 A 1-MHz carrier is amplitude modulated by a pure 200-Hz audio test tone. Which of the following combinations of frequencies represent the total content of the AM signal?

A. 1 MHz and 200 Hz
B. 999.8 kHz and 1000.2 kHz
C. 1 MHz, 999.8 kHz, 1000.2 kHz, and 200 Hz
D. 1 MHz and 1000.2 kHz
E. 999.8 kHz, 1000 kHz, and 1000.2 kHz

Page(s) 316

Q1-083 A test to determine whether an oscillator is generating its output, is to check:

A. that drain current is flowing
B. the value of the signal bias on the gate
C. that source current is flowing
D. the dc value of the drain voltage
E. for a high value of the dc supply voltage

Page(s) 272

Q1-084 For a first offense, the penalty for willfully violating a Rule, Regulation, Restriction or Condition of the Communications Act of 1934, is a:

A. fine of not more than $500.00 for each and every day of the offense
B. fine of not more than $10000.00 or imprisonment for a term not exceeding one year, or both
C. fine of not more than $10000.00 or imprisonment for a term not exceeding two years, or both
D. fine of not more than $25000.00
E. fine of not less than $500.00 for the offense, regardless of its duration

Page(s) 618, 619

Q1-085 The authorized bandwidth for aviation SSSC transmitters operating below 50 MHz, is:

A. 2.8 kHz
B. 3 kHz
C. 5 kHz
D. 4 kHz
E. 8 kHz

Page(s) 553

Q1-086 The very high frequency (VHF) band covers the frequency range of:

A. 30,000 to 300,000 kHz
B. 3 to 30 MHz
C. 300 MHz to 3 GHz
D. 30 to 300 MHz
E. choices A and D are true

Page(s) 443

Q1-087 Marine VHF transmitters use antennas that are:

A. vertically polarized
B. horizontally polarized
C. circularly polarized
D. omnidirectional
E. choices A and D are true

Page(s) 604

Q1-088 Which of the following logic gates corresponds to the waveforms of FIG. 1-10?

A. NOR
B. NAND
C. OR

D. NAND
E. EX-NOR

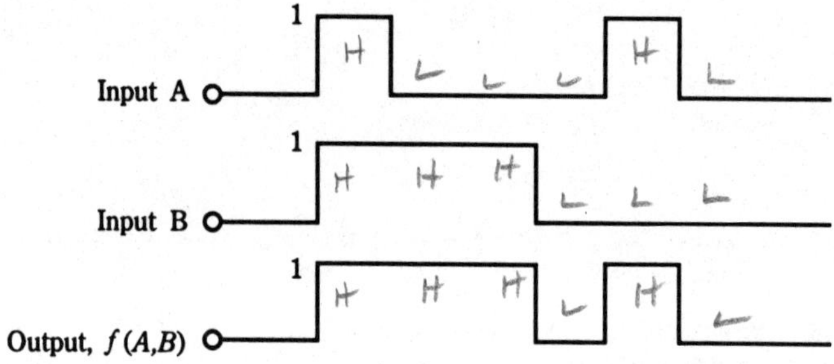

1-10 Waveforms for Question 1-088.

Page(s) 527 to 529

Q1-089 In a PM transmitter, the amplitude of the audio tone is doubled and the modulating frequency is also doubled. The frequency deviation is:

A. unchanged
B. doubled
C. multiplied by 4
D. divided by 4
E. halved

Page(s) 366

Q1-090 Those vessels that are subject to the Bridge-to-Bridge Act, must:

A. have a transmitter with a maximum power capability of 1 W
B. be capable of operating on Channel 16
C. maintain a constant watch on 156.65 MHz when the vessel is within 100 miles of U.S. shores
D. be capable of an emission on 156.8 MHz
E. choices B and C are true

Page(s) 554, 555

Q1-091 The conductance of a 2000-Ω ¼-W resistor is:

A. 2 mS
B. 5 mS
C. 20 mS
D. 50 μS
E. 500 μS

Page(s) 17, 18

Q1-092 Express 3.00 PM Eastern Standard Time (EST) in terms of Universal Time Coordinated (UTC):

A. 2000 hours
B. 1000 hours
C. 0300 hours

D. 2300 hours
E. 1800 hours

Page(s) 442

Q1-093 What is the maximum duration of the test signal transmitted from a marine radiotelephone station?

A. 10 seconds
B. 20 seconds
C. 30 seconds
D. one minute
E. five minutes

Page(s) 610

Q1-094 If the top light of an antenna tower fails, the time allowed for correction of the fault before reporting the failure, is:

A. 15 minutes
B. 30 minutes
C. 60 minutes
D. 90 minutes
E. the fault must be reported immediately

Page(s) 612

Q1-095 The limiter stage of an FM receiver:

A. follows the discriminator stage
B. has a low gain and provides an IF signal with a relatively constant amplitude
C. feeds directly into the de-emphasis circuit
D. provides considerable gain for the IF signal
E. is operated from a high voltage source

Page(s) 384, 385

Q1-096 The "spike" shown in the display of FIG. 1-11 has a shape which is:

A. determined by the narrow bandwidth of the spectrum analyzer's receiver
B. the positive alternation (180°) of a sine wave

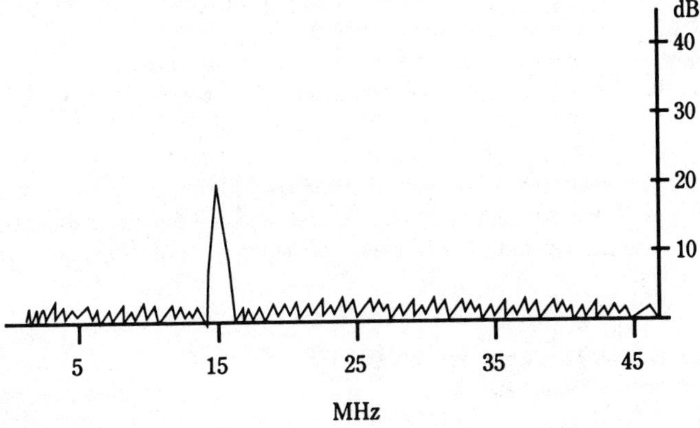

1-11 Display for Question 1-096.

C. one quarter cycle (90°) of a sine wave
D. determined by the characteristic of a narrow bandpass filter
E. choices A and D are true

Page(s) 317, 318

Q1-097 Figure 1-12 shows the phase relationship between a source voltage and the accompanying source current. The circuit across which the source is connected, contains:

A. resistance only
B. inductance only
C. capacitance only
D. resistance and inductance in series
E. resistance and capacitance in series

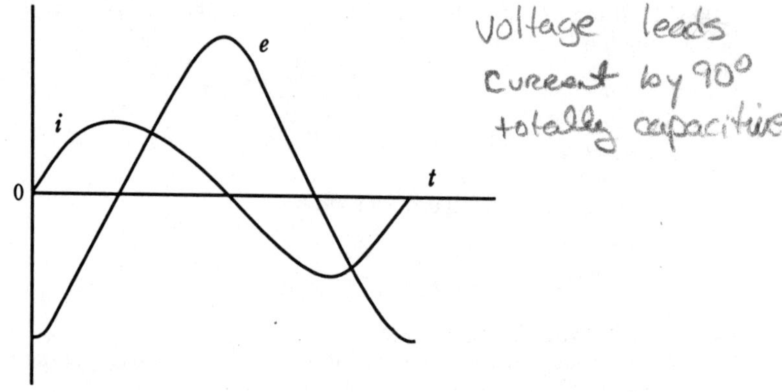

1-12 Waveforms for Question 1-097.

Page(s) 119 to 122

Q1-098 When a compulsory ship has left her port of departure, the operating power of the 2182-kHz transmitter suddenly falls to zero. The operator must immediately:

A. contact the ship's Master
B. switch to Channel 13 and operate with another transmitter
C. switch to Channel 16 and use the VHF transmitter
D. shut down the transmitter and carry out the necessary repairs
E. contact the communications repair installation at the port of destination

Page(s) 609

Q1-099 In an FM transmitter, a frequency deviation of 5 kHz corresponds to 100% modulation. If the transmitter is 50% modulated by a 7000 Hz test tone and the modulating frequency is then reduced to 5000 Hz, the value of the frequency deviation at both frequencies (neglecting pre-emphasis) is:

A. 2.5 kHz at both frequencies
B. 2.5 kHz at 7000 Hz and 1.8 kHz at 5000 Hz
C. 5 kHz at both frequencies
D. 1.8 kHz at 7000 Hz and 2.5 kHz at 5000 Hz
E. 10 kHz at both frequencies

Page(s) 367

Q1-100 When an urgency signal is transmitted by a mobile station, it indicates that:

A. the mobile station is threatened by grave and imminent danger
B. there is a message concerning the safety of navigation or important meteorological warnings
C. there is a message relating to the navigation and safe movement of aircraft engaged in search and rescue operations
D. there is a very important message concerning the safety of the ship, aircraft or other vessel, or the safety of a person
E. there is a message relating to the weather observation information destined for an official meteorological service

Page(s) 600

Element 3
Test 2

Q2-001 The frequency of a transistorized multivibrator is determined primarily by:

A. the collector supply voltage, V_{cc}
B. the junction capacitances of the transistors
C. the collector load resistors
D. the time constants formed by the coupling capacitors and the base resistors
E. the parameters of the transistors

Page(s) 278 to 280

Q2-002 The stage that feeds into the discriminator of an FM receiver is the:

A. local oscillator
B. first IF amplifier
C. mixer stage
D. RF amplifier
E. final IF amplifier, which also acts as a limiter stage

Page(s) 384, 385

Q2-003 The operating frequency of loran C lies within the:

A. LF band
B. VLF band
C. ELF band
D. MF band
E. HF band

Page(s) 439, 443

Q2-004 When a space-wave signal passes over a mountain ridge, a small part of the signal is diffracted down the far side of the mountain. This phenomenon is called:

A. discontinuity scattering
B. tropospheric ducting
C. knife-edge diffraction
D. space-wave refraction
E. refraction in the atmosphere

Page(s) 440

Q2-005 A tunnel diode is used in a microwave oscillator circuit because:

A. it has a negative temperature coefficient of resistance
B. it is lightly doped and has a wide depletion region
C. its equivalent capacitance changes as the applied voltage fluctuates
D. its characteristic contains a negative resistance section
E. its current increases as the applied voltage increases over its operating range

Page(s) 221 to 223

Q2-006 The operating power output of a ship station's radiotelephone transmitter must be determined if the authorized power is less than the manufacturer's rated power output by:

A. 5%
B. 10%
C. 15%
D. 20%
E. 25%

Page(s) 615

Q2-007 If the turns ratio of a step-up power transformer is 1:5:

A. the primary current is 20% of the secondary current
B. the secondary current is 20% of the primary current
C. the primary and secondary currents are equal
D. the secondary voltage is 20% of the primary voltage
E. the secondary current is 500% of the primary current

Page(s) 166 to 168

Q2-008 The emission designation for facsimile (FAX) is:

A. A3E
B. F4E
C. A4E
D. F3C
E. choices A and D are both true

Page(s) 380

Q2-009 The regulations regarding the required daily observations of antenna tower lights are to be found:

A. in FAA Rules and Regulations
B. on the back of the station license
C. in Part 13 of the FCC Rules and Regulations

D. in Part 17 of the FCC Rules and Regulations
E. in Part 80 of the FCC Rules and Regulations

Page(s) 612

Q2-010 Which of the following logic gates corresponds to the truth table of FIG. 2-1?

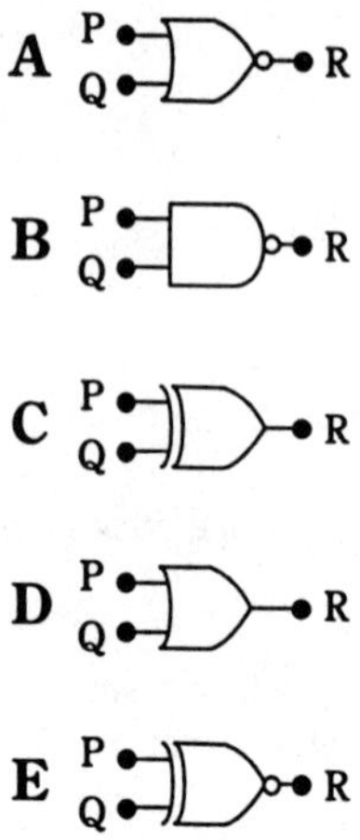

A P Q R

B P Q R

C P Q R

D P Q R

E P Q R

P	*Q*	*R*
False	False	False
False	True	True
True	False	True
True	True	False

2-1 Table for Question 2-010.

Page(s) 536 to 538

Q2-011 Which of the following is an authorized emission for tone paging communications?

A. A2E
B. R2D
C. J3E
D. F2B
E. A1C

Page(s) 612

Q2-012 The extremely high frequency (EHF) band covers the frequency range of:

A. 3 to 30 MHz
B. 30 to 300 MHz
C. 300 to 3000 MHz
D. 3 to 30 GHz
E. 30 to 300 GHz

Page(s) 443

Q2-013 In the circuit of FIG. 2-2A, both indicated voltages are measured, with respect to ground. The value of the potential at point A, with respect to ground, is:

A. +50 V
B. +35 V
C. +20 V
D. −20 V
E. −15 V

Page(s) 33 to 35

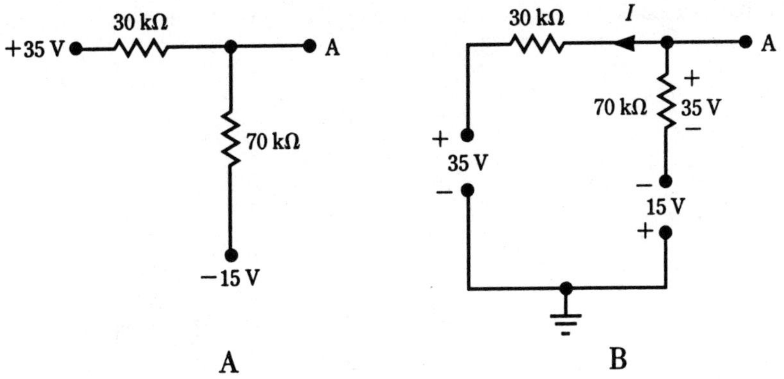

2-2 Circuit for Question 2-013.

Q2-014 The transmitter of a marine station is deviating from its technical requirements. The operator must immediately:

A. switch to the dummy antenna
B. suspend transmission
C. inform the ship's Master, who alone can authorize the transmission to be resumed
D. reduce the percentage of modulation
E. lower the level of the operating power

Page(s) 669

Q2-015 The circuit of FIG. 2-3 represents an AM receiver's:

A. AGC rectifier
B. mixer stage
C. squelch circuit
D. detector stage
E. modulator circuit

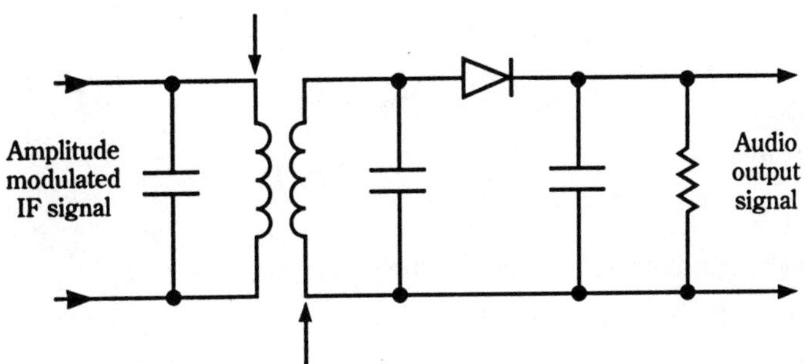

2-3 Circuit for Question 2-015.

Page(s) 352, 353

Q2-016 In the circuit of FIG. 2-4 the reading of the voltmeter connected across the inductor, is:

A. 1 V
B. 100 V
C. 200 V
D. 50 V
E. 1000 V

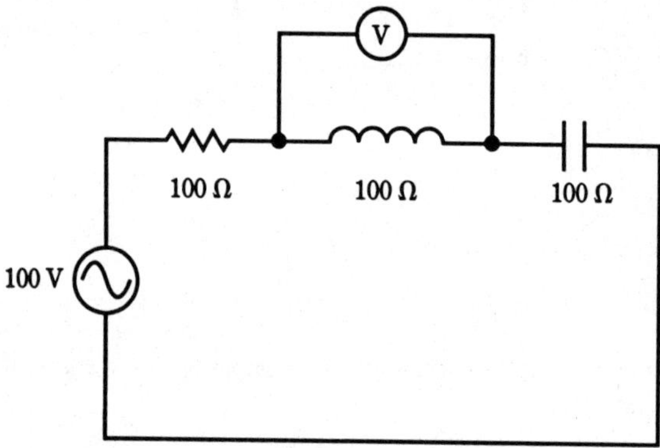

2-4 Circuit for Question 2-016.

Page(s) 149 to 154

Q2-017 Tests of survival craft emergency radio equipment must be conducted:

A. within 24 hours prior to the ship's departure from a port
B. by connecting the transmitter to a dummy antenna
C. at weekly intervals
D. to include the determination of the specific gravity or voltage of any batteries
E. all of the above choices are true

Page(s) 608

Q2-018 The color-coding of a resistor is Brown, Black, Red, Silver. What are the values of its nominal resistance and tolerance?

A. 1 kΩ, 10%
B. 2000 Ω, 10%
C. 100 Ω, 10%
D. 10 Ω, 20%
E. 100 kΩ, 10%

Page(s) 22 to 24

Q2-019 The input signal is introduced into the traveling-wave tube at the:

A. cathode
B. anode
C. control grid of the electron gun
D. cathode end of the helix
E. collector end of the helix

Page(s) 467 to 469

Q2-020 If a radiotelephone operator on duty hears profanity being transmitted over the air, the operator must:

A. take steps to end the transmission
B. enter all relevant details in the station log
C. warn the offender against the use of profanity
D. submit a report of the incident to the FCC
E. all of the above choices are true

Page(s) 603

Q2-021 When measuring a transmitter's frequency against a suitable standard, the frequency to be measured is taken from the:

A. oscillator stage
B. buffer stage
C. intermediate amplifiers
D. final frequency multiplier stage
E. final RF stage

Page(s) 337, 338

Q2-022 When an atom gains an additional electron, the result is:

A. positive ion
B. negative molecule
C. positive molecule
D. negative ion
E. negative neutron

Page(s) 6

Q2-023 For a second offense, the penalty for willfully violating a provision of the Commissions Act of 1934, is a fine of not more than:

A. $ 20000.00, or imprisonment for a term not exceeding two years, or both
B. $ 10000.00, or imprisonment for a term not exceeding two years, or both
C. $ 20000.00, or imprisonment for a term not exceeding one year, or both
D. $ 10000.00, or imprisonment for a term not exceeding one year, or both
E. $ 25000.00

Page(s) 618, 619

Q2-024 The maximum operating power of an aeronautical multicom station is:

A. 50 W
B. 25 W
C. 8 W
D. 10 W
E. 5 W

Page(s) 615

Q2-025 The purpose of a beat frequency oscillator (BFO) is to:

A. generate a 1-kHz note for morse reception
B. aid in the reception of weak voice-modulated signals
C. generate a signal, whose frequency is the same as that of the intermediate frequency

D. generate an output, whose frequency differs from the incoming carrier frequency by the value of the IF
E. generate an output, whose frequency differs from that of the intermediate frequency by 1 kHz

Page(s) 359

Q2-026 Before a newly installed transmitter can be put into normal service, it must:

A. receive type-approval
B. receive type-acceptance
C. Either choice A or B
D. be inspected and certified by the FCC
E. be tested by the Senior General Radiotelephone Operator on board ship

Page(s) 617

Q2-027 A compulsory ship is assigned a working frequency of 1980 kHz. On which frequency must an efficient listening watch be maintained?

A. 1960 kHz
B. 2000 kHz
C. 3960 kHz
D. 2182 kHz
E. 2128 kHz

Page(s) 583, 584

Q2-028 In a transmitter, a constant and stable load for the oscillator can be provided by a:

A. class-C intermediate stage
B. push-pull class-C stage
C. frequency multiplier
D. buffer stage
E. push-push stage

Page(s) 298

Q2-029 If an inductor is added in series with a vertical Marconi antenna:

A. the antenna will be electrically longer
B. resonant frequency will decrease
C. the antenna will be electrically shorter
D. the horizontal radiation pattern will no longer be omnidirectional
E. choices A and B are correct

Page(s) 428

Q2-030 When a calling station has a vital message to send concerning the safety of a passenger or crew member, its transmission is preceded by the word:

A. pan
B. security
C. safety
D. emergency
E. mayday

Page(s) 600

Q2-031 In FIG. 2-5, what is the reading of the meter M3?

A. 5 A
B. 4 A
C. 3 A
D. 2 A
E. 1 A

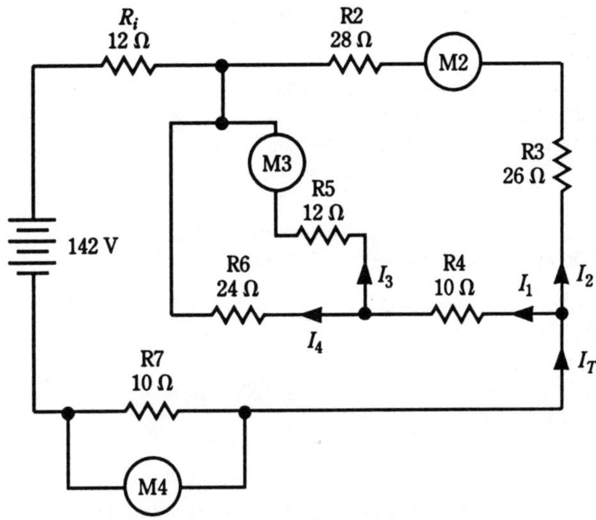

2-5 Circuit for Question 2-031.

Page(s) 43 to 46

Q2-032 In a crystal oscillator the frequency can be varied by a change in the temperature and also by:

A. a change in the value of the dc supply voltage
B. a change in the value of the emitter resistor
C. a change in the value of the inductance in the plate tank circuit
D. a change in the value of the capacitance in the plate tank circuit
E. changing the component values that provide the signal bias

Page(s) 278

Q2-033 An auxiliary ship unit which is associated with a mother ship may communicate with:

A. other auxiliary ship units of the same mothership
B. the mothership
C. all ships within the range of the auxiliary ship's transmitter
D. any auxiliary unit operating on Channel 16
E. choices A and B are true

Page(s) 596

Q2-034 At midnight two ships at sea are 135 miles apart. On which of the following frequencies can communication be established between the two ships?

A. 1.535 MHz
B. 3.548 MHz
C. 2182 kHz
D. 2460 kHz
E. 156.65 MHz

Page(s) 623

Q2-035 Hand-held portable units are used to communicate:

A. from shore
B. with all ships within the transmitter's range
C. with the ship station with which the portable unit is associated
D. with associated ship units of the mothership
E. choices C and D are true

Page(s) 596

Q2-036 When communications are weak or difficult, the radio operator should:

A. overmodulate the transmission
B. turn off the transmitter
C. shout into the microphone
D. switch from the working frequency to the calling frequency
E. use the phonetic alphabet

Page(s) 595

Q2-037 A coil consists of 2500 turns of AWG #26 copper wire and has a self-inductance of 0.3 H. If the air core is replaced by a soft iron core, the new value of the self-inductance is:

A. less than 0.3 H
B. 0.25 H
C. 0.3 H
D. greater than 0.3 H
E. choices A and B are true

Page(s) 64, 65

Q2-038 A transmitter has an assigned frequency of 156.8 MHz and a frequency tolerance of ± 0.002%. The maximum permitted frequency deviation is:

A. 3.136 kHz
B. 3.136 Hz
C. 313.6 Hz
D. 31.36 Hz
E. 3.136 Hz

Page(s) 297

Q2-039 An operator may signify "my transmission is ended and I expect a response from you" by using the word:

A. over
B. out
C. roger
D. wilco
E. clear

Page(s) 591

Q2-040 What is the authorized bandwidth of a marine A3E emission?

A. 8 kHz
B. 4 kHz
C. 10 kHz
D. 5.4 kHz
E. 6 kHz

Page(s) 334

Q2-041 The de-emphasis circuit in an FM receiver is used to:

A. attenuate low-frequency components in order to restore the tonal balance of the audio signal
B. accentuate high-frequency components in order to restore the tonal balance of the audio signal
C. accentuate low-frequency components in order to restore the tonal balance of the audio signal
D. attenuate high-frequency components in order to restore the tonal balance of the audio signal
E. attenuate low audio-frequency components and accentuate high audio-frequency components

Page(s) 388, 389

Q2-042 The symbol of FIG. 2-6 refers to a (an):

A. npn bipolar transistor
B. pnp bipolar transistor
C. p-channel JFET
D. n-channel JFET
E. D MOSFET

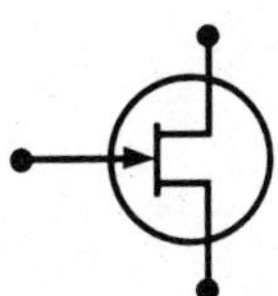

2-6 Symbol for Question 2-042.

Page(s) 253 to 256

Q2-043 A UHF transmitter is used for on-board communications, and is operating on a frequency of 467.825 MHz. Its corresponding repeater station frequency is:

A. 457.525 MHz
B. 457.550 MHz
C. 457.575 MHz
D. 457.600 MHz
E. 457.625 MHz

Page(s) 590

Q2-044 A transformer has an output of 10 W at the fundamental frequency whereas its second harmonic output is 0.1 W. By how much is the second-harmonic output attenuated, with respect to the fundamental output?

A. 3 dB
B. 100 dB
C. 10 dB
D. 20 dB
E. 40 dB

Page(s) 145 to 147

Q2-045 The charge on a capacitor:

A. may be disregarded while carrying out maintenance procedures
B. will only remain for a short while after the capacitor is charged from a dc source
C. is equal to the source voltage divided by the value of the capacitance
D. lasts indefinitely, unless it is deliberately bled off
E. is measured in coulombs per square meter

Page(s) 73, 74

Q2-046 Certain marine transmitters operating in the 156- to 162-MHz band must be equipped with an audio low-pass filter, which is installed between the modulation limiter and the modulated RF stage. This filter must:

A. attenuate audio frequencies above 3 kHz. The degree of attenuation must be at least 10 dB greater than at 1 kHz
B. attenuate audio frequencies above 5 kHz. The degree of attenuation must be at least 15 dB greater than that at 1 kHz
C. attenuate audio frequencies above 20 kHz. The degree of attenuation must be at least 50 dB greater than that at 1 kHz
D. attenuate audio frequencies above 15 kHz. The degree of attenuation must be at least 25 dB greater than that at 5 kHz
E. attenuate audio frequencies above 10 kHz. The degree of attenuation must be at least 20 dB greater than that at 3 kHz

Page(s) 588

Q2-047 The emission designator for a marine SSSC transmitter with a authorized bandwidth of 3 kHz, is:

A. 3K00J3E
B. 3K00R3E
C. 3K00A3E
D. 2K80H3E
E. 2K80J3E

Page(s) 334

Q2-048 The primary frequency standard transmitter that radiates a continuous 20-MHz carrier, is called:

A. WWV
B. WWB
C. WWVH

D. FCCV
E. choices A and C are true

Page(s) 338

Q2-049 A microcomputer has a total memory capacity of 4096 words. If there are 8-bits for each word, the required minimum number of address lines is?

A. 16
B. 8
C. 12
D. 14
E. 11

Page(s) 546, 547

Q2-050 An operator who lost his/her license, has now obtained a duplicate. If the operator finds the original license at a later date, he/she must:

A. destroy the original license immediately
B. destroy the duplicate immediately
C. return the duplicate to the FCC for cancellation
D. return the original to the FCC for cancellation
E. either choice C or D

Page(s) 587

Q2-051 In the circuit of FIG. 2-7 the total equivalent capacitance between the points X and Y is:

A. 1.2 μF
B. 0.8 μF
C. 1.5 μF
D. 1.8 μF
E. 8 μF

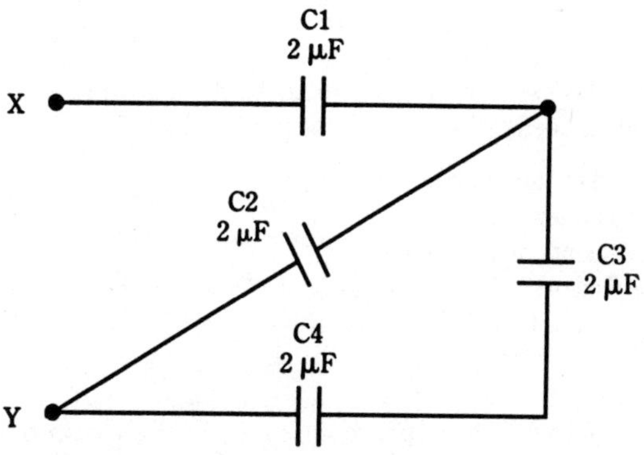

2-7 Circuit for Question 2-051.

Page(s) 75 to 79

Q2-052 The emission designation of a phase-modulated telephony signal is:

A. G3E
B. F3E
C. A3E
D. J3E
E. R3E

Page(s) 380

Q2-053 When an aircraft is descending toward a runway, the ILS Localizer unit indicates the:

A. vertical deviation from the optimum path of descent
B. deviation from the optimum speed of descent
C. azimuth of the aircraft in relation to the axis of the runway
D. horizontal deviation from the optimum path of descent along the axis of the runway
E. vertical angle between the axis of the aircraft and the axis of the runway

Page(s) 582

Q2-054 Which of the following transistorized stages might need to be neutralized?

A. audio amplifiers
B. push-pull audio amplifiers
C. class-C RF power amplifiers
D. frequency multipliers
E. RF oscillators

Page(s) 249 to 251

Q2-055 If a carrier is frequency modulated by a single test tone, the maximum value of the modulation index is directly proportional to the:

A. carrier amplitude
B. carrier frequency
C. modulating frequency
D. amplitude of the tone
E. none of the above choices is true

Page(s) 362

Q2-056 What class of license is required to operate the marine station on a large passenger ship if the station power exceeds 250-W carrier power and 1500-W peak envelope power?

A. Marine Radiotelephone Operator Permit
B. Restricted Radiotelephone Permit
C. General Radiotelephone License
D. Second-Class Radiotelephone License
E. Choices C and D are true

Page(s) 581

Q2-057 Which of the following microphones uses a very light strip of corrugated aluminum suspended in a magnetic field?

A. crystal
B. dynamic
C. velocity

D. carbon
E. ceramic

Page(s) 324, 325

Q2-058 The electrical length of a Marconi antenna can be increased by adding a (an):

A. inductor in series
B. capacitor in series
C. capacitor in parallel
D. resistor in parallel
E. inductor in parallel

Page(s) 428

Q2-059 A marine transmitter is operating on a frequency of 156.8 MHz. The frequency tolerance of this transmitter is:

A. 10 Hz
B. 20 Hz
C. 30 Hz
D. 50 Hz
E. 10 ppm

Page(s) 579

Q2-060 When compared to the full-wave rectifier circuit containing two diodes, the bridge arrangement:

A. provides a lower dc output voltage
B. employs a minimum of three diodes
C. does not require a power transformer for its operation.
D. does not require a center tap on the secondary winding of the power transformer
E. choices C and D are true

Page(s) 208 to 214

Q2-061 After construction of a radio station and the completion of the equipment tests, service tests may be carried out for a period not to exceed:

A. 5 days
B. 10 days
C. 15 days
D. 20 days
E. 30 days

Page(s) 576

Q2-062 In FIG. 2-8 what is the phase relationship between the source voltage, *E*, and the source current, *I*?

A. *E* and *I* are in phase
B. *E* lags *I*
C. *I* leads *E*
D. *E* and *I* are 90° out of phase
E. The phase difference between *E* and *I* is 45°

Page(s) 131 to 133

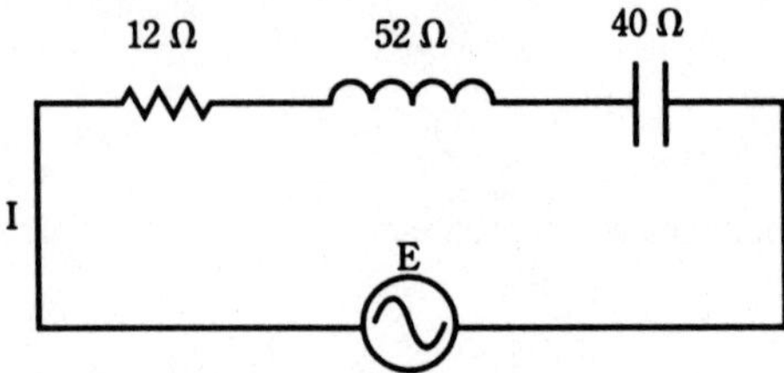

2-8 Circuit for Question 2-062.

Q2-063 If U.S. Coast Guard involvement is not possible, the test of the Emergency Position Indicating Radio Beacon (E.P.I.R.B) is carried out:

A. prior to leaving port
B. monthly during an international voyage
C. once a year
D. during the first five minutes of any hour and must last no longer than three audio sweeps
E. for a period of 15 seconds

Page(s) 573

Q2-064 An emitter-follower circuit can be used to provide:

A. a high voltage gain
B. a high output impedance
C. a low input impedance
D. matching between a low impedance source and a high impedance load
E. a high degree of isolation between two stages

Page(s) 243, 244

Q2-065 Which of the distress frequencies lies within the band of 1605 to 27500 kHz?

A. 2182 kHz
B. 2182 MHz
C. 2.182 MHz
D. 218.2 kHz
E. choices A and C are true

Page(s) 570

Q2-066 When low-level modulation is used in an AM transmitter, the RF stages following the modulated stage, cannot be:

A. harmonic generators
B. operated in class A
C. operated on class B
D. operated in class C
E. choices A and D are true

Page(s) 326

Q2-067 In the MF band of 1605 to 3500 kHz, the radiotelephone distress frequency and the type of emission are:

A. 2128 kHz, A3E
B. 2812 kHz, R3E
C. 2182 kHz, J3E
D. 2.182 MHz, R3E
D. 2.218 MHz, J3E

Page(s) 570

Q2-068 A high-value resistor is added in series with a moving-coil meter movement. The purpose of this resistor is to:

A. swamp out variations in the moving coil's resistance caused by temperature changes
B. prevent the needle from overswinging
C. increase the current range of the meter
D. decrease the current range of the meter
E. extend the voltage range of the meter

Page(s) 87

Q2-069 A common-base arrangement uses a pnp transistor and is biased for linear amplification. On the positive half cycle of the input sine-wave signal:

A. the collector-base voltage decreases
B. the output signal from the collector is a negative half cycle
C. there is a power loss and a current gain
D. the base current decreases
E. the collector current increases

Page(s) 237, 238

Q2-070 In the marine mobile services a radio operator must prevent interference with other channels by:

A. using the highest level of power to ensure good communications
B. using the highest level of modulation required for good communications
C. using selective calling on 2182 kHz
D. turning off the transmitter when not in use
E. allowing no communication to exceed 30 minutes in duration

Page(s) 591

Q2-071 The impedance of an ac circuit is measured in:

A. siemens
B. henrys
C. farads
D. ohms
E. the unit depends on the nature of the components in the circuit

Page(s) 122 to 124

Q2-072 Licensed radio operators are prohibited from:

A. disclosing the content of an intercepted distress message
B. communicating directly with a foreign country
C. divulging for his/her own personal gain the content of an intercepted message

D. disclosing the content of an intercepted message transmitted by an amateur station for the benefit of the general public
E. disclosing the content of an intercepted message to the addressee

Page(s) 604

Q2-073 In the soldering process for electronics work, rosin flux is used to:

A. reduce the temperature of the soldering iron
B. remove any oxide film on the metals being joined
C. eliminate the need for tinning
D. prevent the molten solder from wetting the metals
E. Acid flux, not rosin flux, should be used

Page(s) 102

Q2-074 When calling another ship, a radio operator must identify his/her own ship's radio station by means of its:

A. assigned callsign only
B. callsign and port of origin
C. callsign and port of destination
D. callsign and name of ship
E. callsign, name of ship, and country of registration

Page(s) 558, 559

Q2-075 A vertical Hertz dipole:

A. is omnidirectional in the horizontal plane
B. is omnidirectional in the vertical plane
C. is unidirectional in a vertical plane
D. receives equally well from all horizontal directions
E. choices A and D are true

Page(s) 416, 417

Q2-076 The frequency of the input signal to a double-conversion superhet receiver is 156.7 MHz. If the frequency of the second oscillator is 10.114 MHz, the frequency of the first local oscillator is:

A. 146 MHz
B. 146.664 MHz
C. 20.814 MHz
D. 135.98 MHz
E. 21.4 MHz

Page(s) 382, 383

Q2-077 When initiating a radiotelephone call:

A. never use the distress frequency of 2182 kHz
B. never use the distress frequency of 156.8 MHz
C. the call signal must not continue for more than 30 seconds in each instance
D. do not repeat the call if there is no reply until 10 minutes have elapsed
E. always use the working frequency

Page(s) 557

Q2-078 For an aircraft station operating with F3E emission in the frequency range of 100 to 137 MHz, the frequency tolerance is:

A. 20 ppm
B. 30 ppm
C. 50 ppm
D. 20 Hz
E. 100 ppm

Page(s) 578

Q2-079 What are the station identification requirements for bridge-to-bridge communications?

A. the station callsign is mandatory
B. identification is only required at the end of a transmission
C. identification is only required at the start of a transmission
D. the name of the vessel is used in lieu of the station call sign
E. identification is required every 30 minutes during a long transmission

Page(s) 554, 555

Q2-080 During average peaks of the audio signal, a high level of modulation is necessary in an AM transmitter in order to:

A. provide a high level of signal-to-noise ratio at the receiver
B. provide a high level of audio power for the receiver's loudspeaker
C. widen the bandwidth of the AM signal
D. reduce the bandwidth of the AM signal
E. choices A and B are true

Page(s) 314

Q2-081 The maximum occupied bandwidth that can be used by a marine radio station is called the:

A. authorized bandwidth
B. bandwidth of emission
C. operating bandwidth
D. necessary bandwidth
E. occupied bandwidth

Page(s) 553

Q2-082 Convert the binary number, 11100101111_2, into its equivalent hexadecimal number:

A. $82E_{16}$
B. $72E_{16}$
C. $82F_{16}$
D. $73F_{16}$
E. $72F_{16}$

Page(s) 523

Q2-083 Which of the following frequency bands are assigned to VOR stations?

A. 112.050 to 117.950 MHz
B. 118.050 to 122.950 MHz
C. 108.050 to 111.850 MHz

D. 112.200 to 117.850 MHz
E. 110 to 115 MHz

Page(s) 623

Q2-084 The outer conductor of a coaxial cable is only grounded at:

A. the input end
B. the output end
C. its middle
D. the input end and the output end
E. the outer conductor is never grounded

Page(s) 411

Q2-085 The purpose of the receiver's squelch circuit is to:

A. prevent fluctuations in the AGC bias level
B. overcome fluctuations in the level of the RF signal arriving at the receiving antenna
C. prevent amplified noise from reaching the loudspeaker during the absence of an incoming signal
D. reduce the receiver's sensitivity for all incoming signals
E. reduce the receiver's selectivity for all incoming signals

Page(s) 355

Q2-086 An application for a ship's station license renewal must be filed within _____ days, but not later than _____ days prior to the end of the license term:

A. 60; 15
B. 90; 30
C. 30; 10
D. 60; 10
E. 30; 15

Page(s) 549

Q2-087 An RF stage is coupled to the antenna and precedes the mixer stage of a superhet receiver. One advantage of including this RF stage, is:

A. improved signal-to-noise ratio
B. improved image-channel rejection
C. better selectivity
D. greater sensitivity
E. all of the above choices are true

Page(s) 348

Q2-088 Which of the following is an example of angle modulation?

A. double sideband, amplitude modulation
B. frequency modulation
C. single sideband, amplitude modulation
D. phase modulation
E. choices B and D are correct

Page(s) 366

Q2-089 The local oscillator of a VHF receiver is generating a 167.7-MHz output. If the receiver is tuned to 157.0 MHz, the frequency of the image channel is:

A. 21.4 MHz
B. 178.4 MHz
C. 146.3 MHz
D. 135.6 MHz
E. 189.1 MHz

Page(s) 346

Q2-090 A 36-foot length of wire has a resistance of 12 ohms per foot. If the wire's cross-sectional area is reduced to one third of its original value, the new resistance of the wire is:

A. 144 Ω
B. 432 Ω
C. 3888 Ω
D. 1444 Ω
E. 1296 Ω

Page(s) 22 to 25

Q2-091 In an FM receiver, which stage has the IF signal as its input and the audio signal as its output?

A. limiter
B. discriminator
C. de-emphasis circuit
D. mixer
E. IF amplifier

Page(s) 387, 388

Q2-092 A radar set measures the total time interval for a transmitted pulse to reach the target and its echo to return to the receiver. To determine the radar range in nautical miles, this total time interval in microseconds is divided by:

A. 6.184
B. 12.368
C. 1.15
D. 0.87
E. 24.74

Page(s) 403

Q2-093 Express the decimal number 11_{10} as a binary number to the base 2:

A. 1101_2
B. 1100_2
C. 1110_2
D. 1011_2
E. 1101_2

Page(s) 518, 519

Q2-094 Which electrode of a triode tube can be compared with the base region of a bipolar transistor?

A. cathode
B. plate
C. screen grid
D. control grid
E. filament

Page(s) 225

Q2-095 If a carrier is frequency modulated by a single test tone, the frequency separation between a sideband and its neighboring sideband is equal to:

A. the modulating frequency
B. twice the modulating frequency
C. the carrier frequency divided by the modulation index
D. the frequency deviation
E. the frequency deviation multiplied by the modulation index

Page(s) 363

Q2-096 Three quarters of one cycle of a sine wave cover an angle of:

A. 2π radians
B. π radians
C. 90°
D. 270°
E. 450°

Page(s) 105, 106

Q2-097 Express a distance of 2.3 statute or land miles in terms of nautical miles:

A. 2.65
B. 1.83
C. 2.37
D. 1.91
E. 2.00

Page(s) 402, 403

Q2-098 At microwave frequencies, waveguides are preferred over coaxial cables because their:

A. lower attenuation
B. lower cost
C. greater flexibility
D. smaller size
E. greater frequency range

Page(s) 622

Q2-099 Express 3.00 PM Central Standard Time (CST) in terms of Universal Time Coordinated (UTC):

A. 0900 hrs
B. 1900 hrs
C. 1500 hrs
D. 2100 hrs
E. 2000 hrs

Page(s) 442

Q2-100 During landing, an aircraft is communicating with the control tower, which of the following frequencies would not be used for this procedure?

A. 121.5 MHz
B. 121.6 MHz
C. 121.9 MHz
D. 123.6 MHz
E. 132.0 MHz

Page(s) 570

Element 3
Test 3

Q3-001 All ship stations' radiotelephone transmitters must be capable of reducing the operating carrier power to:

A. 1 watt or less
B. 2 watts or less
C. 3 watts or less
D. 5 watts or less
E. 8 watts or less

Page(s) 615

Q3-002 What values are required to calculate the percentage regulation for a dc generator?

A. values of the output terminal voltage under no-load and full-load conditions
B. values of the armature speed under no-load and full-load conditions
C. values of the field current under no-load and full-load conditions
D. a knowledge of the resistances for both the armature and field windings
E. the number of poles and the number of commutator segments

Page(s) 95, 96

Q3-003 Figure 3-1 shows the phase relationship between a source voltage and the accompanying current. The circuit across which the source is connected, contains:

A. inductance only
B. resistance only
C. capacitance only
D. resistance and capacitance in series
E. inductance and resistance in series

Page(s) 116 to 119

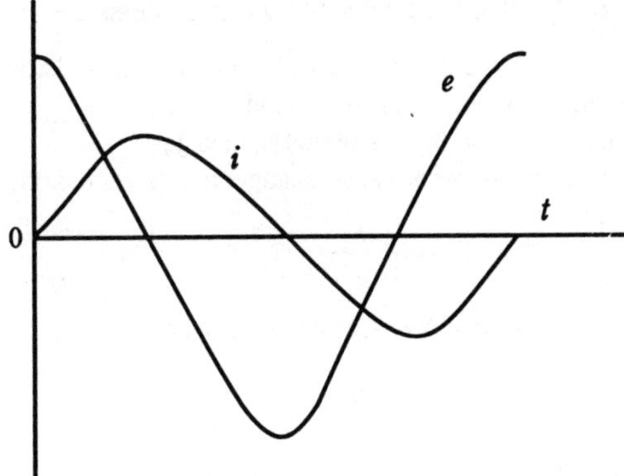

3-1 Waveforms for Question 3-003.

Q3-004 An external frequency check of an AM station revealed that at a particular time, the carrier frequency was 8 Hz low. The transmitter log showed that at the same time, the carrier frequency was 10 Hz high. What was the error in the station's frequency monitor?

A. 2 Hz high
B. 2 Hz low
C. 18 Hz high
D. 18 Hz low
E. none of the above choices are correct

Page(s) 337, 338

Q3-005 If an operator hears an urgency signal, he/she must continue to listen for a minimum period of:

A. 3 minutes
B. 5 minutes
C. 6 minutes
D. 10 minutes
E. 15 minutes

Page(s) 600

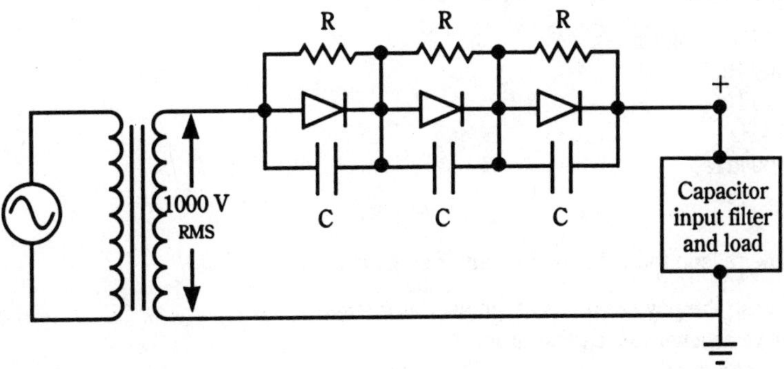

3-2 Circuit for Question 3-006.

Q3-006 In the circuit of FIG. 3-2, the function of the three resistors, *R*, is to:

A. ensure that there is the same forward voltage across each diode
B. reduce the amount of ripple across each diode
C. protect the diodes from the effects of voltage surges
D. ensure that there is the same reverse voltage across each diode
E. choices A and C are true

Page(s) 204, 205

Q3-007 The wavelength of a 500-MHz signal in free space is:

A. 60 m
B. 15 m
C. 60 cm
D. 0.006 m
E. 6 m

Page(s) 402

Q3-008 A reflex klystron is oscillating at the frequency of its resonant cavity. If the reflector voltage is made slightly less negative, the:

A. output power would increase
B. bunching would occur earlier in time
C. oscillation will cease
D. positive feedback will increase
E. the frequency will decrease

Page(s) 466, 467

Q3-009 Crossmodulation in a receiver must be eliminated in the:

A. IF stages
B. mixer stage
C. detector stage
D. audio amplifiers
E. RF stage

Page(s) 357

Q3-010 The reactance modulated oscillator of an FM transmitter operates on 4905 kHz and the output operating frequency is 98.1 MHz. If the output frequency deviation frequency is 5 kHz, the frequency swing at the oscillator stage is:

A. ±5 kHz
B. ±500 Hz
C. ±250 Hz
D. ±1 kHz
E. ±100 kHz

Page(s) 367

Q3-011 One reason for including the buffer stage is to:

A. increase the power output of the oscillator stage
B. behave as a harmonic generator
C. present a varying load to the oscillator stage

D. improve the efficiency of the oscillator stage
E. improve the frequency stability of the oscillator stage

Page(s) 298

Q3-012 Which of the following logic circuits has an operation that corresponds to two or more switches (or relays) in series?

A. AND gate
B. NAND gate
C. OR gate
D. NOR gate
E. EX-OR gate

Page(s) 529, 530

Q3-013 The purpose of the limiter stage in an FM receiver, is to:

A. prevent "blasting" of the loudspeaker
B. detect the IF signal
C. provide the required level of AGC bias
D. substitute for a squelch circuit
E. stop any amplitude modulation of the IF signal from being applied to the discriminator stage

Page(s) 384, 385

Q3-014 In the logic circuit of FIG. 3-3, five entire sequences of the clock input to the flip-flop circuit have been completed. The output of the circuit is:

A. Q
B. $\overline{Q}$
C. 1
D. 0
E. $Q + \overline{Q}$

Page(s) 621, 622

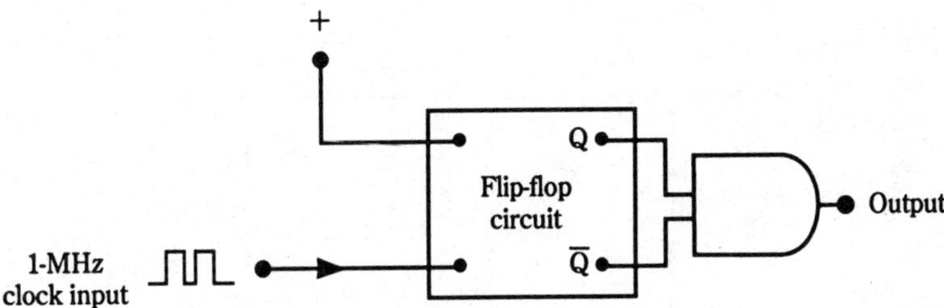

3-3 Circuit for Question 3-014.

Q3-015 In the circuit of FIG. 3-4, an approximate saw-tooth waveform can be monitored between points:

A. A and E
B. E and B
C. A and D

D. C and E
E. A and B

Page(s) 278, 280

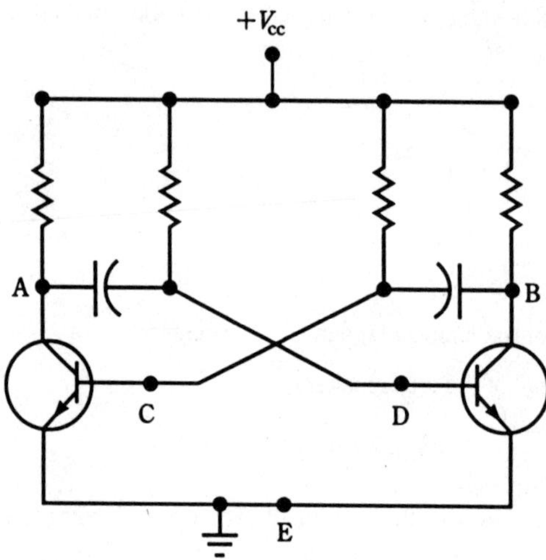

3-4 Circuit for Question 3-015.

Q3-016 If an intermediate light of an antenna tower is extinguished or malfunctioning, the:

A. fact must be entered in the station log
B. FCC regional office must be immediately informed
C. nearest Flight Service station must be informed if the problem cannot be corrected within 30 minutes
D. Office of the Federal Aviation Administration must be informed if the problem cannot be corrected within 30 minutes
E. transmitter must be shut down

Page(s) 612

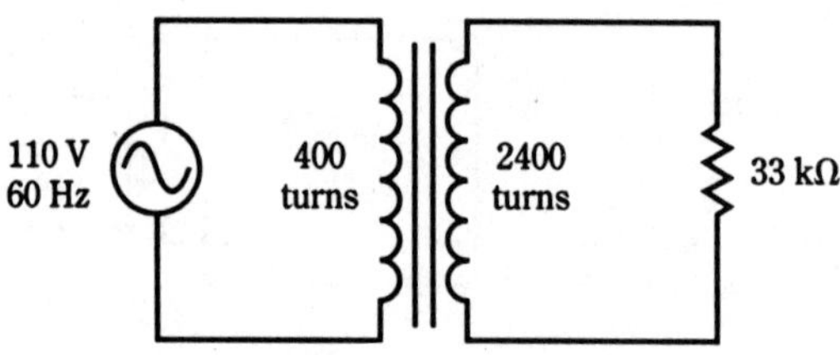

3-5 Circuit for Question 3-017.

Q3-017 In the circuit of FIG. 3-5 the value of the current flowing through the 33-kΩ resistor is:

A. 22 mA
B. 20 mA
C. 0.6 mA

D. 12 mA
E. 132 mA

Page(s) 165 to 168

Q3-018 Immediately prior to sending a test signal, a marine radiotelephone operator hears the word "wait." The operator should:

A. cancel the test completely
B. send his test message as rapidly and as briefly as possible
C. after waiting an appropriate interval of time, repeat his callsign followed by the word "test" and then see if there is a further response
D. switch to the nearest channel on which no communication is taking place
E. The situation, as described, is impossible because a test transmission would never be interrupted by the word "wait"

Page(s) 610

Q3-019 In the circuit of FIG. 3-6, $R_1 = 20\ \Omega$, $C = 40\ \mu F$, $L = 0.1$ H; the reading of V is 40 V and the reading of A is 3 A. The power can be calculated from:

A. the product of the readings of V and A
B. $V^2/(R_1 + R_2)$ watts
C. (*reading of* $A)^2 \times (R_1 + R_2)$ watts
D. the product of the readings of V and A multiplied by the power factor
E. The power cannot be calculated, but must be measured by a wattmeter

Page(s) 80, 81

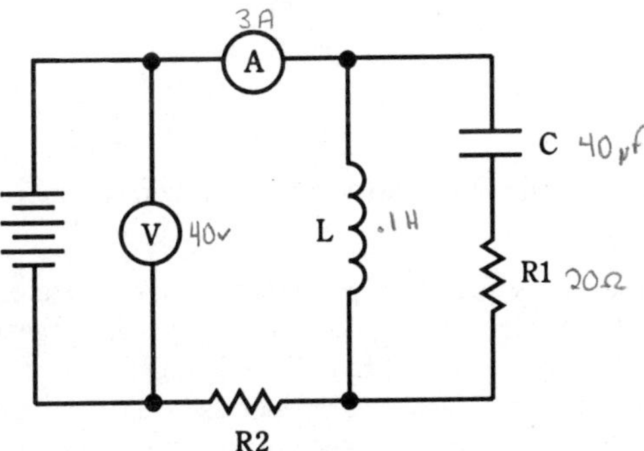

3-6 Circuit for Question 3-019.

Q3-020 Upon receipt of a Notice of Suspension of his/her license, the licensee must normally mail his/her application for a hearing within:

A. 5 days
B. 10 days
C. 15 days
D. 30 days
E. 60 days

Page(s) 608

Q3-021 When a communications receiver is tuned to a strong signal, the AGC bias is measured and found to be zero. The fault cannot be caused by a (an):

A. defective IF stage
B. open circuit in the AGC's filter capacitor
C. defective local oscillator
D. short circuit across the AGC's filter capacitor
E. defective RF stage

Page(s) 354

Q3-022 For a marine station one receiver must be tuned to the international radiotelephone distress frequency:

A. only during the silent period
B. from 0900 to 2100 UTC
C. only when the ship is in international waters
D. only when initiating a call on 2182 kHz
E. on a continuous basis

Page(s) 583

Q3-023 A transmitter's output frequency is 16 MHz with a tolerance of $\pm$ 0.002%. There are three doubler stages between the final amplifier and the oscillator. The maximum permitted frequency deviation at the oscillator is:

A. 320 Hz
B. 400 Hz
C. 40 Hz
D. 80 Hz
E. 160 Hz

Page(s) 297, 301

Q3-024 Which of the following is arranged in the correct priority of communications in the marine mobile service?

A. distress calls, safety signals, urgency signals, and radio direction-finding communications
B. distress calls, radio direction-finding communications, urgency signals, and safety signals
C. distress calls, urgency signals, radio direction-finding communications, and safety signals
D. distress calls, urgency signals, safety signals, and radio direction-finding communications
E. distress calls, safety signals, urgency signals, and radio direction-finding communications

Page(s) 499, 500

Q3-025 Which of the following frequencies falls within the band allocated to marine J3E emissions?

A. 500 kHz
B. 10 MHz
C. 20 MHz
D. 30 MHz
E. choices B and C are true

Page(s) 335

Q3-026 The circuit of FIG. 3-7 has a:

A. very high input impedance
B. low output impedance
C. high voltage gain
D. high output impedance
E. choices A and B are true

Page(s) 253 to 256

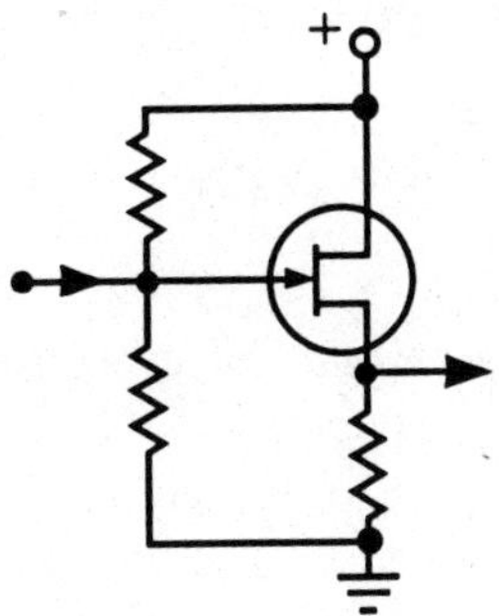

3-7 Circuit for Question 3-026.

Q3-027 If a transmitter has received "type approval":

A. the manufacturer has tested the transmitter to ensure that the specifications have been met
B. a General Radiotelephone licensee on board the ship has tested the transmitter to ensure that the specifications have been met
C. the transmitter was built by a manufacturer who is licensed by the U.S. Government
D. the FCC has conducted tests on the transmitter to ensure that the specifications have been met
E. "type approval" is the preliminary step toward "type acceptance"

Page(s) 617

Q3-028 The radiated carrier power from a transmitter is 500 W. If the radiated power of the second harmonic component is 0.5 W, the degree of the harmonic attenuation relative to the carrier is:

A. 5 dB
B. 8 dB
C. 30 dB
D. 20 dB
E. 50 dB

Page(s) 303, 304

Q3-029 The circuit component which has the highest failure rate (is the most unstable) under normal conditions, is the:

A. air cored inductor
B. choke
C. transformer

D. capacitor
E. resistor

Page(s) 73, 74

Q3-030 An antenna system is operating in the HF band and is radiating a signal toward the ionosphere. If the frequency is increased and the antenna system is still resonant, the:

A. skip distance increases
B. amount of bending in the ionosphere is increased
C. skip distance decreases
D. skip distance remains the same
E. choices A and B are true

Page(s) 440 to 442

Q3-031 An aviation transmitter must have its output operating frequency checked:

A. during the initial installation
B. when any change in the transmitter is made that could affect the operating frequency
C. upon receipt of an official notice of off-frequency operation
D. on a monthly basis
E. choices A, B, and C are true

Page(s) 614

Q3-032 When a carrier is frequency modulated by a test tone, the percentage of modulation can be determined by:

A. observing the waveform of the FM signal
B. using a deviation meter
C. creating a trapezoidal display on an oscilloscope
D. taking readings of the frequency monitor
E. using a frequency counter

Page(s) 362

Q3-033 A radiotelephone transmission that is preceded by the word "security" is:

A. concerned with the safety of navigation
B. concerned with important meteorological warnings
C. sent by a ship or aircraft that is threatened by serious or imminent danger
D. concerned with the safety of some person on board a ship or aircraft
E. either choice A or B is true

Page(s) 600

Q3-034 The inductance of a coil with an air core is directly proportional to the:

A. number of turns
B. cross-sectional area of the wire
C. square of the number of turns
D. length of the core
E. choices A and B are true

Page(s) 64, 65

Q3-035 A tank circuit is caused to resonate at 12 MHz by its tuning capacitor. The circuit is now retuned to 24 MHz. The ratio of the new capacitance to the original capacitance is:

A. 1:4
B. 1:2
C. 4:1
D. 2:1
E. 1:8

Page(s) 160, 161

Q3-036 A compulsory ship has one main transmitter and eight hand-held portable transmitters. The number of radio station licenses required is:

A. 9
B. 1
C. 2
D. 3
E. 5

Page(s) 596

Q3-037 An A3E transmitter has a bandwidth of 10 kHz. If the emission designation is changed to H3E, but the modulating signal remains the same, the new bandwidth is:

A. 3 kHz
B. 2.8 kHz
C. 4 kHz
D. 5 kHz
E. 6 kHz

Page(s) 334

Q3-038 A licensee operates 10 marine utility stations in the same area. The number of licenses required is:

A. 10
B. 5
C. 2
D. 1
E. marine utility stations do not require a license

Page(s) 595, 596

Q3-039 Pre-emphasis is used in FM transmitters to improve the signal-to-noise ratio of:

A. low modulating frequencies
B. all modulating frequencies
C. high modulating frequencies
D. the carrier
E. all the significant sidebands

Page(s) 370

Q3-040 If a mobile station on a U.S. ship visits a foreign country, the government of that country may, under the 1959 Geneva Treaty:

A. inspect the station logs
B. request full details of the radio installations
C. require that the transmitter is kept "off the air" for the duration of the visit

D. require that the station license be produced for inspection
E. demand a list of the frequencies that the station will be using during the visit

Page(s) 582

Q3-041 Class-C operation produces frequency multiplication because:

A. the stage is highly efficient
B. the collector load is a tank circuit
C. the emitter-base forward bias is very high
D. the collector current waveform is severely distorted and therefore contains components which are harmonics of the input frequency
E. the input signal is badly distorted

Page(s) 250

Q3-042 Marine radiotelephone transmitters with single sideband emissions have a frequency tolerance of:

A. 20 Hz
B. 20 ppm
C. 30 Hz
D. 50 Hz
E. 10 ppm

Page(s) 579

Q3-043 An AM receiver's ability to accept the wanted signal while rejecting unwanted signals on nearby frequencies, is called its:

A. image-channel rejection
B. adjacent-channel rejection
C. channel sensitivity
D. intermodulation rejection
E. crossmodulation rejection

Page(s) 358

Q3-044 For 100% modulation the frequency deviation of Marine transmitters which operate in the 156- to 162-MHz band and use F3E or G3E emission, is:

A. 3 kHz
B. 8 kHz
C. 20 kHz
D. 5 kHz
E. 6 kHz

Page(s) 588

Q3-045 In the circuit of FIG. 3-8, the total self-inductance between points P and Q is:

A. 20 H
B. 30 H
C. 2.5 H
D. 5 H
E. 3.3 H

Page(s) 64 to 68

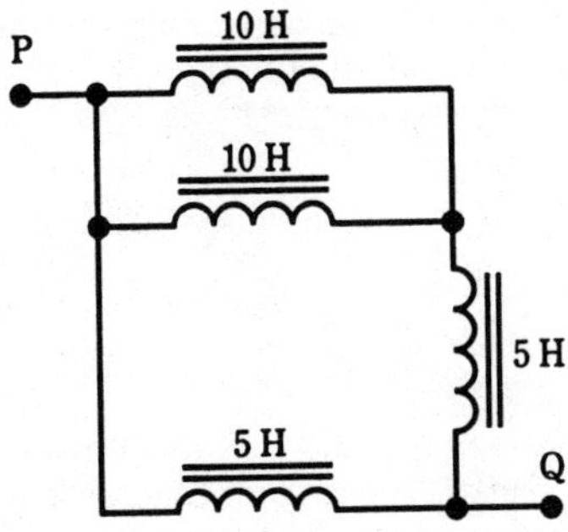

3-8 Circuit for Question 3-045.

Q3-046 A Class-S Emergency Position-Indicating Radio Beacon (E.P.I.R.B):

A. must be capable of floating or being secured to a survival craft
B. must have its battery replaced after emergency use
C. must have its battery replaced before the expiration date established by the manufacturer
D. may be tested during the first five minutes of any hour
E. all of the above choices are true

Page(s) 574

Q3-047 In terms of dBm, a power level of 0.1 mW is equal to:

A. −10 dBm
B. +10 dBm
C. +20 dBm
D. −20 dBm
E. 0 dBm

Page(s) 145 to 147

Q3-048 Who of the following is not eligible to apply for a new General Radiotelephone License?

A. an alien who is ineligible for employment in the U.S.
B. a person who is unable to communicate in the English language
C. a person who is afflicted with complete deafness
D. a person who is afflicted with complete muteness
E. all of the above choices are true

Page(s) 571

Q3-049 The circulating or fly-wheel current in a tank circuit recreates the sinusoidal voltage waveform in:

A. class-A audio amplifiers
B. class-AB audio amplifiers
C. phase inverters
D. class-B push-pull audio amplifiers
E. class-C RF power amplifiers

Page(s) 249, 256

Q3-050 A Citizen's Band transmitter is causing interference with TV channels 2 through 6. This is as a result of:

A. intermodulation
B. crossmodulation
C. spurious oscillations
D. parasitic oscillations
E. harmonic interference

Page(s) 330

Q3-051 The radiotelephone distress and calling frequency in the MF band, is:

A. 2182 kHz
B. 500 kHz
C. 2128 kHz
D. 2812 kHz
E. 2218 kHz

Page(s) 570

Q3-052 A carrier is phase modulated by a test tone. If the amplitude and the frequency of the tone are both doubled, the amount of frequency deviation is:

A. doubled
B. multiplied by four
C. unchanged
D. halved
E. divided by four

Page(s) 366

Q3-053 Which of the following must be included in the transmission of a distress message?

A. ship's name, port of origin, port of destination, nature of distress
B. ship's name, Master's name, port of destination, nature of help requested
C. ship's name, position, nature of distress, nature of help requested
D. ship's name, owner's name, position, nature of help requested
E. ship's name, course and speed (if any), nature of distress, nature of help requested

Page(s) 568

Q3-054 Express 9:00 AM Mountain Standard Time (MST), in terms of Universal Time Coordinated (UTC).

A. 0200 hrs
B. 1600 hrs
C. 0900 hrs
D. 1700 hrs
E. 1500 hrs

Page(s) 442

Q3-055 Which of the following frequency bands does an aircraft control tower use to communicate with aircraft during their landing?

A. 118.000 to 121.400 MHz
B. 121.600 to 121.925 MHz
C. 123.600 to 128.800 MHz

D. 132.025 to 135.975 MHz
E. all of the above choices are true

Page(s) 564

Q3-056 In amplitude modulation, sidebands:

A. represent undesirable distortion of the carrier wave
B. are the audio frequencies contained in the AM signal
C. contain the intelligence that is present in the AM signal
D. are created by the effect of the audio modulation on the amplitude of the RF signal in the modulated stage
E. choices and D are true

Page(s) 316, 317

Q3-057 Express the binary number 1101_2 as a decimal number to the base 10:

A. 12_{10}
B. 13_{10}
C. 8_{10}
D. 11_{10}
E. 14_{10}

Page(s) 517, 518

Q3-058 Which of the following services requires that maintenance work on the transmitters be carried out by the holder of a General Radiotelephone License?

A. CB radios
B. AM broadcast
C. FM broadcast
D. two-way police communications
E. marine

Page(s) 580, 581

Q3-059 For test purposes, a 100-W marine FM transmitter is 80% modulated by a 2-kHz tone. Including the carrier and sidebands, the total power in the modulated FM signal is:

A. 200 W
B. 132 W
C. 11.6 W
D. 164 W
E. 100 W

Page(s) 362, 363

Q3-060 A working frequency:

A. is used to establish the initial radio contact between two marine stations
B. is used for test purposes only
C. is the frequency to which all stations generally listen
D. may have an assigned value of 2182 kHz
E. none of the above choices is true

Page(s) 557

Q3-061 Receiver interference is not reduced by including a (an):

A. insulating enclosure around the receiver
B. crystal filters
C. wave trap
D. RF stage
E. noise limiter

Page(s) 341, 342

Q3-062 A 1-MΩ resistor and a 0.002-μF capacitor are connected in series across a sine-wave voltage source whose frequency is 60 Hz. The value of the circuit's impedance is:

A. 1 MΩ
B. 2.33 MΩ
C. 1.33 MΩ
D. 1.66 MΩ
E. 2.66 MΩ

Page(s) 127, 128

Q3-063 Who of the following is allowed to operate bridge-to-bridge transmitters? Only:

A. the holder of a Marine Operator Permit
B. the holder of a General Radiotelephone License
C. the Master of the vessel
D. the person in charge of navigation
E. choices C and D are true

Page(s) 554, 555

Q3-064 Class-B operation is associated with:

A. a practical efficiency between 50% and 60%
B. a *Q* point near cut-off
C. elimination of even harmonic distortion in push-pull audio amplifiers
D. the requirement for a matched pair of transistors in an audio push-pull amplifier
E. all of the above choices are true

Page(s) 247, 248

Q3-065 The bandwidth that is occupied by the carrier, both sidebands and harmonics, is called the:

A. bandwidth of emission
B. authorized bandwidth
C. occupied bandwidth
D. operating bandwidth
E. choices A and C are true

Page(s) 554

Q3-066 Why is nitrogen gas sometimes used in waveguides?

A. to increase the distributed capacitance
B. to keep the waveguide dry
C. to reduce the skin effect at the walls of the guide

D. to lower the voltage rating
E. to raise the guide's wave impedance

Page(s) 452 to 455

Q3-067 The test of the keying device for the automatic alarm system is conducted:

A. prior to the vessel's departure from each port
B. on each day that the vessel is outside a harbor or port
C. only once if the vessel is in two or more ports within one day
D. either before arrival or after departure if the vessel is in port for less than one day
E. all of the above choices are true

Page(s) 551

Q3-068 A 250-W 4-MHz transmitter is amplitude modulated by a 1.5-kHz tone, which possesses a strong second harmonic. The required bandwidth is:

A. 1.5 kHz
B. 3 kHz
C. 6 kHz
D. 12 kHz
E. 24 kHz

Page(s) 317

Q3-069 The diagram of FIG. 3-9 is a:

A. pre-emphasis circuit
B. de-emphasis circuit
C. limiter
D. high-pass filter
E. band-pass filter

Page(s) 388

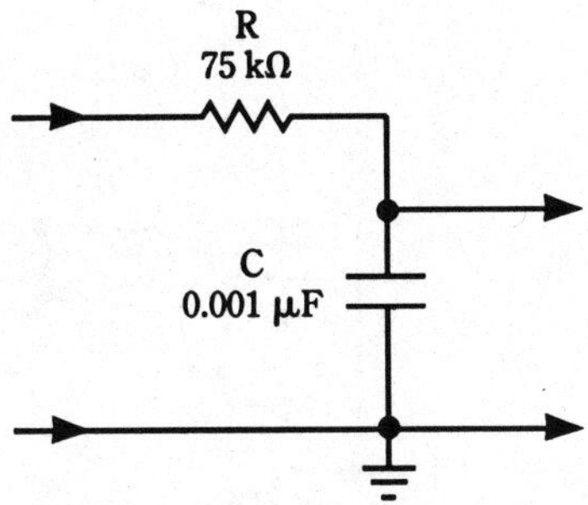

3-9 Circuit for Question 069.

Q3-070 In a power supply, the bleeder resistor burns out. What effect does this have on the circuit during normal operation?

A. there is a considerable increase in the amount of ripple in the output voltage
B. the percentage regulation increases significantly
C. the diodes could be destroyed

D. the power transformer will be damaged unless it is protected by a fuse
E. there is no appreciable effect on the output dc voltage

Page(s) 207

Q3-071 Which of the following is an advantage of an FM receiver over an AM receiver?

A. simpler alignment procedure
B. better signal-to-noise ratio
C. smaller audio range
D. lower bandwidth
E. operation at low carrier frequencies

Page(s) 384, 385

Q3-072 In which of the following may a radio operator not engage?

A. unnecessary transmissions
B. unidentified transmissions
C. superfluous communications
D. personal communications
E. all of the above choices are true

Page(s) 592

Q3-073 In FIG. 3-10 the coupling between L_1 and L_2 is increased up to the critical value. As a result, the:

A. bandwidth of the response curve increases
B. value of the coupling factor decreases
C. stage's voltage gain decreases

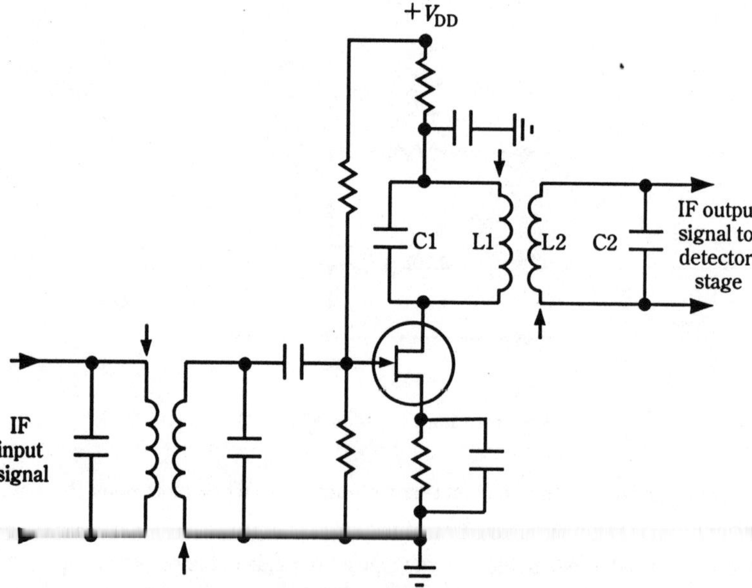

3-10 Circuit diagram for an intermediate-frequency amplifier. Circuit for Question 3-073.

D. amount of RF power transferred to the following stage is decreased
E. response at the IF frequency is reduced

Page(s) 350

Q3-074 A relay coil has a resistance of 600 Ω and operates with a current of 0.1 A. The relay coil is connected in series with a protection (dropping) resistor across a 100 Vdc source. The required resistance for the dropping resistor is:

A. 50 Ω
B. 500 Ω
C. 5 Ω
D. 5 Ω
E. 0.5 Ω

Page(s) 35

Q3-075 In QUES. 3-74, the power dissipated in the protection resistor is:

A. 5 W
B. 6 W
C. 11 W
D. 60 W
E. 0.6 W

Page(s) 35

Q3-076 A radio operator may signify "this conversation is ended and no response is expected" by using the word:

A. clear
B. roger
C. over
D. out
E. either choice A or C is true

Page(s) 591

Q3-077 The super high frequency (SHF) band covers the frequency range of:

A. 3 to 30 MHz
B. 30 to 300 MHz
C. 3 to 30 GHz
D. 300 to 3000 MHz
E. 30 to 300 GHz

Page(s) 443

Q3-078 Which of the following stages has an appreciable voltage gain, an input impedance of the order of 100 Ω or less, a relatively high output impedance, its input and output signals in phase and little possibility of self-oscillation?

A. common emitter amplifier
B. common collector stage
C. common base amplifier

D. JFET amplifier
E. MOSFET amplifier

Page(s) 237, 238

Q3-079 For an on-board communications transmitter, the operator must possess a:

A. Marine Operator Permit
B. Restricted Radiotelephone Permit
C. General Radiotelephone License
D. Second-Class Radiotelephone License
E. no license is required by the operator assigned to the control point

Page(s) 590

Q3-080 If a sine-wave voltage has an effective value of 20 V, its peak value is:

A. 28.3 V
B. 14.1 V
C. 56.6 V
D. 20 V
E. 7.07 V

Page(s) 109, 110

Q3-081 The operating power of a compulsory ship's main transmitter is determined by:

A. the product of the plate voltage and the dc level of the plate current
B. the product of the plate voltage and the antenna current
C. the product of the antenna current and the associated antenna resistance
D. the product of the $(\text{antenna current})^2$ and the antenna resistance
E. none of the above choices is true

Page(s) 599

Q3-082 The operating frequency of the Omega navigational system is:

A. 100 kHz
B. 102 kHz
C. 2182 kHz
D. 10.2 kHz
E. 1.02 kHz

Page(s) 439

Q3-083 Each U.S. cargo ship which is equipped with a radiotelephone station for compliance with Chapter IV of the Safety Convention, shall, while on watch, maintain a continuous watch on:

A. 2182 kHz
B. 500 kHz
C. 156.65 MHz
D. 156.8 MHz
E. choices A and D are true

Page(s) 583, 584

Q3-084 Which of the following statements is true for the combinatorial logic circuit of FIG. 3-11?

A. point A is "low," but points B and C are both "high"
B. point A is "high," but points B and C are both "low"
C. points A and B are both "high," but point C is "low"
D. points A and B are both "low," but point C is "high"
E. points A and C are both "high," but point B is "low"

Page(s) 543 to 545

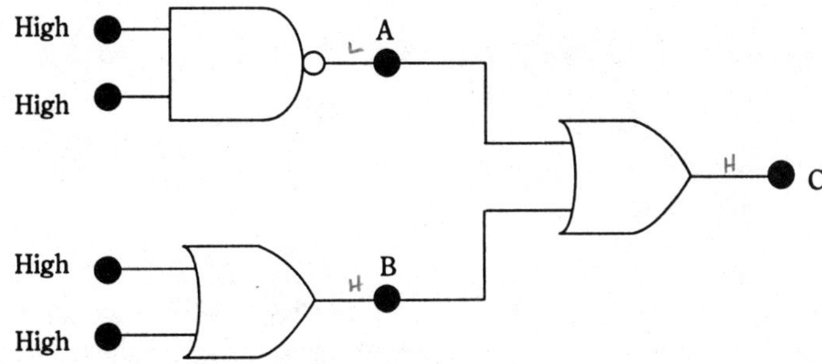

3-11. Logic circuit for Question 3-084.

Q3-085 In FIG. 3-12 identify pin 9 of the microchip:

A. a
B. b
C. c
D. d
E. e

Page(s) 226

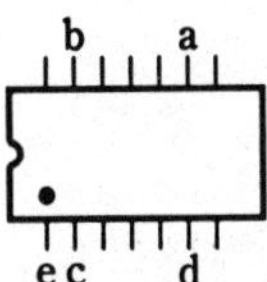

3-12 Pin identification for Question 3-085.

Q3-086 Which of the following groups of frequencies can be used to synthesize an approximation to a 25-MHz symmetrical square wave?

A. 25 MHz, 75 MHz, 125 MHz, 175 MHz, 225 MHz
B. 25 MHz, 50 MHz, 75 MHz, 100 MHz, 125 MHz
C. 25 MHz, 50 MHz, 100 MHz, 150 MHz, 200 MHz
D. 25 MHz, 12.5 MHz, 6.25 MHz, 3.125 MHz, 1.5625 MHz
E. 25 MHz, 125 MHz, 225 MHz, 325 MHz, 400 MHz

Page(s) 192 to 194

Q3-087 When a bipolar transistor is operating as a linear amplifier device, the:

A. emitter-base junction and the collector-base junction are both forward biased
B. emitter-base junction and the collector-base junction are both reverse biased

C. emitter-base junction is forward biased and the collector-base junction is reverse biased
D. emitter-base junction is reverse biased and the collector-base junction is forward biased
E. emitter-base junction is forward biased and the collector-emitter junction is reverse biased

Page(s) 225, 226

Q3-088 A $\lambda/4$ Marconi antenna radiates a signal whose frequency is 520 kHz. The frequency of the fifth harmonic is:

A. 2600 MHz
B. 104 kHz
C. 2.6 MHz
D. 2600 kHz
E. choices C and D are true

Page(s) 426 to 430

Q3-089 What part of the Instrument Landing System (ILS) is used to indicate the horizontal deviation of an aircraft from its optimum path of descent along the axis of the runway?

A. Distance-Measuring Equipment (DME)
B. VOR system
C. glide path unit
D. localizer unit
E. racon station

Page(s) 582

Q3-090 A receiver's antenna system consists of stacked elements. As a result the:

A. selectivity of the array is increased
B. sensitivity of the array is increased
C. resonant frequency of the array is reduced
D. signal-to-noise ratio is lowered
E. array will not respond to harmonics

Page(s) 422 to 424

Q3-091 The circuit in FIG. 3-13 represents a:

A. two-section constant-k high-pass filter
B. constant-k band-pass filter
C. constant-k band-stop filter
D. two-section m-derived filter
E. two-section constant-k low-pass filter

Page(s) 180 to 183

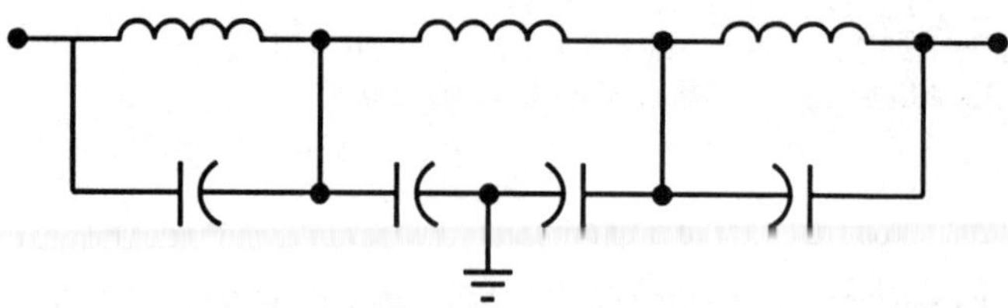

3-13 Circuit for Question 3-091.

Q3-092 In the circuit of FIG. 3-14:

A. the transistor is used in a common collector configuration
B. there is no phase change between the input and output signals
C. the transistor is used in a common base configuration
D. there is a 180° phase change between the input and output signals
E. the amplifier is incorrectly biased

Page(s) 239, 240

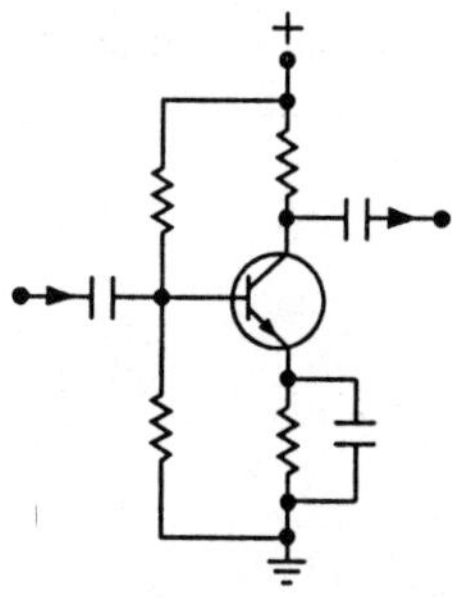

3-14 Circuit for Questions 3-092 and 3-093.

Q3-093 The circuit of FIG. 3-14 has:

A. a low input impedance and a low voltage gain
B. a low input impedance and a high voltage gain
C. a high input impedance and a low voltage gain
D. a high input impedance and a high voltage gain
E. equal input and output impedances

Page(s) 239, 240

Q3-094 The total length of a Hertz dipole is increased from 2.5 feet to 2.8 feet. As a result, the antenna's:

A. input impedance is capacitive
B. radiated power increases
C. resonant frequency decreases
D. power gain increases
E. input impedance falls

Page(s) 412

Q3-095 The presence of standing waves on a transmission line is the result of:

A. a high level of attenuation on the line
B. terminating the line by a resistive load equal in value to the surge impedance
C. reducing the input power to below its critical level
D. an impedance mismatch between the load and the line
E. a reflection coefficient of zero at the terminating load

Page(s) 405 to 410

Q3-096 The purpose of bridge-to-bridge transmitters is:

A. general ship-to-shore communications
B. on-board communications
C. for communicating only outside 100 miles of U.S. shore
D. navigational only
E. restricted to communications with foreign ships

Page(s) 554, 555

Q3-097 The total time taken for a radio pulse to travel to the target and back to the receiver, is 62 μs. The range of the target in nautical miles is:

A. 4.4
B. 5.0
C. 5.8
D. 10.0
E. 2.5

Page(s) 403

Q3-098 A varistor is a semiconductor device:

A. whose capacitance varies with the applied voltage
B. that can be used to achieve voltage regulation
C. that has a high positive temperature coefficient of resistance
D. whose resistance is controlled by the applied voltage
E. choices B and D are true

Page(s) 218

Q3-099 Shouting by a radio operator into a microphone could cause:

A. possible interference with the transmissions of other stations on adjacent frequencies
B. overloading of the microphone
C. overmodulation of the transmitted signal
D. severe distortion of the voice signal so that the message is unintelligible
E. all of the above choices are true

Page(s) 567

Q3-100 In FIG. 3-15, the resistor and the capacitor are connected in series across a sine-wave voltage source whose angular frequency, $\omega = 2\pi f = 1000$ rad./s. The total impedance of the circuit is:

A. 1 MΩ
B. 2 MΩ
C. $\frac{1}{\sqrt{2}}$ MΩ
D. $\sqrt{2}$ MΩ
E. 1.5 MΩ

Page(s) 127, 128

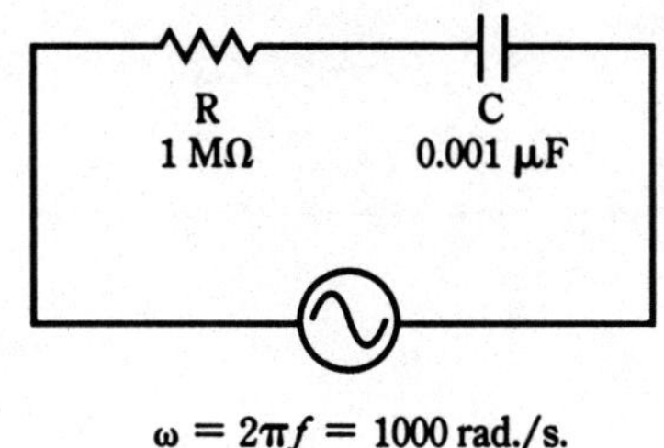

3-15 Circuit for Question 3-100.

Element 3
Test 4

Q4-001 Which of the following permits a microwave signal to travel in one direction with virtually no loss, but severely attenuates any signal attempting to travel in the reverse direction?

A. wave trap
B. isolator
C. tunnel diode
D. circulator
E. diplexer

Page(s) 470

Q4-002 In the circuit of FIG. 4-1, the voltage across the resistor, R3, is:

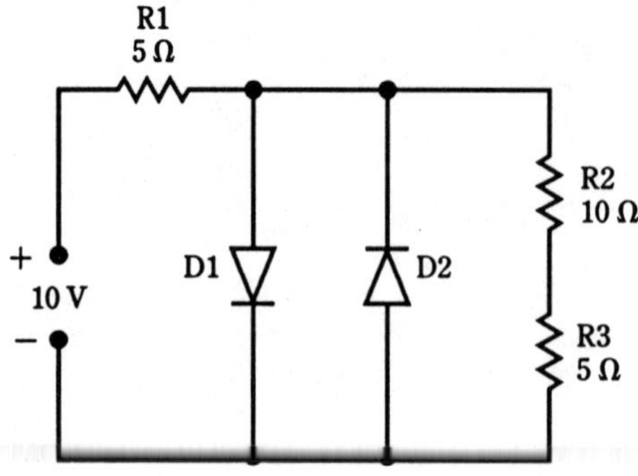

4-1 Circuit for Question 4-002.

A. 2.5 V
B. 0.7 V
C. 1.8 V
D. 0.23 V
E. 3.33 V

Page(s) 621, 622

Q4-003 Under which of the following conditions must a radiotelephone transmission contain the callsign and the name of the ship?

A. bridge-to-bridge-communications
B. all communications should contain this information
C. when calling on 2182 kHz
D. when the transmission is a distress call
E. for on-board communications

Page(s) 568

Q4-004 An alternator operates with a separately excited rotor. Without changing the frequency, the output voltage can be raised by increasing the:

A. rotor's speed
B. number of commutator segments
C. number of poles
D. number of brushes
E. rotor's field current

Page(s) 196, 197

Q4-005 The emission designation, J3E, stands for:

A. single sideband, suppressed carrier, telegraphy
B. single sideband, reduced carrier, telephony
C. single sideband, full carrier, telephony
D. double sideband, telephony
E. single sideband, suppressed carrier, telephony

Page(s) 332 to 334

Q4-006 In a class-C amplifier stage with a tank circuit as its load, the:

A. output current waveform is severely distorted
B. output voltage waveform is severely distorted
C. efficiency is low
D. input signal is small
E. choices A and B are true

Page(s) 249, 250

Q4-007 The carrier frequency of an aviation transmitter must be checked:

A. during the initial installation
B. when any change is made in the transmitter that may influence the operating frequency
C. upon receipt of an official notice of off-frequency operation

D. before the transmitter is removed or replaced
E. choices A, B, and C are true

Page(s) 577

Q4-008 For a communications receiver, image-channel interference must be eliminated in the:

A. RF stage
B. IF amplifiers
C. detector stage
D. audio amplifiers
E. squelch circuit

Page(s) 346, 348

Q4-009 If the lights of an aviation tower are not monitored by automatic means, such lights must be checked:

A. at 9 AM and at 9 PM
B. between sunset and sunrise, local time
C. at the beginning of each hour
D. once every 24 hours
E. once every three months

Page(s) 612

Q4-010 A varactor diode is used:

A. to generate frequency modulation (FM)
B. to generate phase modulation (PM)
C. for frequency multiplication in the microwave region
D. as a control device in an AFC circuit
E. all of the above choices are true

Page(s) 319, 320

Q4-011 A marine radiotelephone transmitter may be tested

A. during the experimental period between 12 midnight local time and local sunrise
B. after receiving official authorization from the regional FCC office
C. as required, in order to ensure proper operation of the equipment
D. only on low power
E. under the authority of the ship's Master

Page(s) 610

Q4-012 In a frequency-modulated transmitter, the number of sidebands:

A. increases with a higher value of the modulation index
B. decreases with an increase in the modulating frequency
C. increases with the amplitude of the modulating signal
D. increases with a higher degree of pre-emphasis
E. all of the above choices are true

Page(s) 363

Q4-013 Measurements have shown that the signal from a marine transmitter contains strong harmonics that exceed their authorized limits. The operator must immediately:

A. measure the operating carrier power
B. add low-pass filters to the antenna's circuitry
C. suspend transmission
D. measure the bias level on the final stage
E. adjust the position of the Faraday screen

Page(s) 609

Q4-014 The base in an RF amplifier is grounded in order to:

A. raise the input impedance
B. lower the output impedance
C. obtain maximum power output
D. raise the amplifier's efficiency
E. avoid the requirement of neutralizing the stage

Page(s) 301

Q4-015 In the circuit of FIG. 4-2, what is the voltage across the capacitor, C, after the switch, S, has been closed for a time interval of 50 ms?

A. 7.56 V
B. 3.78 V
C. 5 V
D. 12 V
E. 0 V

Page(s) 79 to 84

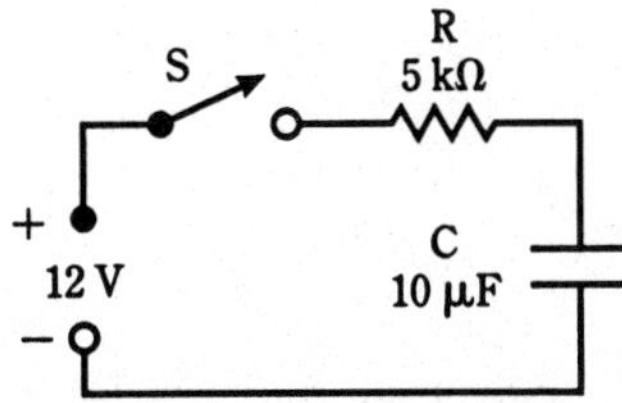

4-2 Circuit for Question 4-015.

Q4-016 If an FM transmitter is producing strong harmonics, how would its signal be heard on an FM receiver that is tuned to the second harmonic of the carrier frequency?

A. only odd harmonics are generated by an FM transmitter
B. the audio signal on the loudspeaker would be unintelligible
C. the signal is received and is intelligible, but the modulation index is halved
D. the signal is received and is intelligible, but the frequency deviation is doubled
E. the signal is received and is intelligible, but its bandwidth is reduced

Page(s) 382, 383

Q4-017 For an aeronautical SSSC transmitter, the carrier of its J3E emission must be suppressed below the peak envelope power by at least:

A. 20 dB
B. 30 dB
C. 40 dB

D. 50 dB
E. 60 dB

Page(s) 605

Q4-018 Convert the hexadecimal number, $A6B_{16}$, into its equivalent binary number.

A. 110110010110_2
B. 1010111001001_2
C. 101001101001_2
D. 101001101011_2
E. 101011011001_2

Page(s) 522, 523

Q4-019 During the soldering process, the leads of the components are normally tinned to:

A. prevent any movement of the parts being soldered
B. aid the connections between the metals and decrease the amount of time required for the heating process
C. wet the metals so that the solder can stick
D. prevent the leads from breaking
E. make the leads more flexible

Page(s) 102

Q4-020 A voltage phasor whose RMS value is 3 V, leads a second voltage phasor by 90°. If the RMS value of the second phasor is 4 V, the effective value of their phasor sum is:

A. 7 V
B. 5 V
C. 3.5 V
D. 1 V
E. 6 V

Page(s) 112 to 114

Q4-021 Where are the positions of maximum, minimum values of effective voltage and current on a resonant Hertz dipole?

A. maximum voltage and current exist at the center of the antenna
B. maximum voltage and current exist at the ends of the antenna
C. maximum voltage and minimum current exist at the center of the antenna
D. minimum voltage and maximum current exist at the center of the antenna
E. minimum voltage and minimum current exist at the ends of the antenna

Page(s) 413

Q4-022 Which of the following stages in an FM receiver is responsible for drastically reducing the effect of static noise during the reception of a signal?

A. de-emphasis circuit
B. limiter stage
C. Foster-Seeley discriminator
D. mixer stage
D. squelch circuit

Page(s) 384, 385

Q4-023 The frequency tolerance of a marine J3E transmitter in the band of 1650 to 27500 kHz is:

A. ± 10 Hz
B. ± 20 Hz
C. ± 20 ppm
D. ± 10 ppm
E. ± 5 ppm

Page(s) 335

Q4-024 An operator is permitted to divulge the contents of an intercepted message when:

A. authorized to do so by the Master of the ship
B. the message is specifically a police communication
C. the message is specifically a government communication
D. the message relates to an aircraft in distress
E. an operator is never permitted to divulge the contents of an intercepted message

Page(s) 563

Q4-025 If a capacitor is added in series with a Marconi antenna:

A. the length of the antenna will be electrically shorter
B. the input impedance will be unchanged
C. its resonant frequency will increase
D. the radiation pattern will become more unidirectional
E. choices A and C are true

Page(s) 428

Q4-026 In an FM transmitter, the amplitude of the modulating test tone is doubled, but its frequency is halved. If the effect of pre-emphasis is neglected, the frequency deviation is:

A. halved
B. doubled
C. unchanged
D. quadrupled
E. quartered

Page(s) 361, 362

Q4-027 The Urgency signal must only be sent from a mobile station on the authority of the:

A. General Radiotelephone Licensee
B. senior radio operator
C. Master of the vessel
D. person in charge of the mobile station
E. Choices C and D are true

Page(s) 600

Q4-028 The phenomenon of knife-edge diffraction refers to:

A. total refraction in the ionosphere
B. total refraction caused by a temperature inversion
C. the bending around a mountain ridge by a UHF signal

D. the bending around the earth by a ground-wave signal
E. the scattering of a VHF signal from the troposphere

Page(s) 440

Q4-029 Which of the following may contain a pre-emphasis circuit?

A. FM receiver
B. VHF AM transmitter
C. single-sideband transmitter
D. AM receiver
E. FM transmitter

Page(s) 370

Q4-030 The system that measures the range from an aircraft's interrogator to the transponder of a radio beacon, is called:

A. Interrogatory Friend or Foe (IFF)
B. omega (Ω)
C. long-range navigation (LORAN)
D. Interrogator-Transponder Transit (ITT)
E. Distance-Measuring Equipment (DME)

Page(s) 620

Q4-031 The solder grade primarily used for electronics work, is:

A. 60% tin, 40% lead
B. 50% tin, 50% lead
C. 70% tin, 30% lead
D. 40% tin, 60% lead
E. 30% tin, 70% lead

Page(s) 101

Q4-032 If a transmitter has received "type acceptance":

A. the manufacturer has tested the transmitter to ensure that the specifications have been met
B. a General Radiotelephone licensee on board ship has tested the transmitter to ensure that the specifications have been met
C. the transmitter was built by a manufacturer who is licensed by the U.S. Government
D. the FCC has conducted tests on the transmitter to ensure that the specifications have been met
E. "type acceptance" is the step which follows "type approval"

Page(s) 617

Q4-033 The operating carrier power of marine transmitters with G3E or F3E emission in the 156- to 162-MHz frequency band, must not exceed:

A. 1 W
B. 3 W
C. 5 W

D. 10 W
E. 25 W

Page(s) 615

Q4-034 The rods of a vertical Hertz antenna are shortened in length. As a result, the:

A. antenna behaves as an inductive load
B. impedance of the antenna decreases
C. resonant frequency of the antenna increases
D. radiated power from the antenna increases
E. directivity of the antenna in the horizontal plane increases

Page(s) 412

Q4-035 A class-C RF amplifier stage:

A. operates with a high level of forward bias
B. provides minimum distortion of the collector current waveform
C. produces a collector output voltage which consists of narrow pulses
D. has a high level of efficiency
E. uses a resistor as its collector load

Page(s) 249, 250

Q4-036 An RF amplifier may be operated under linear class-B conditions (as opposed to class C) in order to:

A. amplify an AM signal
B. generate only even harmonics
C. generate only odd harmonics
D. increase the efficiency
E. increase the harmonic content in the output signal

Page(s) 326

Q4-037 The Urgency signal:

A. is preceded by the word PAN spoken three times
B. may be transmitted only on the authority of the Master of the ship carrying the marine station
C. has priority over all other communications except distress
D. is intercepted by mobile stations, which must continue to listen for at least three minutes
E. all of the above choices are true

Page(s) 600

Q4-038 Pre-emphasis in an FM transmitter means that:

A. the higher audio frequencies, above about 2000 Hz, are progressively accentuated as the audio frequency is increased
B. audio frequencies in the vicinity of 2000 Hz are accentuated
C. the higher audio frequencies above about 2000 Hz, are progressively attenuated as the audio frequency is increased
D. the frequency band between 2000 Hz and 15000 Hz is uniformly accentuated
E. frequencies up to 2000 Hz are accentuated, but higher frequencies are attenuated

Page(s) 370

Q4-039 Accurate measurements of resistance can be obtained by using a(n):

A. ohmmeter
B. voltmeter
C. ammeter
D. combination of a voltmeter and an ammeter
E. Wheatstone bridge

Page(s) 46 to 50

Q4-040 In an ac circuit, the effective values of the source voltage and the source current are kept constant. Initially, the voltage and the current are in phase, but as they move out of phase, the:

A. apparent power increases
B. reactive power decreases
C. true power is unchanged
D. power factor increases
E. true power decreases

Page(s) 124

Q4-041 Hand-held portable ship units are identified by:

A. callsign only
B. callsign and name of mothership
C. name of ship only
D. callsign and appropriate unit designator
E. appropriate unit designator only

Page(s) 596

Q4-042 Which of the following logic gates corresponds to the truth table of FIG. 4-3?

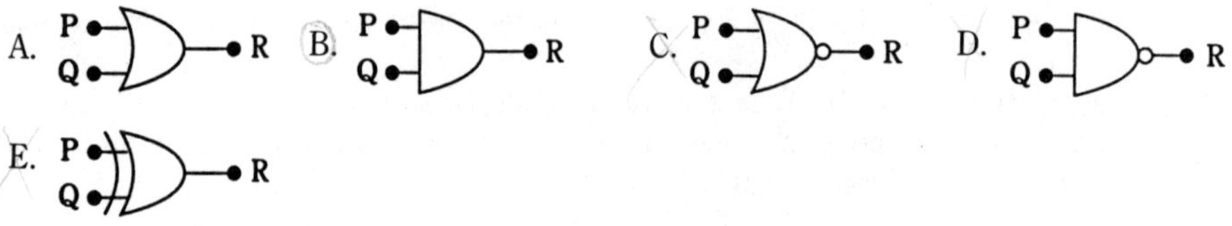

P	*Q*	*R*
Low	Low	Low
Low	High	Low
High	Low	Low
High	High	High

4-3 Truth table for Question 4-042.

Page(s) 325, 330

Q4-043 A - Alpha, B - Bravo, C - Charlie are part of the:

A. semantic system of communications
B. phonetic alphabet
C. morse vocabulary
D. telephonic dictionary
E. symbolic code

Page(s) 595

Q4-044 Two 0.1-μF capacitors are connected in series across a 120-Vdc source. The source is then removed and a third uncharged 0.1-μF capacitor is subsequently connected across the two series capacitors. What is the voltage across the third capacitor?

A. 120 V
B. 60 V
C. 80 V
D. 40 V
E. 0 V

Page(s) 75 to 77

Q4-045 In which of the following may a radio operator not engage?

A. communications containing obscene or profane words
B. transmission of false callsigns
C. willful or malicious interference
D. signals not addressed to a particular station
E. all of the above choices are true

Page(s) 592

Q4-046 An operator normally exhibits his/her authority to operate a marine station by:

A. posting a valid operator license or permit in the Master's cabin
B. posting a valid operator license or permit at the control point of the transmitter
C. keeping the original license or permit in his/her possession and posting a photostat copy at his/her place of duty
D. depositing the original license or permit in the ship's safe
E. keeping the original license on his/her person and exhibiting a "posting statement" at his/her place of work

Page(s) 598

Q4-047 A radio operator may request "Communication is difficult. Please send every phrase twice" by using the word(s):

A. repeat
B. words twice
C. say again
D. retransmit
E. message twice

Page(s) 591

Q4-048 Routine station logs are normally required to be retained for a period of:

A. 1 year
B. 2 years
C. 3 years
D. 5 years
E. these logs must be retained until the FCC authorizes their destruction

Page(s) 585, 586

Q4-049 Which of the following carrier frequencies is assigned to an on-board mobile communications unit?

A. 2182 kHz
B. 243 MHz
C. 156.8 MHz
D. 156.65 MHz
E. 467.75 MHz

Page(s) 590

Q4-050 Which of the following stages has a very high input impedance, a low output impedance, a voltage gain of approximately 0.98 and no phase change between its input and output signals?

A. common-collector stage
B. common-emitter amplifier
C. common-base amplifier
D. emitter follower
E. choices A and D are true

Page(s) 243, 244

Q4-051 At frequencies in the VHF band and the lower part of the UHF band, waveguides are not practical owing to excessive:

A. copper loss
B. dielectric loss
C. radiation loss
D. standing waves
E. size

Page(s) 453

Q4-052 When a marine transmitter uses double-sideband emission, the peak modulation must be maintained between:

A. 50% to 90%
B. 60% to 95%
C. 70% to 100%
D. 75% to 100%
E. 80% to 100%

Page(s) 588

Q4-053 The emission designation for frequency-shift keying (FSK) is:

A. A1A
B. A1B

C. F1A
D. F1B
E. F2C

Page(s) 380

Q4-054 The main advantage of an m-derived filter over the corresponding prototype circuit, is its:

A. simplicity of design
B. ability to be terminated by a high resistance load
C. sharper cutoff characteristic
D. low *Q* value
E. low resonant frequency

Page(s) 180 to 182

Q4-055 A dc supply voltage to a transmitter's final stage is 1220 V and the associated dc level of current is 320 mA. If the output carrier power is 250 W, the efficiency factor is:

A. 0.69
B. 0.59
C. 0.66
D. 0.73
E. 0.64

Page(s) 303, 304

Q4-056 Twelve nickel-cadmium cells are connected in series-aiding. What is the total available value of the EMF?

A. 1.25 V
B. 2.05 V
C. 12 V
D. 24 V
E. 15 V

Page(s) 51

Q4-057 In radio circuits, leads should be kept as short as possible so that:

A. skin effect is reduced
B. there is less hysteresis effect
C. stray coupling is minimized
D. there is less eddy current loss
E. there is less dielectric loss

Page(s) 174, 175

Q4-058 When a radio operator is required to "stand watch" on the International Radiotelephone Distress frequency, under which of the following circumstances may the operator cease to listen?

A. when the station is being used for transmission on 2182 kHz
B. when there is poor reception due to severe conditions of static and fading
C. when all received signals are badly distorted and barely intelligible

D. when the station is being used for communication on other channels
E. choices A and D are true

Page(s) 583

Q4-059 A 500-W transmitter is 100% amplitude modulated by a pure tone. The amount of the power in the lower sideband is:

A. 250 W
B. 125 W
C. 62.5 W
D. 500 W
E. 50 W

Page(s) 316, 317

Q4-060 In the circuit of FIG. 4-4, V_i = + 5 V, V_{ref} = + 3 V, V = 12 V. The value of V_o is:

A. +5 V
B. +3 V
C. +8 V
D. +12 V
E. −12 V

Page(s) 289, 290

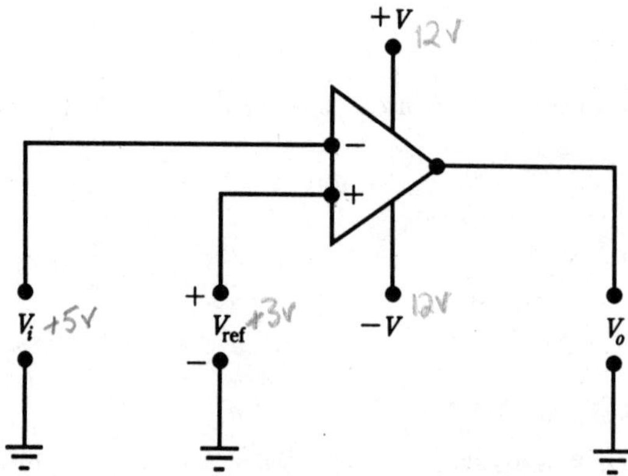

4-4 Circuit for Question 4-060.

Q4-061 An Emergency Locator Transmitter is operating on a frequency of 243 MHz with a tolerance of 50 parts per million (ppm). Which of the following frequencies lies within the quoted tolerance?

A. 243.012 MHz
B. 242.968 MHz
C. 243.013 MHz
D. 242.987 MHz
E. all of the above choices are within tolerance

Page(s) 572

Q4-062 Nitrogen gas is used in rigid coaxial cables in order to:

A. increase the value of the surge impedance
B. decrease the value of the surge impedance
C. increase the dielectric strength of the insulator
D. exclude moisture and avoid oxidation
E. reduce the value of the relative permittivity

Page(s) 399

Q4-063 For aircraft stations employing single-sideband transmissions, the frequency tolerance is:

A. 20 ppm
B. 30 ppm
C. 50 ppm
D. 20 Hz
E. 30 Hz

Page(s) 578, 579

Q4-064 On a matched transmission line, the voltage between the conductors at any position is equal to the:

A. product of the line current and the surge impedance
B. square root of the power divided by the surge impedance
C. power divided by the square of the surge impedance
D. result of dividing the line current by the surge impedance
E. square of the power divided by the square of the surge impedance

Page(s) 402

Q4-065 Upon completion of construction of a radio station, equipment tests may be carried out during a period not to exceed:

A. 5 days
B. 10 days
C. 15 days
D. 20 days
E. 30 days

Page(s) 576, 577

Q4-066 The system that contains a crystal oscillator, a varactor diode and an audio correction network is the:

A. AM transmitter
B. SSB transmitter
C. direct FM transmitter
D. indirect FM transmitter
E. PM receiver

Page(s) 376

Q4-067 De-emphasis in an FM receiver means that:

A. the higher audio frequencies, above about 2000 Hz, are progressively attenuated as the audio frequency is increased

B. audio frequencies in the vicinity of 2000 Hz are attenuated
C. the higher audio frequencies, above about 2000 Hz, are progressively accentuated as the audio frequency is increased
D. the frequency band between 2000 Hz and 15000 Hz is uniformly attenuated
E. frequencies up to 2000 Hz are attenuated, but higher frequencies are accentuated

Page(s) 388, 389

Q4-068 The Emergency Position Indicating Radio Beacon (E.P.I.R.B) must have its battery replaced:

A. when 50% of its useful life has expired
B. before the expiration date established by the manufacturer
C. once a year
D. after carrying out an operational test
E. choice A or choice B, whichever is earlier

Page(s) 573

Q4-069 In the circuit of FIG. 4-5, what is the voltage across the capacitor C, after the switch, S, has been closed for a time interval of 500 ms?

A. 0 V
B. 7.56 V
C. 3.78 V
D. 5 V
E. 12 V

Page(s) 79, 80

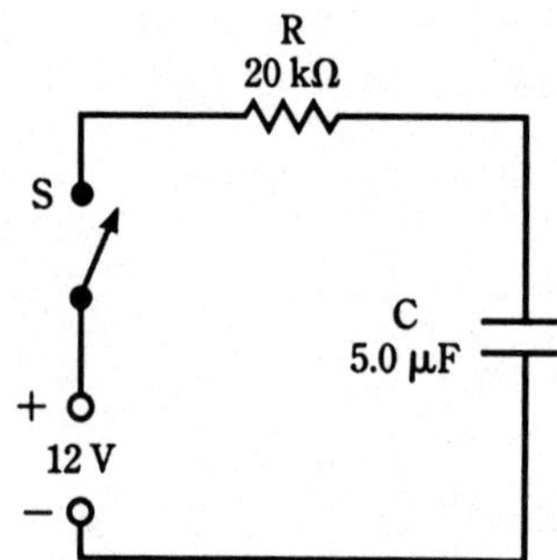

4-5 Circuit for Question 4-069.

Q4-070 The frequency range of the low-frequency (LF) band is:

A. 3 to 300 kHz
B. 30 to 300 Hz
C. 30 kHz to 3000 kHz
D. 30 to 300 kHz
E. 300 to 3000 kHz

Page(s) 443

Q4-071 Who of the following has the authority to order the transmission of a distress call?

A. the ship's radio operator
B. the holder of a General Radiotelephone License
C. the ship's Master
D. the ship's owner, if on board
E. choices C and D are true

Page(s) 568

Q4-072 To reduce high-frequency parasitic oscillation:

A. the circuit must be neutralized
B. low-value damping resistors are connected to the active device
C. RF chokes are connected in series with the low-value damping resistors
D. an additional resistor is connected between the input and output circuits of the active device
E. choices B and C are true

Page(s) 1

Q4-073 A callsign:

A. is a marine station's name and identification
B. is transmitted by a station so that other monitoring stations can easily identify the station of origin
C. must be sent clearly and distinctly so that unnecessary repetition of the call letters is avoided
D. consists of letters or a combination of letters and digits
E. all of the above choices are true

Page(s) 558, 559

Q4-074 A series L, C, R circuit consists of a 6-Ω resistor, a 5-μH inductor and a 5-pF capacitor. The resonant frequency of this circuit is:

A. 3.18 MHz
B. 31.8 MHz
C. 318 kHz
D. 31.8 kHz
E. 318 MHz

Page(s) 152

Q4-075 Bridge-to-bridge communications on Channel 13 are identified by:

A. name of the vessel in lieu of the callsign
B. callsign and country of registration
C. callsign, name of vessel, and country of registration
D. name of vessel and port of origin
E. name of vessel and port of destination

Page(s) 554, 555

Q4-076 A gain of 10 dB is equivalent to a power ratio of:

A. 2
B. 20
C. 10

D. 100
E. 5

Page(s) 145 to 147

Q4-077 If the carrier frequency is 2182 kHz with a frequency tolerance of ±10 ppm, the maximum permitted deviation is:

A. 218.2 Hz
B. 2.182 kHz
C. 21.82 Hz
D. 2.182 Hz
E. 0.2182 Hz

Page(s) 297

Q4-078 What is the international bridge-to-bridge frequency?

A. Channel 13
B. Channel 16
C. 156.65 MHz
D. 156.8 MHz
E. choices A and C are true

Page(s) 555

Q4-079 In the circuit of FIG. 4-6, the voltage across the resistor, R1, is:

A. 3 V
B. 4 V
C. 0.7 V
D. 6 V
E. 9 V

Page(s) 215, 216

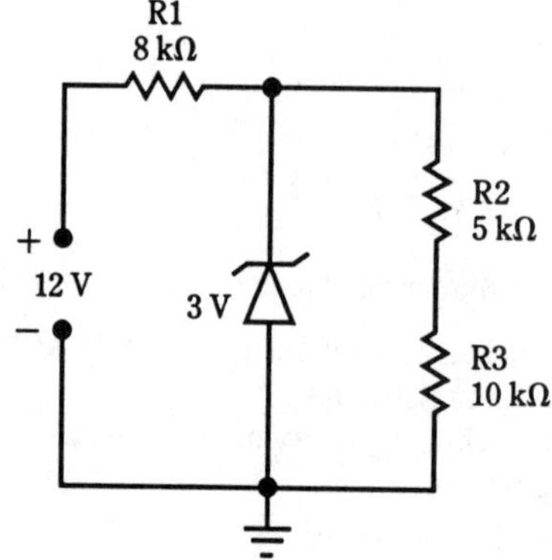

4-6 Circuit for Questions 4-079 and 4-080.

Q4-080 In QUES. 4-079, the voltage across the resistor, R2, is

A. 3 V
B. 2 V

C. 1 V
D. 0.7 V
E. 3.7 V

Page(s) 215, 216

Q4-081 It is required to increase the resonant frequency of an end-fed Marconi antenna. This may be achieved by:

A. adding a capacitor in series
B. adding an inductor in series
C. adding an inductor in parallel
D. reducing the physical length of the antenna
E. choices A and D are true

Page(s) 428

Q4-082 In FIG. 4-7, the ratio of the power dissipated in the parallel circuit to the power dissipated in the series circuit is:

A. 2:1
B. 1:2
C. 4:1
D. 1:4
E. 3:1

Page(s) 26 to 28, 36 to 38

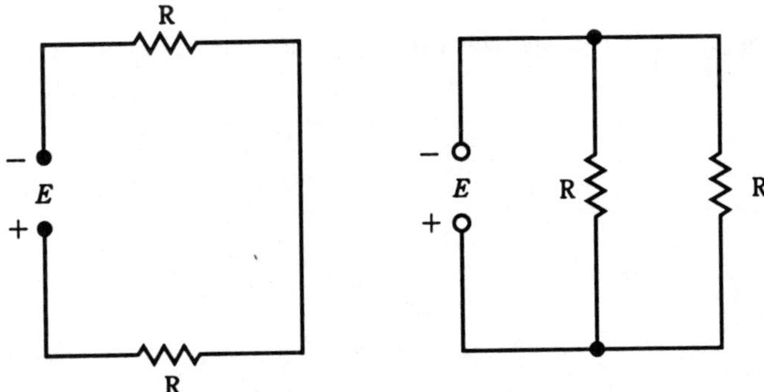

4-7 Circuit for Question 4-082.

Q4-083 Express a frequency tolerance of ± 10 ppm as a percentage.

A. ± 1%
B. ± 0.1%
C. ± 0.01
D. ± 0.001%
E. ± 0.0001%

Page(s) 297

Q4-084 When requesting an inspection of a Compulsory Ship Station, how long before the proposed inspection date must FCC Form 801 be submitted?

A. at least 3 days
B. at least 5 days
C. at least 10 days
D. at least 15 days
E. at least 30 days

Page(s) 549

Q4-085 The purpose of the radiotelephone auto-alarm system is to provide an alert that either a:

A. distress signal is about to follow
B. or a transmission of an urgent cyclone warning is about to follow
C. or there is information about the loss of a person or persons overboard
D. or an important safety message is about to follow
E. all of the above choices are true

Page(s) 551

Q4-086 A radiotelephone distress message from a ship's station, shall contain the following:

A. the word MAYDAY, spoken three times, followed by the words THIS IS
B. callsign of the station in distress, spoken three times
C. name of the ship in distress and ship's position
D. nature of distress and kind of assistance required. Details of any other information that may facilitate rescue
E. all of the above choices are true

Page(s) 568

Q4-087 In the circuit of FIG. 4-8, how many watts are supplied from the sine-wave voltage source?

A. 0 W
B. 1 W
C. 10 W
D. 20 W
E. 30 W

Page(s) 124

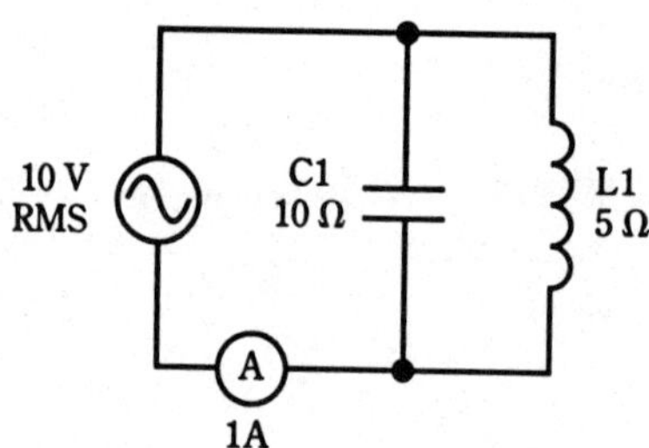

4-8 Circuit for Question 4-087.

Q4-088 Radiotelephone stations that use a shared channel:

A. should listen in on the channel first to avoid disrupting any communication that is already in progress
B. must decrease their operating powers by 20% to reduce the possibility of harmful interference
C. must limit each transmission to a period not exceeding five minutes
D. must leave an interval between calls
E. choices A and D are true

Page(s) 565

Q4-089 A communications superhet is receiving an A3E 2-MHz transmission in which the highest audio frequency is 4 kHz. The required bandwidth for the IF stages is at least:

A. 4 kHz
B. 2004 kHz
C. 2008 kHz
D. 2 kHz
E. 8 kHz

Page(s) 350

Q4-090 If a dc voltage across a resistance is doubled, by what factor must the resistance be multiplied if the dissipated power is unchanged?

A. 0.5
B. 4
C. 0.25
D. 2
E. none of the above choices is true

Page(s) 18 to 20

Q4-091 For successful operation, a Hartley oscillator requires:

A. sufficient positive feedback to overcome the circuit losses
B. a very low-*Q* tank circuit
C. indirect capacitive feedback from the output circuit to the input circuit
D. a tank coil that is grounded at its midpoint
E. a capacitive voltage divider

Page(s) 271, 272

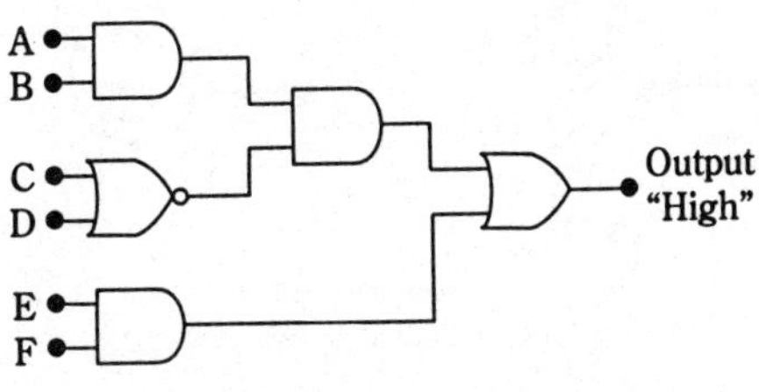

4-9 Circuit for Question 4-092.

Q4-092 Which of the following provides a high output from the logic circuit of FIG. 4-9?

A. A "high," B "low," C "low," D "low," E "high," F "high"
B. A "high," B "low," C "high," D "low," E "high," F "low"
C. A "high," B "high," C "low," D "high," E "high," F "low"
D. A "high," B "low," C "low," D "low," E "high," F "low"
E. A "high," B "low," C "low," D "low," E "high," F "low"

Page(s) 543 to 545

Q4-093 When a communications receiver is tuned to a strong signal, the delayed AGC bias is measured and found to be −2.4 V. If the receiver is now retuned to a very weak signal, the new bias is:

A. −2.4 V
B. −1.5 V to −2.0 V
C. −1.0 V to −1.5 V
D. −0.5 V to −1.0 V
E. 0

Page(s) 354

Q4-094 In FIG. 4-10, which of the symbols represents a DE MOSFET?

A. a
B. b
C. c
D. d
E. e

Page(s) 260 to 264

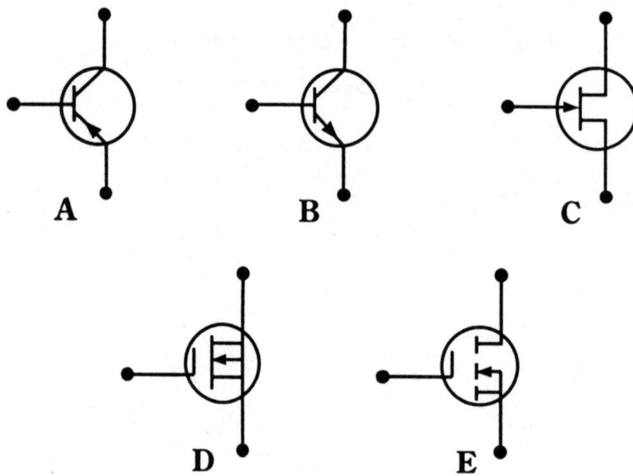

4-10 Symbols for Questions 4-094 and 4-095.

Q4-095 In FIG. 4-10, which of the symbols represents an E MOSFET?

A. a
B. b

C. c
D. d
E. e

Page(s) 260 to 264

Q4-096 A marine station's callsign is transmitted:

A. at the beginning of a communication
B. at the end of a communication
C. at 15-minute intervals during a lengthy communication
D. in the English language
E. all of the above choices are true

Page(s) 558, 559

Q4-097 A superhet receiver has an IF of 455 kHz and is experiencing image-channel interference on a frequency of 1570 kHz. The receiver is tuned to:

A. 1115 kHz
B. 660 kHz
C. 2025 kHz
D. 2480 kHz
E. 910 kHz

Page(s) 346

Q4-098 The circuit of FIG. 4-11:

A. will not provide voltage amplification
B. represents a common-emitter stage
C. uses a pnp transistor
D. is improperly grounded
E. introduces a 180° phase change between the input and output signals

Page(s) 237, 238

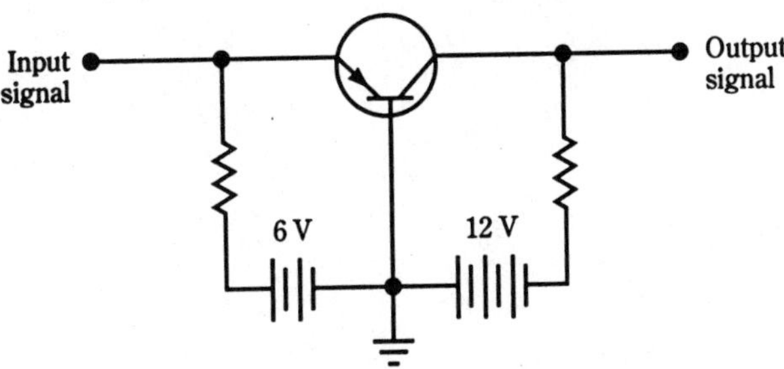

4-11 Circuit for Question 4-098.

Q4-099 The input impedance to an infinite length of RF transmission line:

A. has a phase angle of +90°
B. has a phase angle of −90°
C. is equal to $\sqrt{C/L}$ Ω

D. is equal to the surge impedance
E. choices C and D are true

Page(s) 397

Q4-100 Just before making a soldering connection, it is common practice to place a small amount of solder on the tip of a soldering iron. The purpose of this procedure is to:

A. decrease the amount of flux
B. reduce the temperature of the soldering iron's tip
C. allow the solder to wet the metals so that the solder can stick
D. remove any oxide film that may be present
E. none of the above is true

Page(s) 101, 102

Element 3
Test 5

Q5-001 A capacitor is charged to 100 V and is then switched across a resistor. When the voltage across the capacitor has fallen to 14 V, the duration of the discharge as measured in time constants, is approximately:

A. 0.3
B. 1.0
C. 2.0
D. 2.5
E. 3.0

Page(s) 621

Q5-002 Which of the following frequency groups are contained in the harmonic analysis of a 250-kHz symmetrical square wave?

A. 250 kHz, 500 kHz, 750 kHz, and all harmonic frequencies
B. 250 kHz, 500 kHz, 1000 kHz, and additional even harmonic components
C. 250 kHz, 125 kHz, 62.5 kHz, 31.25 kHz
D. 250 kHz, 750 kHz, 1250 kHz, 1750 kHz, and additional odd harmonic components
E. 250 kHz, 500 kHz, 1000 kHz, 2000 kHz, 4000 kHz.

Page(s) 192 to 194

Q5-003 Convert the decimal number, 5693_{10}, into its equivalent octal number.

A. 12674_8
B. 13075_8
C. 12973_8
D. 12563_8
E. 12773_8

Page(s) 520 to 521

Q5-004 For a radio wave traveling in free space, its velocity:

A. is constant
B. increases in the microwave region
C. is equal to the velocity of light
D. is constant only for frequencies above the VHF band
E. choices A and C are true

Page(s) 402

Q5-005 The limiter stage of an FM receiver:

A. limits the amplitude of the IF signal to the required level
B. removes all AM noise from the IF signal
C. behaves as a low-pass filter
D. behaves as a high-pass filter
E. choices A and B are true

Page(s) 384, 385

Q5-006 On the frequency of 2182 kHz, a radiotelephone silent period shall be observed for:

A. three minutes, commencing at the hour and the half hour
B. three minutes, commencing at the hour only
C. three minutes, commencing at 15 minutes and at 45 minutes past the hour
D. three minutes, commencing at the half hour only
E. five minutes, commencing at 15 minutes and at 45 minutes past the hour.

Page(s) 583, 584

Q5-007 A bipolar transistor is operated with both the emitter-base junction and the collector-base junction in the reverse biased condition. As a result, the:

A. transistor is cut off
B. transistor is in its saturation mode
C. transistor is acting as a linear amplifying device
D. transistor could be ruined
E. choices B and D are true

Page(s) 225, 226

Q5-008 The radiotelephone Urgency signal consists of the word:

A. pan, spoken three times
B. mayday, spoken three times
C. urgent, spoken three times
D. safety, spoken three times
E. security, spoken three times

Page(s) 600

Q5-009 The circuit in FIG. 5-1 represents a (an):

A. constant-k high-pass filter
B. constant-k low-pass filter
C. m-derived high-pass filter
D. constant-k band-pass filter
E. m-derived low-pass filter

Page(s) 177, 178

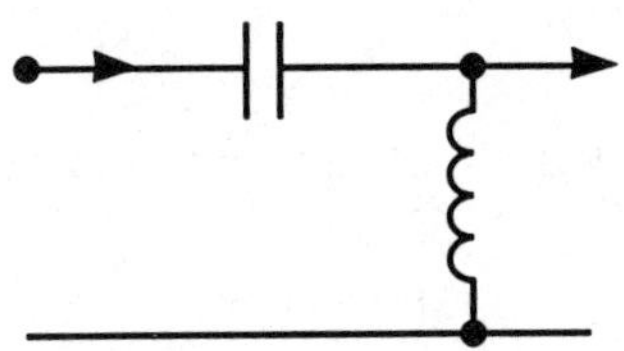

5-1 Circuit for Question 5-011

Q5-010 For a first offense, the penalty for willfully violating a provision of the Communication Act of 1934, is:

A. cancellation of the operator's license
B. a fine of not more than \$500.00 for each provision violated
C. a fine of not more than \$10000.00, or imprisonment for a term not exceeding two years, or both
D. a fine of not more than \$10000.00, or imprisonment for a term not exceeding one year, or both
E. a fine of not more than \$25000.00

Page(s) 618, 619

Q5-011 An AM transmitter has an assigned carrier frequency of 25 MHz. Measurements reveal that the actual carrier frequency under unmodulated conditions is 25.00025 MHz, but it shifts to 24.99950 MHz when the modulation is applied. Which of the following statements is correct?

A. if the allowed frequency tolerance is 0.003%, the transmission is illegal
B. if the allowed frequency tolerance is 0.001%, the transmission is legal
C. if the allowed frequency tolerance is 0.002%, the transmission is illegal
D. if the authorized frequency tolerance is 0.0005%, the transmission is legal
E. the question is in error because the carrier frequency cannot change when the modulation is applied

Page(s) 316, 317

Q5-012 The following information appears on the name plates of type-accepted transmitters:

A. name of the manufacturer
B. operating frequency
C. type of emission
D. FCC ID number
E. choices A and D are true

Page(s) 617

Q5-013 The antennas of two AM transmitters are close together. As a result the two modulated signals are mixed in the final RF stages of both transmitters. The resultant effect on other stations is called:

A. intermodulation interference
B. harmonic interference

C. spurious interference
D. crossmodulation interference
E. parasitic interference

Page(s) 326

Q5-014 Which of the following logic circuits corresponds to the truth table of FIG. 5-2?

A. NAND operation
B. NOR operation
C. OR operation
D. AND operation
E. NOT operation

Page(s) 532, 533

Input	Output
High Low	Low High

5-2 Truth table for Question 5-014.

Q5-015 In the marine service, which of the following has a higher priority than communications preceded by the urgency signal?

A. communications preceded by the safety signal
B. distress calls, distress messages and distress traffic
C. government radio telegrams
D. communications that relate to the navigation and safe movement of aircraft
E. communications that relate to radio-direction finding

Page(s) 599, 600

Q5-016 In the circuit of FIG. 5-3, V_i = + 2.7 V, V_{ref} = + 1.3 V, V = 15 V. The value of V_o is:

A. +2.7 V
B. +1.3 V

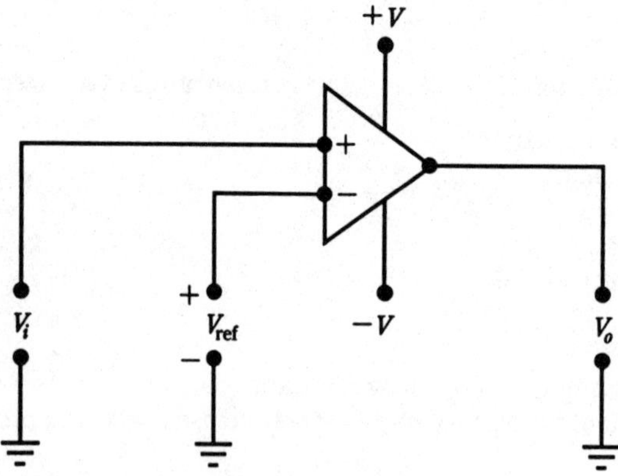

5-3 Circuit for Question 5-016.

C. −14 V
D. −15 V
E. +14 V

Page(s) 289, 290

Q5-017 A marine transmitter is connected to ground through:

A. a single copper conductor
B. AWG #22, #24, or higher gauge wire
C. multistrand wire, whose length is as short as possible
D. multistrand wire with each strand insulated from its neighbors
E. a braided copper strip

Page(s) 154, 155

Q5-018 An electrical circuit operated with a power of 242 W for a time of 31 hours. The amount of energy consumed is:

A. 242 W
B. 750 Wh
C. 7.5 kWh
D. 2.7×10^4 J
E. choices B and D are correct

Page(s) 13 to 15

Q5-019 A class-C collector current waveform contains a:

A. dc level together with ac fundamental and even harmonic components
B. dc level together with ac fundamental and odd harmonic components
C. dc level together with ac fundamental and harmonic components, both odd and even
D. dc level and only an ac fundamental component
E. dc level and subharmonic components

Page(s) 249, 250

Q5-020 Hand-held portable transmitters are identified:

A. by the callsign of the vessel followed by the appropriate unit designation
B. every 10 minutes
C. every 15 minutes
D. the name of the vessel followed by the appropriate unit designator
E. choices A and C are true

Page(s) 596

Q5-021 Express 6:00 PM Pacific Standard Time (PST) in terms of Universal Time Coordinated (UTC):

A. 1000 hrs
B. 0200 hrs
C. 0600 hrs
D. 1400 hrs
E. 2200 hrs

Page(s) 442

Q5-022 A word list that is useful in identifying letters or words that sound like other letters or words of different meaning, is known as the:

A. morse alphabet
B. radio alphabet
C. phonetic alphabet
D. telephonic vocabulary
E. word alphabet

Page(s) 595

Q5-023 To correct the circuit of FIG. 5-4:

A. reverse the diode, D4
B. reverse the diode, D2
C. reverse both the diodes, D2 and D4
D. reverse both the diodes, D1 and D3
E. reverse the diode, D1

Page(s) 210 to 214

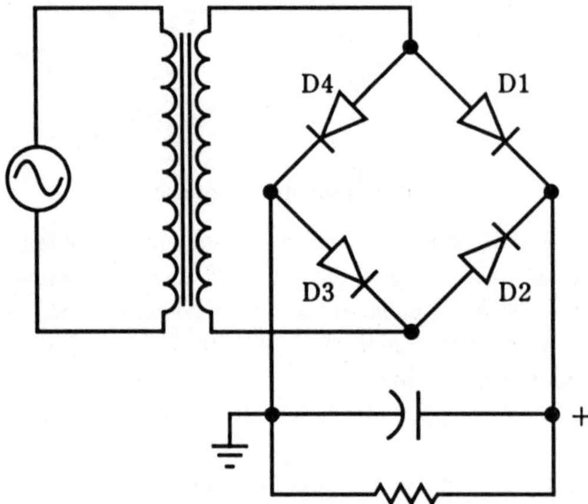

5-4 Circuit for Question 5-023.

Q5-024 The known values for a transmitter are as follows: dc supply voltage to the final stage is 600 V, associated dc level of current for the final stage is 0.3 A, antenna current at the feedpoint is 3 A, and antenna resistance at resonance is 15 Ω. Calculate the value of the efficiency factor:

A. 0.75
B. 0.80
C. 0.72
D. 0.65
E. 0.55

Page(s) 303

Q5-025 The word "Roger" is used by an operator to signify that:

A. "I have received all of your last transmission"
B. "your last message received, understood and will be complied with"

C. "my transmission is ended and I expect a response from you"
D. "the transmission is ended and no response is expected"
E. "part of the transmission has been sent and there will be a pause before sending the remainder of the message"

Page(s) 591

Q5-026 The rate at which the frequency swings in an FM transmitter is determined by the:

A. amplitude of the modulating signal
B. modulating frequency
C. carrier frequency
D. phase angle of the modulating signal
E. carrier amplitude

Page(s) 361, 362

Q5-027 Which of the following is not grounds for suspension of operator licenses?

A. malicious interference with other radio communications
B. violation of any provision of any act or treaty binding on the United States
C. willful damage to radio equipment
D. knowingly transmitting false or deceptive signals
E. transmission of superfluous radio communications

Page(s) 608

Q5-028 Which of the following could cause packing of the granules in a carbon microphone?

A. connecting the microphone to the battery with the polarity reversed
B. moisture
C. too high a level of current
D. speaking close to the microphone in a loud voice
E. choices B and C are true

Page(s) 323, 324

Q5-029 The purpose of an FM discriminator stage is to:

A. convert amplitude variations of the IF signal into audio information
B. improve the signal-to-noise ratio of the audio signal
C. convert frequency variations of the IF signal into audio information
D. de-emphasize the FM signal before its detection
E. reverse the pre-emphasis process which occurred in the FM transmitter

Page(s) 387, 388

Q5-030 The frequency of a crystal oscillator is shifted slightly if:

A. a resistor is added in series with the crystal
B. an inductor is added in series with the crystal
C. an capacitor is added in series with the crystal
D. an inductor is added in parallel with the crystal
E. a capacitor is added in parallel with the crystal

Page(s) 278

Q5-031 When a 100-W signal is fed to an attenuator, the power level of the output signal is only 1 mW. The loss provided by the attenuator is:

A. 100 dB
B. 50 dB
C. 30 dB
D. 20 dB
E. 10 dB

Page(s) 145 to 147

Q5-032 To call another ship when the working frequency lies in the 1605- to 3500-kHz band,

A. the first step is to monitor the working frequency
B. if the working frequency is clear, initiate the call on the frequency of 1282 kHz
C. the callsignal should not continue for more than 30 seconds
D. if there is no reply to the call, the callsignal shall not be repeated until after an interval of two minutes
E. all of the above choices are true

Page(s) 557

Q5-033 The frequency range of the very low frequency (VLF) band is:

A. 3 to 30 MHz
B. 30 to 300 kHz
C. 3 to 30 kHz
D. 3 to 30 Hz
E. 300 to 3000 Hz

Page(s) 443

Q5-034 The durable nameplate mounted on a marine transmitter indicates the:

A. date on which the transmitter was placed into service
B. dates on which the transmitter was inspected
C. assigned frequency
D. assigned power
E. name of manufacturer and model number

Page(s) 617

Q5-035 In the vicinity of a receiver, the modulation of an unwanted signal is transferred to the desired carrier. This effect is called:

A. image-channel interference
B. adjacent-channel interference
C. crossmodulation
D. intermodulation
E. modulation mixing

Page(s) 357

Q5-036 Which of the following is the operating frequency of the main transmitter on a compulsory ship?

A. 500 kHz
B. 2182 kHz
C. 156.8 MHz
D. 156.65 MHz
E. 121.5 MHz

Page(s) 616

Q5-037 The beam intensity of a cathode ray tube is primarily controlled by the:

A. heater voltage
B. grid-to-cathode voltage
C. horizontal accelerating voltage
D. second anode voltage
E. horizontal deflection voltage

Page(s) 189, 190

Q5-038 A 1-mW signal is the input to an attenuator which provides a loss of −40 dB. The power output of the attenuator is:

A. 0.1 μW
B. 1 μW
C. 10 μW
D. 0.1 mW
E. 0.01 μW

Page(s) 145 to 147

Q5-039 When an input signal is present, the circuit of FIG. 5-5 is operated as a class-B stage. In the absence of an input signal, the forward bias applied to the emitter-base junction is:

A. 15 V
B. 5 V
C. 4.3 V
D. 0.7 V
E. 10 V

Page(s) 233, 234

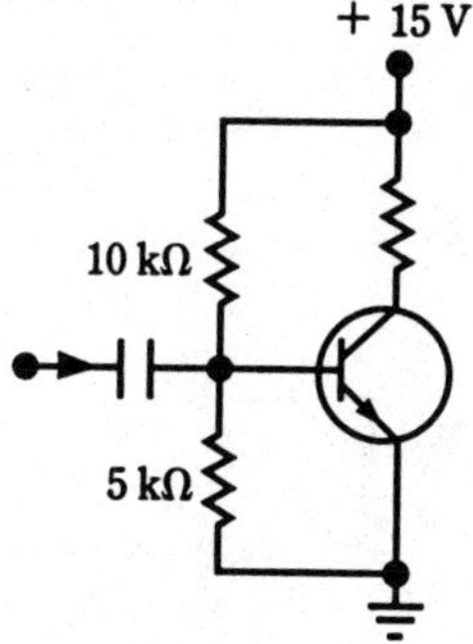

5-5 Circuit for Question 5-039.

Q5-040 Except for distress, urgency or safety messages, marine stations licensed to transmit radiotelephony must observe a silent period:

A. for three minutes after 15 minutes past the hour
B. for three minutes after 45 minutes past the hour
C. for three minutes after the hour

D. for three minutes after the half-hour
E. choices C and D are true

Page(s) 583, 584

Q5-041 A transmitter has an assigned frequency of 50 MHz, but its operating frequency is 50.01 MHz. The percentage of variance is:

A. 0.02%
B. 0.002%
C. 0.001%
D. 0.01%
E. 0.05%

Page(s) 301

Q5-042 In the circuit of FIG. 5-6, calculate the value of the maximum power that can be developed in the load, R_L:

A. 30 W
B. 7.5 W
C. 15 W
D. 20 W
E. 25 W

Page(s) 115

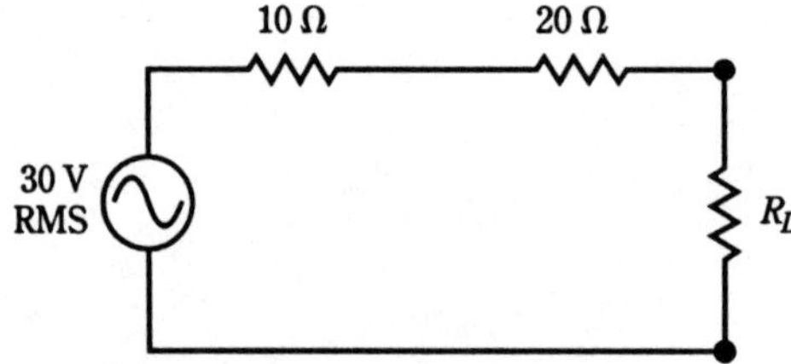

5-6 Circuit for Question 5-042.

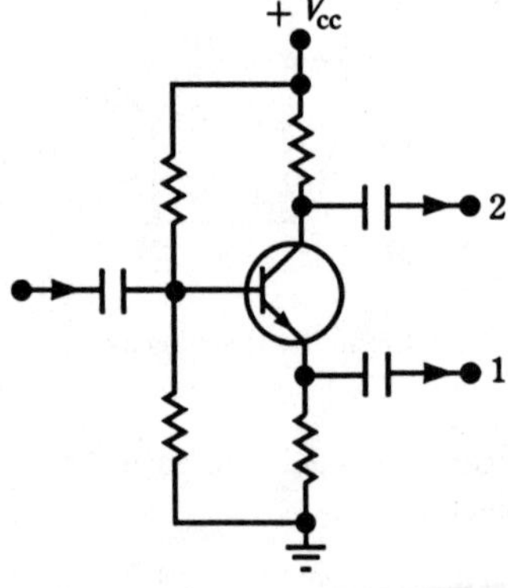

5-7 Circuit for Question 5-043.

Q5-043 The circuit shown in FIG. 5-7 is a:

A. signal doubler
B. balanced collector-emitter amplifier
C. phase inverter
D. collector feedback amplifier
E. collector-emitter follower

Page(s) 244, 245

Q5-044 Which of the following best describes the ILS instrument system? It is:

A. an aircraft's cockpit instrument which provides two separate items of information in relation to the runway
B. a system of vertical guidance only
C. a system of horizontal guidance only
D. an aircraft's cockpit instrument, which provides three separate items (height, horizontal deviation, and bearing) of information in relation to the runway
E. part of the DME system

Page(s) 582

Q5-045 An FM broadcast receiver is experiencing interference from an airport tower's transmitter which is operating on 121.4 MHz. If the receiver is tuned to a station whose carrier frequency is close to 100 MHz, the most likely reason for the problem is:

A. mistuning of the transmitter's wave traps
B. intermodulation
C. misalignment of the receiver's intermediate frequency amplifiers
D. image-channel interference
E. harmonic interference

Page(s) 382

Q5-046 A marine transmitter is operating on a frequency of 216 MHz. The frequency tolerance of this transmitter is:

A. 5 ppm
B. 10 ppm
C. 10 Hz
D. 20 Hz
E. 100 Hz

Page(s) 579

Q5-047 The emission, R3E, stands for:

A. single sideband, suppressed carrier, telephony
B. double sideband, reduced carrier, telephony
C. single sideband, full carrier, telephony
D. double sideband, telephony
E. single sideband, reduced carrier, telephony

Page(s) 332 to 334

Q5-048 The operating carrier frequencies of marine transmitters shall be determined:

A. when a transmitter is originally installed
B. when any change or adjustment is made that could affect a transmitter's operating frequency or its stability
C. upon receipt of an official notice of off-frequency operation
D. before the transmitter is removed prior to replacement
E. choices A, B, and C are true

Page(s) 577

Q5-049 The operating frequency of the loran C navigational system is:

A. 10.2 kHz
B. 100 MHz
C. 100 kHz
D. 102 kHz
E. 2182 kHz

Page(s) 439

Q5-050 On which of the following frequencies do class-A and class-B EPIRBs operate?

A. 156.8 MHz
B. 156.75 MHz
C. 121.5 MHz
D. 243 MHz
E. choices C and D are true

Page(s) 573, 574

Q5-051 The tuned-primary and tuned-secondary circuits of an IF amplifier are tightly coupled. As a result:

A. the amplifier has a narrow bandwidth
B. the secondary response at the intermediate frequency is increased
C. the amplifier has a wide frequency response
D. there is maximum power transfer from the primary circuit to the secondary circuit
E. the amplifier's overall *Q* is increased

Page(s) 350

Q5-052 The Emergency Position Indicating Radio Beacon (E.P.I.R.B) should be checked to ensure proper operation:

A. prior to leaving port
B. daily
C. only after its use in an emergency situation
D. once a month
E. once a year

Page(s) 573, 574

Q5-053 The frequency range of the microwave region is generally regarded as extending from:

A. 1 to 500 MHz
B. 1000 to 10000 GHz
C. 1 to 1000 GHz
D. 10 to 100 GHz
D. 300 to 3000 MHz

Page(s) 448

Q5-054 Under which of the following conditions may the output power of a bridge-to-bridge transmitter exceed 1 W?

A. when communicating with a coastal station and the vessel is more than 100 miles away from U.S. shores
B. when transmitting on a frequency other than the international bridge-to-bridge frequency
C. when rounding a bend in a river
D. when the transmitter is not being used for a navigational purpose
E. the output power of a bridge-to-bridge transmitter must never exceed 1 W

Page(s) 554, 555

Q5-055 In order to correct the common emitter amplifier circuit of FIG. 5-8,

A. reverse the collector battery
B. reverse both batteries
C. reverse the base battery
D. the ground point must be shifted
E. the circuit is correct as shown

Page(s) 239, 240

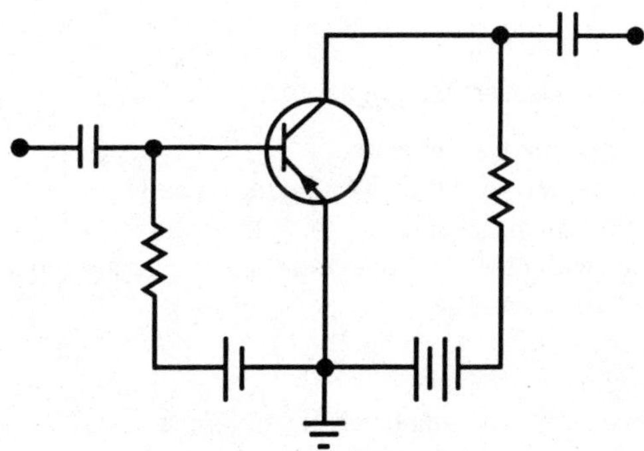

5-8 Circuit for Question 5-055.

Q5-056 A communications system for the transmission of fixed images that are recorded in a permanent form, is called:

A. teletype
B. telegraphy
C. facsimile
D. image projection
E. radio photography

Page(s) 380

Q5-057 In the VHF band of 156 to 162 MHz, the radiotelephone distress frequency and type of emission are:

A. 156.65 MHz, G3E
B. 156.8 MHz, J3E

C. 158.6 MHz, F3E
D. 156.8 MHz, G3E
E. 156.6 MHz, J3E

Page(s) 570

Q5-058 The frequency of the fifth harmonic of a 520-kHz signal is:

A. 2650 kHz
B. 2600 Hz
C. 2.6 MHz
D. 104 kHz
E. 2.6 kHz

Page(s) 106, 107

Q5-059 The percentage of modulation for an AM transmitter is increased from 50% to 80%. The percentage increase in the antenna current is:

A. 6.5%
B. 8.3%
C. 10.6%
D. 11.5%
E. 12.4%

Page(s) 330, 331

Q5-060 Overmodulation of a transmitted signal could:

A. be caused by the transmitter's circuitry
B. be caused by the operator shouting into the microphone
C. cause severe distortion of the audio signal at the receiver
D. cause interference with other stations operating on nearby frequencies
E. all of the above choices are true

Page(s) 567

Q5-061 Two 0.1-μF capacitors are connected in parallel across a 120-Vdc source. The voltage source is then removed and a third uncharged 0.1-μF capacitor is connected across the parallel combination. The voltage across the third capacitor is:

A. 80 V
B. 120 V
C. 60 V
D. 0 V
E. 40 V

Page(s) 76, 77

Q5-062 For a particular transmitter, the details of its type of emission are shown:

A. on the durable nameplate which is attached to the transmitter
B. on the front page of the station log
C. in CFR Title 47 of the FCC Rules and Regulations
D. on the back of the radio station's license
E. details on the type of emission are provided by the FCC upon application

Page(s) 576

Q5-063 Which of the following is the symbol for a zener diode?

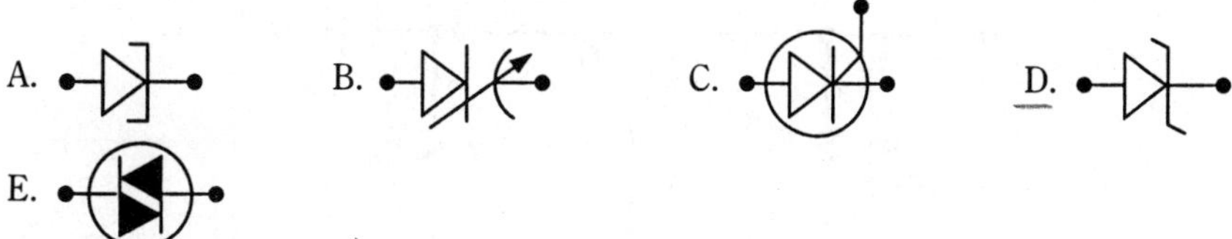

Page(s) 215, 216

Q5-064 A Marconi antenna radiates a fundamental power output of 500 W. If the power output at the second harmonic is 0.5 W, the attenuation of the second harmonic component, when compared with the fundamental component, is:

A. 1000 dB
B. 5 dB
C. 20 dB
D. 30 dB
E. 10 dB

Page(s) 426 to 430

Q5-065 A vessel maintains a simultaneous watch on both calling and common working frequencies. When communicating with this vessel, the initial call is made on:

A. 2128 kHz
B. 156.8 MHz
C. the calling frequency
D. the common working frequency
E. Channel 13

Page(s) 559

Q5-066 A voltmeter on its 0-50 V range has a total resistance of 50 kΩ. The value of the instrument's sensitivity is:

A. 1000 Ω/V
B. 1000 V/Ω
C. 5.000 Ω/V
D. 5000 V/Ω
E. 10000 Ω/V

Page(s) 87, 88

Q5-067 Which of the following represents the correct procedure for calling another station?

A. KXYZ - KXYZ - KXYZ. This is KABC - KABC - KABC. Over
B. KXYZ - KXYZ - KXYZ. This is KABC. Over
C. KXYZ. This is KABC. Over
D. KXYZ - KXYZ - KXYZ. This is KABC - KABC - KABC. Out
E. KXYZ - KXYZ - KXYZ. This is KABC. Out

Page(s) 558

Q5-068 What, if anything, is wrong with the circuit of FIG. 5-9?

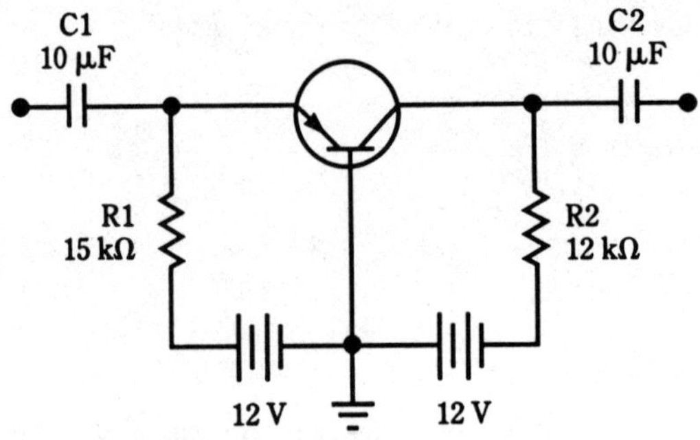

5-9 Circuit for Question 5-068.

A. the emitter-base bias battery must be reversed
B. the collector-base bias battery must be reversed
C. the voltage of the emitter-base bias battery is too large
D. the voltage of the collector-base bias battery is too large
E. the circuit is correct as shown

Page(s) 237, 238

Q5-069 At sea, the best frequency to use for bridge-to-bridge communications is:

A. 2450 kHz
B. 121.5 MHz
C. 243 MHz
D. 156.65 MHz
E. 157.75 MHz

Page(s) 554, 555

Q5-070 Which of the following statements are true for the combinatorial logic circuit of FIG. 5-10?

A. points A and B are both "low," but point C is "high"
B. point A is "high," but points B and C are both "low"

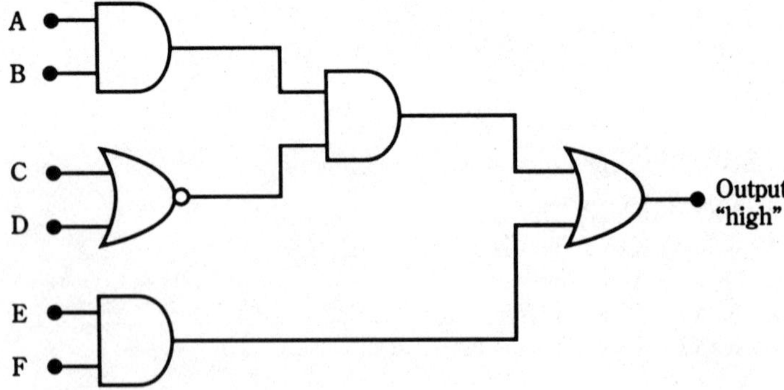

5-10 Logic circuit for Question 5-070.

C. points A and C are "low," but point B is "high"
D. points A, B, and C are all "high"
E. points A and B are both "high," but point C is "low"

Page(s) 543 to 545

Q5-071 The emission designation for FM telephony is:

A. G3E
B. J3E
C. F3E
D. R3E
E. H3E

Page(s) 380

Q5-072 What is the minimum power capability of a bridge-to-bridge transmitter?

A. 500 mW
B. 400 mW
C. 0.7 W
D. 1 W
E. 3 W

Page(s) 554, 555

Q5-073 The effect of adding parasitic elements to a Hertz dipole, is to:

A. increase the antennas's power gain
B. make the antenna more omnidirectional
C. make the antenna more unidirectional
D. reduce its resonant frequency
E. choices A and C are true

Page(s) 421, 422

Q5-074 A vessel with a compulsory ship station is at sea. Which of the following systems must be active when no radio operator is on watch?

A. Emergency Position-Indicating Radio Beacon
B. the auto-alarm system
C. emergency transmitter
D. bridge-to-bridge transmitter
E. portable ship units

Page(s) 551

Q5-075 A transmitter has an assigned carrier frequency of 16 MHz with a tolerance of ±200 ppm. Between the final amplifier and the oscillator are three doubler stages. The maximum permitted frequency deviation at the oscillator is:

A. 40 Hz
B. 400 Hz
C. 800 Hz
D. 1600 Hz
E. 3200 Hz

Page(s) 301

Q5-076 A dc voltage is applied across a certain value of resistance. If the resistance value is halved, by what factor must the voltage be multiplied if the dissipated power is unchanged?

A. 0.5
B. 4
C. 0.25
D. 2
E. 0.707

Page(s) 18

Q5-077 If a voltage difference exists between two points, but there is no current flowing:

A. there is no electric field intensity between the points
B. an electrostatic field exists between the points
C. an arc will ultimately occur
D. a magnetic field exists between the points
E. the voltage cannot exist without a current flowing

Page(s) 71

Q5-078 Test transmissions of a marine radiotelephone installation are sent:

A. in order to find out whether other stations are maintaining their required testing watch
B. to ensure that the radio equipment is functioning normally
C. in order to assess the FCC's monitoring capabilities
D. with the use of an unmodulated carrier
E. choices A, B, and C are true

Page(s) 610

Q5-079 In FIG.5-11 identify pin 10 of the microchip:

A. a
B. b
C. c
D. d
E. e

Page(s) 226

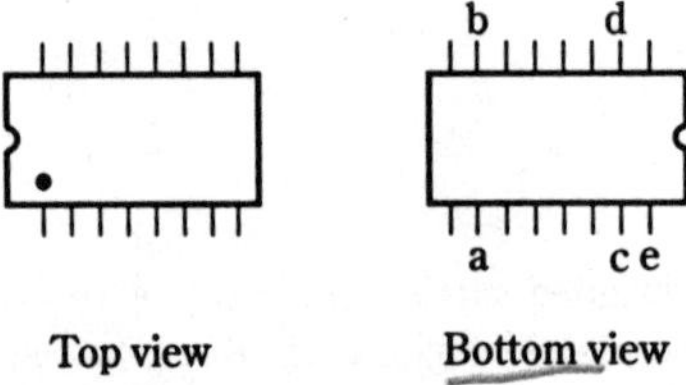

5-11 Pin identification for Question 5-079.

Q5-080 Which of the following is the ferrite device that buffers a microwave source from the effects of a varying load, and thereby prevents the formation of standing waves on the connecting waveguide?

A. circulator
B. isolator

C. diplexer
D. duplexer
E. inhibitor

Page(s) 470

Q5-081 All flashing or rotating beacons and automatic lighting control devices must be inspected:

A. every 24 hours
B. once every week
C. once every month
D. once every three months
E. once every six months

Page(s) 612

Q5-082 The deviation ratio of an FM transmitter is the ratio of the:

A. maximum frequency swing to the highest modulating frequency
B. operating frequency to the assigned frequency
C. frequency swing to the modulating frequency
D. highest modulating frequency to the minimum frequency deviation
E. lowest modulating frequency to the maximum frequency deviation

Page(s) 362

Q5-083 A crystal-controlled marine transmitter must have its output carrier frequency checked at least once every:

A. day
B. week
C. month
D. three months
E. year

Page(s) 615

Q5-084 Which of the following is best for long distance FM communications?

A. narrow-band system
B. A UHF carrier frequency, as opposed to one in the VHF band
C. a single-sideband FM system
D. wide-band system
E. few frequency multiplier stages in the transmitter

Page(s) 372

Q5-085 If the Hertz antenna is too short, this dipole can be brought to resonance by:

A. adding a capacitor in series with the antenna
B. lowering the frequency of the transmitter
C. adding an inductor in series with the antenna
D. adding a capacitor in parallel with the antenna
E. using a short length of transmission line

Page(s) 412

Q5-086 One disadvantage of a TRF receiver is:

A. unsatisfactory reception of strong signals
B. poor sensitivity at low frequencies
C. the requirement of a local oscillator for the reception of telephony
D. poor selectivity at high frequencies
E. the requirement for a detector stage

Page(s) 342, 343

Q5-087 A voltage source has a no-load terminal PD of 660 V and a full-load terminal PD of 600 V. The value of the percentage regulation is:

A. 9%
B. 10%
C. 11%
D. 12%
E. 15%

Page(s) 521

Q5-088 If a marine transmitter is left unattended by a radio operator:

A. all power must be removed from the transmitter
B. the microphone must be removed
C. the antenna must be disconnected from the transmitter
D. the transmitter must be rendered inaccessible to all unauthorized personnel
E. choices A and D are true

Page(s) 618

Q5-089 A 100-Ω 10-W resistor and a 50-Ω 10-W resistor are connected in parallel across a dc source. Without exceeding the wattage rating of either resistor, what is the maximum power that this circuit can safely dissipate?

A. 20 W
B. 10 W
C. 13.3 W
D. 15 W
E. 12.5 W

Page(s) 36 to 40

Q5-090 The known values for a transmitter are as follows: dc supply voltage to the final stage = 500 V, associated dc level of current for the final stage = 0.4 A, antenna current at the feedpoint = 3.2 A, antenna resistance at resonance = 15 Ω, efficiency factor = 0.7. Calculate the value of the operating power by the direct method:

A. 140 W
B. 154 W
C. 200 W
D. 173 W
E. 168 W

Page(s) 303

Q5-091 An RF transmission line whose surge impedance is 100 Ω, conveys a power of 200 watts. Assuming that the line is loss-free and is matched to a resistive load, the value of the line current is:

A. 2 A
B. 4 A
C. 1 A
D. 1.4 A
E. 0.71 A

Page(s) 402

Q5-092 The international radiotelephone alarm signal consists of:

A. two sinusoidal audio tones with frequencies of 2300 and 1200 Hz
B. two sinusoidal audio tones that are transmitted alternately, each with a duration of 200 ms
C. A combination of two tones which must be transmitted continuously for at least 20 seconds
D. two sinusoidal audio tones with frequencies of 2200 and 1300 Hz
E. two sinusoidal audio tones that are transmitted alternately, each with a duration of 300 ms

Page(s) 551

Q5-093 An electrical current in a copper wire is equivalent to a flow of:

A. negative ions
B. positive ions
C. valence electrons
D. positive neutrons
E. protons

Page(s) 6, 7

Q5-094 Express a distance of 1.74 nautical miles in terms of land or statute miles:

A. 2.00
B. 2.15
C. 1.50
D. 1.62
E. 1.13

Page(s) 402, 403

Q5-095 In FIG. 5-12, the local oscillator is generating a frequency of 2675 kHz. The receiver is tuned to a carrier frequency of:

A. 2220 kHz
B. 1765 kHz
C. 3030 kHz
D. 3585 kHz
E. 90 kHz

Page(s) 345, 346

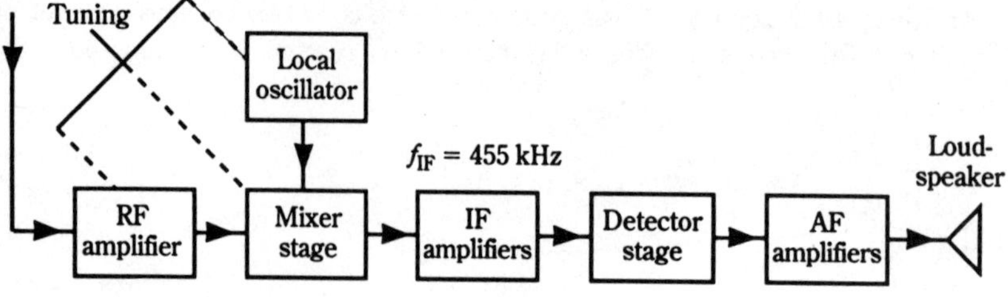

5-12 Block diagram For Question 5-095.

Q5-096 A varactor diode can be used in a(an):

A. direct FM modulator circuit
B. AFC circuit in a direct FM transmitter
C. frequency-multiplier device in the microwave region
D. phase-modulator circuit
E. all of the above choices are true

Page(s) 369, 372

Q5-097 High selectivity occurs when the degree of coupling between a receiver's RF stages, is:

A. tight
B. critical
C. adjusted for maximum power transfer
D. adjusted for maximum voltage gain
E. loose

Page(s) 348

Q5-098 The main advantage of frequency-shift keying over on/off keying is:

A. its narrower bandwidth
B. the improvement in the receiver's quieting
C. the receiver's AGC bias is maintained at a less constant level
D. its greater power requirement
E. choices B and C are true

Page(s) 378, 379

Q5-099 The maximum range in nautical miles of marine VHF transmissions, is normally:

A. 15
B. 20
C. 30
D. 40
E. 50

Page(s) 439, 440

Q5-100 On a compulsory ship, a radiotelephone communications system can be installed in lieu of a radiotelegraph system, provided that the ship's tonnage does not equal or exceed:

A. 300
B. 600
C. 900
D. 1200
E. 1600

Page(s) 562

Element 3
Test 6

Q6-001 An RF transmission line is used to connect a transmitter to its antenna. If the power output of the transmitter to the line is 1000 W and the line introduces an attenuation of 20 dB, the amount of power reaching the antenna is:

A. 10 W
B. 50 W
C. 1 W
D. 500 W
E. 100 W

Page(s) 400

Q6-002 When applying for a new ship station license, how many days before the license is needed, must the application be submitted?

A. at least 3 days
B. at least 10 days
C. at least 15 days
D. at least 30 days
E. at least 60 days

Page(s) 549

Q6-003 A choke joint:

A. has two flanges that are mechanically separated by a half wavelength
B. provides a loss of 0.3 dB
C. is used with rotating waveguide sections
D. is used when two waveguide sections are joined in parallel
E. presents an inductive reactance to the waveguide

Page(s) 455, 456

Q6-004 In bridge-to-bridge communications, the power output of the transmitter is limited to 1 watt:

A. when there is an emergency
B. when rounding a bend in a river
C. when a ship fails to respond to a call
D. under normal navigational conditions
E. when the vessel is navigating through a blind spot

Page(s) 554, 555

Q6-005 Four complete sequences of a square wave occur in 100 ms. How many complete cycles of the square wave occur in 790°?

A. 1
B. 2
C. 3
D. 4
E. 5

Page(s) 621

Q6-006 The RF power output of a transmitter is 25 W, but as a result of an impedance mismatch, the reflected power is 5 W. What value of power is entered in the transmitter's log?

A. 25 W
B. 5 W
C. 20 W
D. 30 W
E. 15 W

Page(s) 408

Q6-007 A bridge-to-bridge transmitter is operating on Channel 13 with a power output of 15 W. This is legal if:

A. the ship being called on low power fails to respond
B. the ship is rounding a bend in a river
C. there is an emergency situation
D. the ship is navigating through a blind spot
E. all of the above choices are true

Page(s) 554, 555

Q6-008 The ratio of a modulated signal to the noise level is 20:1. This is equivalent to:

A. 20 dB quieting
B. 10 dB quieting
C. 3 dB quieting
D. 30 dB quieting
E. 13 dB quieting

Page(s) 321

Q6-009 The percentage modulation of an FM transmitter is determined by the:

A. amplitude of the carrier
B. modulating frequency
C. carrier frequency
D. amplitude of the modulating signal
E. phase angle of the modulating signal

Page(s) 362

Q6-010 The time constant of an RC circuit is the:

A. time taken by the capacitor to charge completely after the source voltage is initially applied
B. time taken by the capacitor to charge to 39.3% of the source voltage
C. time taken for the capacitor to discharge to 50% of its initial voltage
D. time taken by the capacitor to charge to 63.2% of the source voltage
E. time taken for the capacitor to discharge to 63.2% of its initial voltage

Page(s) 77, 78

Q6-011 A unit of electrical energy is the:

A. joule
B. watt-second
C. watt-hour
D. kilowatt-hour
E. all of the above are true

Page(s) 10

Q6-012 What defect, if any, exists in the circuit of FIG. 6-1?

A. the RFC choke is not required
B. the diode, D1, must be reversed
C. the diode, D2, must be reversed
D. C1 should be removed
E. the circuit is grounded at the wrong point

Page(s) 388

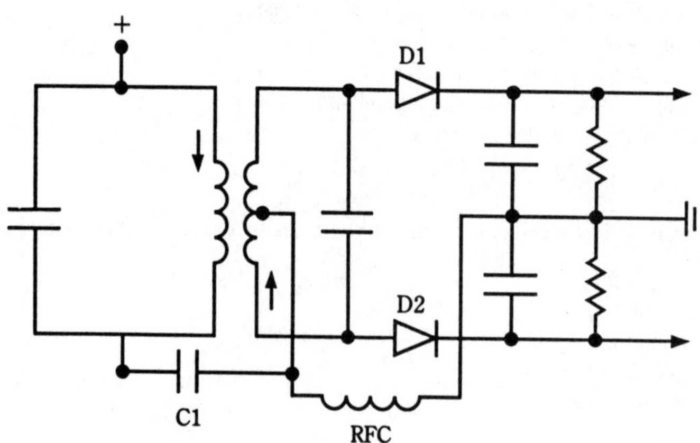

6-1 Circuit for Question 6-010.

Q6-013 The frequency tolerance of a 2-MHz oscillator is ± 0.002%. Between the crystal oscillator and the output amplifier of the transmitter are the three doubler stages. The maximum permitted deviation of the output frequency is:

A. 3.2 kHz
B. 320 Hz
C. 32 kHz
D. 0.32 MHz
E. 32 Hz

Page(s) 301

Q6-014 The circuit of FIG. 6-2 represents a crystal oscillator that is operating on the third overtone. If the crystal has a fundamental frequency of 1 MHz, the output frequency is:

A. 1 MHz
B. 2 MHz
C. 3 MHz
D. 4 MHz
E. 333 kHz

Page(s) 273 to 278

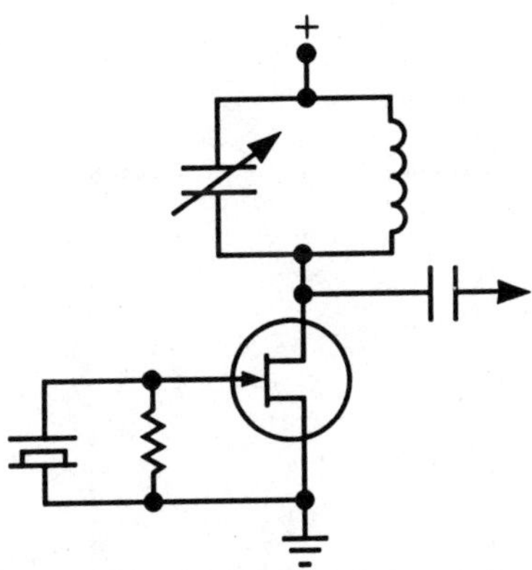

6-2 Circuit for Question 6-014.

Q6-015 The transmission of the radiotelephone auto-alarm signal is tested:

A. daily
B. prior to leaving port
C. by feeding the alarm signal to a dummy antenna
D. by operating on a frequency other than 21.82 kHz
E. all of the above choices are true

Page(s) 551

Q6-016 A mobile receiver experiences "dead" areas of reception as a result of:

A. atmospheric absorption
B. tropospheric scatter
C. shading of the RF signal by hills and trees

D. knife-edge refraction
E. sporadic E

Page(s) 439, 440

Q6-017 If there is a malfunction in the automatic actuation switch controlled by the photocell, the antenna tower lights must burn:

A. continuously
B. from 6 PM to 6 AM
C. from local sunset to 8:30 AM
D. from local sunset to local sunrise
E. from 6 PM to local sunrise

Page(s) 612

Q6-018 In the circuit of FIG. 6-3, the true power can be calculated from:

A. the product of V and A
B. the product of A^2 and $(R_1 + R_2)$
C. the power factor times the product of V and A
D. the result of dividing V^2 by $(R_1 + R_2)$
E. the true power cannot be calculated, but must instead be measured by a wattmeter

Page(s) 124

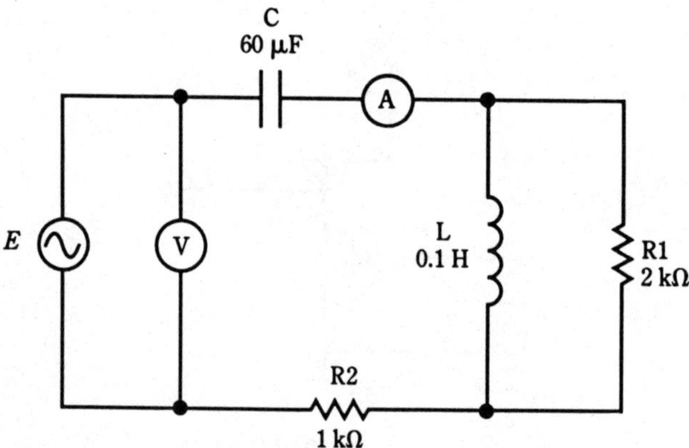

6-3 Circuit for Question 6-018.

Q6-019 The lights of an antenna tower must be displayed:

A. from 9 PM to 9 AM, local time
B. on a continuous basis
C. from 12 midnight to local sunrise
D. from sunset to sunrise
E. from 6 PM to 6 AM, local time

Page(s) 612

Q6-020 The time of 2300 hours Universal Time Coordinated (UTC) is equivalent to:

A. 3:00 PM PST
B. 11:00 PM PST
C. 5:00 PM MST

D. 5:00 PM EST
E. 4:00 PM CST

Page(s) 442

Q6-021 On the frequency of 2182 kHz or 156.8 MHz in a region of heavy traffic, what is the minimum period of time that must elapse before a test transmission is repeated?

A. 1 minute
B. 2 minutes
C. 3 minutes
D. 4 minutes
E. 10 minutes

Page(s) 610

Q6-022 Eddy currents are:

A. the result of skin effect in the transformer's windings
B. due to the effect of hysteresis in the iron core
C. produced as a result of the alternating magnetic flux cutting the iron core of a power transformer
D. reduced as the frequency is increased
E. reduced by the use of a solid iron core

Page(s) 167

Q6-023 Signal bias in a JFET oscillator:

A. is the result of the time constant provided by the resistor, capacitor combination in the gate-source circuit
B. depends on the flow of source current to generate the bias
C. depends on the amplitude of the oscillation
D. prevents any flow of the drain current
E. both choices A and C are true

Page(s) 272, 273

Q6-024 Marine emergency radio equipment on a survival craft must be tested:

A. on full power with the transmitter connected to its normal antenna
B. only when the ship is more than 100 miles from U.S. shores
C. prior to departure
D. at weekly intervals while at sea
E. choices C and D are true

Page(s) 607, 608

Q6-025 The radiated carrier power from a transmitter is 1 kW. If the second harmonic component has been attenuated to 40 dB below the carrier power, the power in the second harmonic is:

A. 0.4 W
B. 0.1 W
C. 10 W
D. 4 W
E. 1.4 W

Page(s) 303, 304

Q6-026 During the silent period, a radiotelephone ship station may not transmit on 2182 kHz except for:

A. distress calls
B. urgency signals
C. safety signals
D. government communications
E. choices A, B, and C are true

Page(s) 583

Q6-027 The frequency range of the medium frequency (MF) band is:

A. 300 to 3000 Hz
B. 3 to 30 MHz
C. 300 kHz to 3 MHz
D. 300 to 3000 kHz
E. choices C and D are true

Page(s) 443

Q6-028 Which of the following has the first priority of communications?

A. safety signals
B. urgency signals
C. weather warnings
D. distress signals
E. navigational warnings

Page(s) 599, 600

Q6-029 When aligning an FM receiver, the first step is to introduce the test signal at the:

A. base of the first stage
B. antenna circuit
C. gate of the limiter stage
D. base of the RF stage
E. output point of the discriminator circuit

Page(s) 390

Q6-030 A compulsory ship is equipped with a radiotelegraph installation. Its associated radiotelephone installation must be capable of not less than:

A. 25 W carrier power (A3E) or 60 W peak envelope power (H3E)
B. 20 W carrier power (A3E) or 50 W peak envelope power (H3E)
C. 60 W peak envelope power for A3E and H3E emissions
D. 50 W peak envelope power for J3E emissions on 1282 kHz
E. 50 W peak envelope power for H3E and J3E emissions

Page(s) 562

Q6-031 Which of the following waveforms represents the output from the logic circuits shown in FIG. 6-4?

Page(s) 577

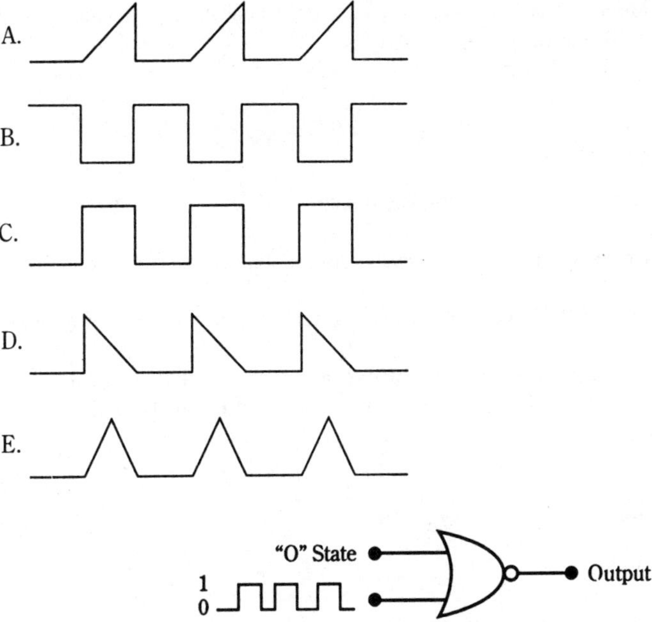

6-4 Logic circuit for Question 6-031.

Q6-032 Which of the following is arranged in the correct order of communications priority for the marine mobile service?

A. distress, urgency, safety signals
B. distress, safety, urgency signals
C. urgency, safety, distress signals
D. safety, distress, urgency signals
E. safety, urgency, distress signals

Page(s) 599, 600

Q6-033 During tuning and testing procedures that must be carried with minimum radiation (radio silence), the transmitter is coupled to a (an):

A. quarter-wave antenna
B. loop antenna
C. shortened Hertz antenna
D. array of parasitic elements
E. dummy antenna

Page(s) 434

Q6-034 The dc power input to the final stage of a transmitter is calculated by:

A. multiplying the RMS value of the input signal by the dc level of output current
B. multiplying the operating power by the efficiency factor
C. multiplying the dc supply voltage by the RMS value of the antenna current

D. multiplying the antenna resistance by the square of the final stage's dc current and dividing the result by the efficiency factor
E. none of the above choices is true

Page(s) 303, 304

Q6-035 In a push-push doubler stage:

A. the two bases are fed 180° out of phase and the collectors are joined together to one end of the tank circuit
B. the two bases are fed in phase and the collectors are joined together to one end of the tank circuit
C. the two bases are fed 180° out of phase and the tank circuit is connected between the collectors
D. the two bases are fed in phase and the tank circuit is connected between the collectors
E. the two bases are fed 180° out of phase and the emitters are joined together to one end of the tank circuit

Page(s) 250, 251

Q6-036 A class-C amplifier stage:

A. has a low level of efficiency
B. has a small input signal
C. operates with a bias near to the cut-off value
D. causes the waveform of the collector current to be severely distorted
E. has a low power output, when compared with class-A or class-B stages

Page(s) 249, 250

Q6-037 The electrical length of a Marconi antenna can be shortened by adding a (an):

A. parallel LC resonant circuit in series
B. series LC resonant circuit
C. capacitor in series
D. inductor in series
E. inductor in parallel

Page(s) 428

Q6-038 A message that gives an important meteorological warning is preceded by the word(s):

A. weather alert
B. security
C. danger
D. met warning
E. met alert

Page(s) 600

Q6-039 The tendency for high-frequency alternating currents to retreat towards the surface of a conductor, rather than exist across the entire cross-sectional area, is called:

A. proximity effect
B. surface attraction
C. skin effect
D. perimeter effect
E. reluctance

A. 35 μV/m
B. 140 μV/m
C. 70 μV/m
D. 2240 μV/m
E. 1120 μV/m

Page(s) 418

Q6-060 A 500-W 3-MHz transmitter is 80% amplitude modulated by a pure tone. The total power in the sidebands is:

A. 320 W
B. 400 W
C. 200 W
D. 160 W
E. 80 W

Page(s) 317

Q6-061 Which of the following is the symbol for a varactor diode?

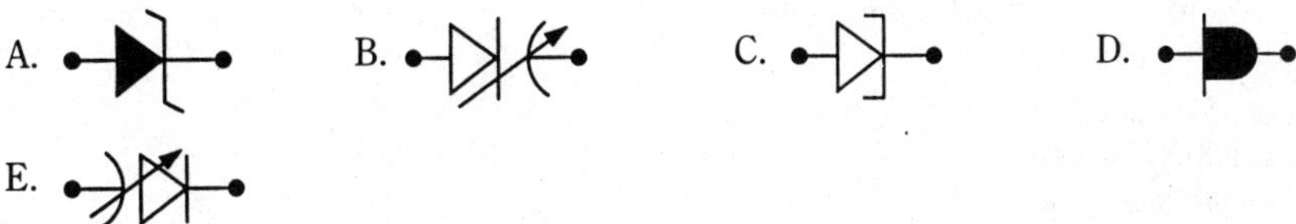

Page(s) 219 to 221

Q6-062 Which of the following represents the highest degree of selectivity for an AM receiver?

A. −70 dB adjacent-channel sensitivity
B. −50 dB for 20-kHz adjacent-channel rejection
C. −40 dB for 30-kHz adjacent-channel rejection
D. −60 dB for 20-kHz adjacent-channel rejection
E. 60 dB for 30-kHz adjacent-channel rejection

Page(s) 358

Q6-063 Two 0.1-μF capacitors are connected in series across a 120-Vdc source. These capacitors are subsequently disconnected from the source and are then carefully joined in parallel. If a third uncharged 0.1-μF capacitor is now connected in parallel with the other two capacitors, the voltage across the third capacitor is:

A. 60 V
B. 40 V
C. 120 V
D. 0 V
E. 80 V

Page(s) 75, 76

Q6-064 The input to a circuit is 120 mV and its output is 120 μV. Assuming that the input and the output resistances are the same, the amount of the attenuation is:

A. 10 dB
B. 20 dB
C. 30 dB
D. 12 dB
E. 40 dB

Page(s) 145 to 147

Q6-065 The holder of a General Radiotelephone Operator's License, is not required to be on board a ship in order to:

A. operate a ship's radar system, provided that the system can be operated by using external controls only and contains a fixed-frequency pulsed magnetron
B. operate a bridge-to-bridge communications system
C. operate on-board communications
D. operate a mobile station that is intended solely for survival purposes
E. all of the above choices are true

Page(s) 554, 555, 590, 607, 608

Q6-066 Which of the following logic gates corresponds to the truth table of FIG. 6-7?

A. NOR gate
B. NAND gate
C. AND gate
D. EX-NOR gate
E. OR gate

Page(s) 533 to 535

P	*Q*	*R*
False	False	True
False	True	False
True	False	False
True	True	False

6-7 Truth table for Question 6-066.

Q6-067 The frequency tolerance of aeronautical stations operating in the band of 100 to 2450 MHz is:

A. 20 ppm
B. 20 Hz
C. 10 ppm
D. 5 ppm
E. 30 ppm

Page(s) 578

Q6-068 The circuit of FIG. 6-8:

A. provides a 180° phase reversal between the input and output signals
B. provides no phase change between the input and output signals
C. represents a common base configuration

D. has a very low input impedance
E. represents a common collector configuration

Page(s) 239, 240

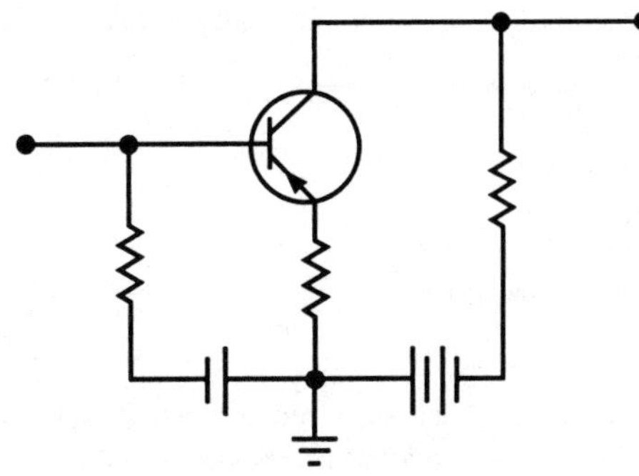

6-8 Circuit for Question 6-068.

Q6-069 The carrier frequency of a ship-borne transmitter must be measured:

A. on a daily basis with the aid of a dummy antenna
B. on a weekly basis with reduced carrier power
C. on a monthly basis in conjunction with the U.S. Coast Guard
D. prior to leaving port
E. frequency measurements are not carried out, unless some change is made to the transmitter that affects its operating frequency

Page(s) 577

Q6-070 If the temperature of a transistor increases, the:

A. surrounding circuit is not affected
B. base current decreases
C. emitter current decreases
D. collector current increases.
E. value of β_{dc} is unchanged

Page(s) 231 to 234

Q6-071 Which of the following combinations represent the first three words in the modern phonetic alphabet?

A. Alpha, Bravo, Charlie
B. Able, Baker, Charlie
C. Ack, Beer, Charlie
D. Alpha, Beta, Charlie
E. Alpha, Baker, Charline

Page(s) 339, 340

Q6-072 A class-S Emergency Position-Indicating Radio Beacon (E.P.I.R.B) is tested:

A. with the aid of a dummy antenna, whose load is the same as that of the EPIRB's antenna
B. by using a manually activated test switch
C. without the radiation exceeding 25 μV/m at a distance of 150 feet

D. during the first five minutes of any hour
E. choices A, B, C are true

Page(s) 573, 574

Q6-073 The input to a detector stage is an amplitude-modulated (A3E) IF signal. The output from the stage is:

A. a lower frequency carrier
B. the audio voice information
C. a morse-code signal
D. the upper or lower set of sidebands
E. none of the above choices is true

Page(s) 352, 353

Q6-074 Under no-load conditions a half-wave rectifier circuit with a capacitor input filter, has a dc output voltage of 9 V. What is the effective value of the ac voltage input to the rectifier circuit?

A. 9 V
B. 12.7 V
C. 6.4 V
D. 7.3 V
E. 5.8 V

Page(s) 201 to 207

Q6-075 What is the carrier frequency and purpose of Channel 16?

A. 156.65 MHz. Bridge-to-bridge communications
B. 457.525 MHz. Survival craft station
C. 156.8 MHz. Distress and calling frequency
D. 2182 kHz. Distress and calling frequency
E. 121.5 MHz. Distress and calling frequency

Page(s) 570

Q6-076 In FIG. 6-9 the transistor is:

A. reverse-biased on the base
B. forward-biased on the collector
C. reverse-biased on the emitter
D. forward-biased
E. reverse-biased

Page(s) 225, 226

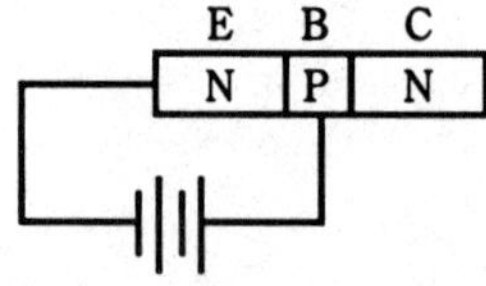

6-9 Circuit for Question 6-076.

Q6-077 Which of the following meters is most frequently used to determine the presence of an open circuit or a short circuit?

A. ohmmeter
B. voltmeter
C. ammeter
D. wattmeter
E. electrometer

Page(s) 41 to 43

Q6-078 An ideal inductor and an ideal capacitor have no resistive losses and are connected in parallel across a sine-wave voltage source. Which of the following statements is true?

A. the power factor of the circuit is always unity
B. the phase angle of the circuit is zero degrees and is independent of the frequency
C. the source current is in phase with the source voltage
D. the source current is 180° out of phase with the source voltage
E. the power factor of the circuit is zero

Page(s) 138 to 140

Q6-079 If a ship has foundered and is sinking, the radiotelephone operator would send the distress signal of:

A. pan, spoken three times
B. SOS, spoken three times
C. security, spoken three times
D. mayday, spoken three times
E. disaster, spoken three times

Page(s) 568, 599

Q6-080 In the circuit of FIG. 6-10, $V_i = +4$ V, $V = 12$ V. The value of V_o is:

A. +4 V
B. −4 V
C. +12 V
D. −12 V
E. −8 V

Page(s) 289, 290

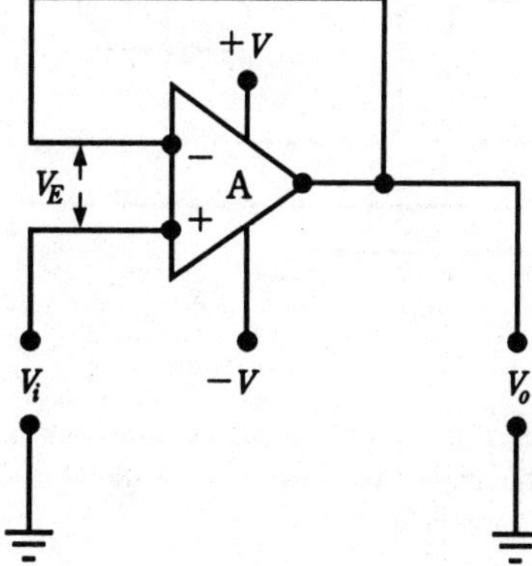

6-10 Circuit for Question 6-080.

Q6-081 Which of the following vessels are required to install compulsory radiotelegraph communications equipment?

A. cargo ships of 1600 gross tons and upward
B. all large passenger ships
C. cargo ships of 300 gross tons and upward but less than 1600 tons on international voyages
D. small passenger boats that transport six or more passengers
E. choices A and B are true

Page(s) 562

Q6-082 The circuit of FIG. 6-11:

A. provides AGC bias
B. represents a second detector stage
C. is used for frequency conversion
D. combines RF and IF amplifiers into one stage
E. contains a Colpitts oscillator

Page(s) 348, 349

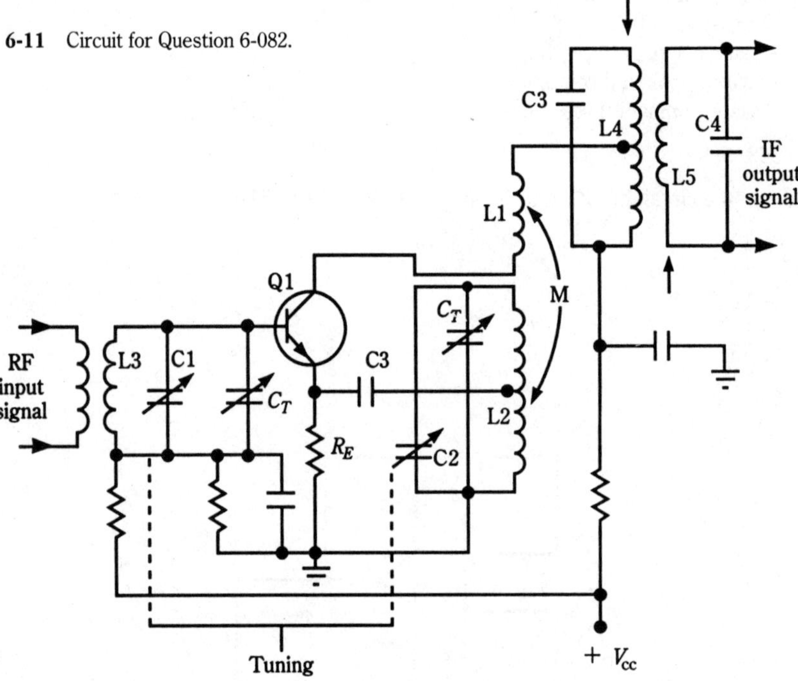

6-11 Circuit for Question 6-082.

Q6-083 A resistor and a capacitor are connected in series across a sine-wave voltage source. If the resistance is 100 Ω and the capacitive reactance is 100 Ω the phase difference between the source voltage and the source current is:

A. 0°
B. +90°

C. −90°
D. +45°
E. −45°

Page(s) 128

Q6-084 A variable resistor (such as a rheostat) and a fixed value resistor are connected in series across a dc voltage source. If the value of the variable resistor is decreased:

A. the amount of power dissipated will decrease
B. the value of the source voltage will increase
C. the value of the current will increase
D. the voltage drop across the fixed value resistor decreases
E. the voltage drop across the variable resistor increases

Page(s) 33 to 35

Q6-085 In a marine R3E emission, the carrier is reduced below the peak envelope power by:

A. 8 dB
B. 10 dB
C. 12 dB
D. 15 dB
E. 18 dB

Page(s) 334

Q6-086 Upon the sale of a vessel, the correct procedure regarding the radio transmitter's license, involves:

A. renewing the existing license when it expires
B. the new owner submitting an application for a new license
C. surrendering the existing license for cancellation upon receipt of the new license
D. an inspection of the transmitter within 30 days by the FCC
E. choices B and C are true

Page(s) 560

Q6-087 Which of the following emission designators has the greatest necessary bandwidth?

A. 160HA1A
B. 300HJ2B
C. 2K66A2A
D. 2K80H3E
E. 1K40H2A

Page(s) 334

Q6-088 A 100-V 60-Hz supply voltage is connected to a relay whose resistance is 4 Ω. If the relay current is 0.2 A, the impedance of the relay is:

A. 4 Ω
B. 20 Ω
C. 50 Ω
D. 20 Ω
E. 500 Ω

Page(s) 122 to 125

Q6-089 When operating with a J3E transmitter on 2182 kHz or a VHF G3E transmitter on 156.8 MHz:

A. the initial calling signal must not last longer than 30 seconds
B. a call must not be repeated until a two-minute interval has elapsed
C. there must be a 15-minute waiting period after three attempts at calling have been made
D. the transmitter is switched from the calling frequency to the working frequency as soon as contact is made
E. all of the above choices are true

Page(s) 557

Q6-090 A conductor is composed of copper wire with a circular cross-sectional area. If the diameter of the wire is doubled, but the length remains the same, the new resistance of the wire is:

A. doubled
B. halved
C. quadrupled
D. quartered
E. unchanged

Page(s) 22 to 25

Q6-091 The commercial line voltage has a frequency of 60 Hz. Its phasor rotates with an angular velocity of:

A. 60 rad./s
B. 3600 rad./s
C. 377 rad./s
D. 189 rad./s
E. 755 rad./s

Page(s) 112, 113

Q6-092 If a steady current of 3.5 A exists at a given point for a period of 30 minutes, calculate the amount of charge in coulombs flowing past that point:

A. 6300 C
B. 12600 C
C. 3150 C
D. 2250 C
E. 4500 C

Page(s) 10 to 12

Q6-093 A two-way communications system is which both stations operate on the same frequency, is called:

A. simplex
B. uniplex
C. duplex
D. biplex
E. diplex

Page(s) 326, 327

Q6-094 In the month of December, 3 PM Eastern Standard Time is equivalent to:

A. 1900 UTC
B. 2000 UTC
C. 2100 UTC
D. 1800 UTC
E. 2200 UTC

Page(s) 622

Q6-095 It is discovered that the signal from a marine transmitter is severely distorted. The operator must, immediately:

A. lower the percentage of modulation
B. suspend transmission
C. lower the value of the operating power
D. commence to use the phonetic alphabet
E. speak more softly into the microphone

Page(s) 609

Q6-096 A receiver is connected to a number of stacked antennas which are positioned at various angles to each other. The purpose of this antenna array is to:

A. provide an omnidirectional reception pattern
B. increase the magnitude of the received signal
C. provide a unidirectional reception pattern
D. increase the size of the major lobe at the expense of the side lobes
E. choices B, C, and D are true

Page(s) 422 to 424

Q6-097 When aiming a ship-borne microwave antenna at a geostationary satellite, the azimuth is:

A. the angle of aim in the vertical plane
B. the angle of aim in the horizontal plane
C. normally measured from magnetic North
D. the angle between the vertical and the line of aim
E. an angle that can never exceed 90°

Page(s) 422 to 424

Q6-098 The FCC requires that all radiotelephone transmissions from a ship's station are identified by the:

A. name of the ship
B. callsign
C. working frequency
D. name of the operator
E. home port

Page(s) 558

Q6-099 In FIG. 6-12, $R_1 = 10\ \Omega$ and $R_2 = 1000\ \Omega$. When the bridge is balanced, the value of R_3 is adjusted to $5.7\ \Omega$. What is the value of the unknown resistor, R_x?

A. 5.7 Ω
B. 5700 Ω
C. 570 Ω
D. 0.057 Ω
E. 0.57 Ω

Page(s) 49, 50

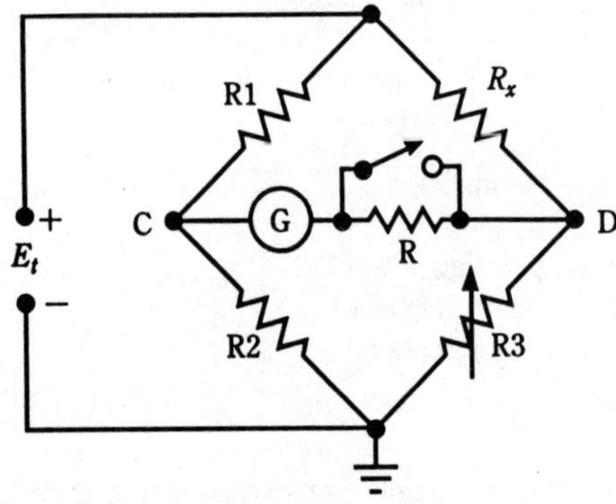

6-12 Circuit for Question 6-099.

Q6-100 What details are contained in the station (technical) log of a compulsory ship?

A. signature of each licensed operator responsible for the operation of the transmitting equipment
B. hours of duty for each licensed operator responsible for the operation of the transmitting equipment
C. listing of the frequencies used
D. power input to the transmitter's final stage
E. all of the above choices are true

Page(s) 585, 586

Element 3
Test 7

Q7-001 In the circuit of FIG. 7-1, E is held at a constant level, but the frequency is steadily increased. The output voltage V_o, will:

A. decrease steadily
B. rise to a maximum value and then subsequently decrease
C. fall to a minimum value and then subsequently rise
D. stay the same
E. increase steadily

Page(s) 137, 138

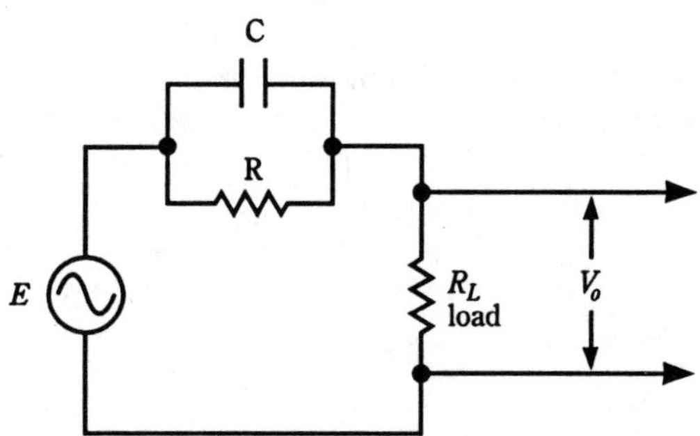

7-1 Circuit for Question 7-001.

Q7-002 The lights of an antenna tower are not monitored by automatic means. These lights must be visually inspected:

A. whenever the manual control is used
B. once every two days
C. on a weekly basis
D. once every 24 hours
E. between sunset and sunrise, local time.

Page(s) 612

Q7-003 Which electrode of a triode tube can be compared with the collector region of a bipolar transistor?

A. plate
B. control grid
C. cathode
D. filament
E. screen grid

Page(s) 225

Q7-004 Which of the following shall be included in the voice announcement at the conclusion of a test transmission?

A. the operating power of the testing station
B. the official callsign of the testing station
C. the frequency on which the test was conducted
D. the name of the ship on which the marine testing station is located
E. choices B and D are true

Page(s) 610

Q7-005 One reason for including a buffer stage in a transmitter is to:

A. provide a low output impedance to the intermediate power amplifiers
B. stabilize the power supply to the oscillator stage
C. stop the oscillator from generating parasitic oscillations
D. present a constant load to the oscillator stage
E. present a low input impedance to the oscillator stage

Page(s) 298

Q7-006 For a marine station producing a J3E emission, the carrier must be suppressed below the peak envelope power by at least:

A. 3 dB
B. 10 dB
C. 20 dB
D. 30 dB
E. 40 dB

Page(s) 605

Q7-007 A duplexer circuit allows a transmitter and a receiver to operate from the same antenna with virtually no interaction. This circuit may be replaced by a (an):

A. circulator
B. lossy waveguide
C. isolator

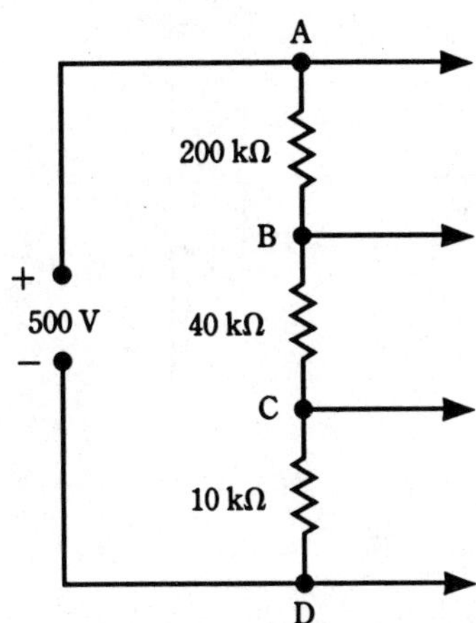

7-4 Circuit for Question 7-014.

C. distress messages from ships or aircraft
D. messages regarding the navigation of ships
E. all of the above choices are true

Page(s) 604

Q7-016 The true power is calculated by knowing the:

A. RMS values of the source voltage and the source current
B. apparent power and the form factor
C. cosine of the phase angle
D. average value of the source voltage and the source current
E. both Choices A and C are required

Page(s) 124

Q7-017 One hertz is equivalent to an angular frequency of:

A. π radians/second
B. 2π cycles/second
C. π cycles/second
D. 2π radians/second
E. π meters/second

Page(s) 105 to 108

Q7-018 A marine station which hears an emergency signal, must:

A. immediately alert all ships in the vicinity
B. immediately inform the Master of the vessel
C. continue to listen for a period of not less than three minutes
D. cease all transmissions for at least 30 minutes
E. ignore the signal if it is not addressed to the ship on which the marine station is located

Page(s) 599, 600

Q7-019 In the circuit of FIG. 7-5, $V_i = +2.5$ V, $V_{ref} = +4.0$ V, $V = +6$ V. The value of V_o is:

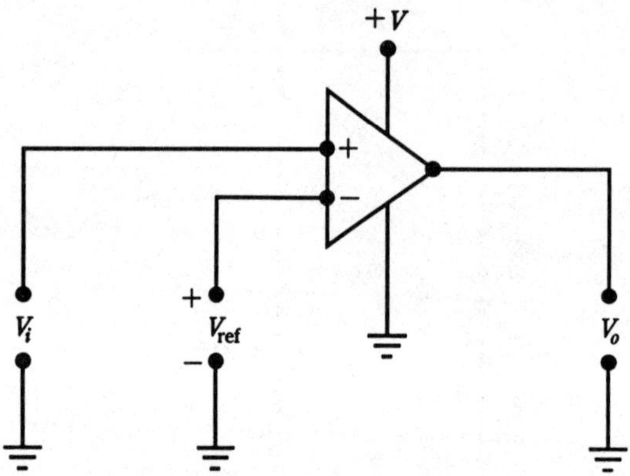

7-5 Circuit for Questions 7-019 and 7-020.

A. +2.5 V
B. +4.0 V
C. +1.5 V
D. 0 V
E. +6 V

Page(s) 289, 290

Q7-020 In the circuit of FIG. 7-5, V_i = +4. 0 V, V_{ref} = + 2.5 V, V = +6 V. The value of V_o is:

A. +2.5 V
B. +4.0 V
C. +1.5 V
D. 0 V
E. +6 V

Page(s) 289, 290

Q7-021 For willfully violating a provision of the Communications Act of 1934 for commercial advantage or private financial gain, the penalty is a fine of not more than:

A. $ 25000.00 or imprisonment for a term not exceeding one year, or both
B. $ 20000.00 or imprisonment for a term not exceeding one year, or both
C. $ 10000.00 or imprisonment for a term not exceeding two years or both
D. $ 10000.00 or imprisonment for a term not exceeding one year, or both
E. $ 25000.00 or imprisonment for a term not exceeding two years, or both

Page(s) 618, 619

Q7-022 Three land or statute miles is equivalent to:

A. 3.45 nautical miles
B. 2.61 nautical miles
C. 2.45 nautical miles
D. 2.52 nautical miles
E. 3.61 nautical miles

Page(s) 622, 623

Q7-023 A cargo ship of 100 gross tons is sailing on an international voyage. Her compulsory radiotelephone installation must be capable of a daytime minimum range of:

A. 250 nautical miles
B. 200 nautical miles
C. 150 nautical miles
D. 100 nautical miles
E. 50 nautical miles

Page(s) 616

Q7-024 A crystal oscillator is operated at its fundamental frequency of 184 kHz. If the transmitter's output frequency is 2208 kHz, the required combination of harmonic generators is:

A. three doubler stages
B. three doubler stages and a tripler stage
C. one doubler stage and two tripler stages
D. one doubler stage and one quadrupler stage
E. two doubler stages and one tripler stage

Page(s) 300, 301

Q7-025 The semiconductor device whose capacitance is voltage-controlled, is the:

A. varactor diode
B. reactance diode
C. tunnel diode
D. zener diode
E. avalanche diode

Page(s) 219, 220

Q7-026 The signal sent by an aircraft that is threatened by serious and imminent danger is preceded by the word:

A. mayday
B. danger
C. pan
D. security
E. emergency

Page(s) 599

Q7-027 If a carrier is frequency modulated by a test tone, the amount of the frequency deviation is mainly determined by the:

A. amplitude of the tone
B. modulating frequency
C. carrier amplitude
D. carrier frequency
E. both choices A and B are true

Page(s) 362

Q7-028 When transmitted by radiotelephony, the safety signal is indicated by the word:

A. safety
B. mayday
C. security
D. pan
E. SOS

Page(s) 600

Q7-029 The diagram of FIG. 7-6 refers to the:

A. mixer stage
B. RF amplifier
C. AF amplifier
D. oscillator stage
E. detector stage

Page(s) 342

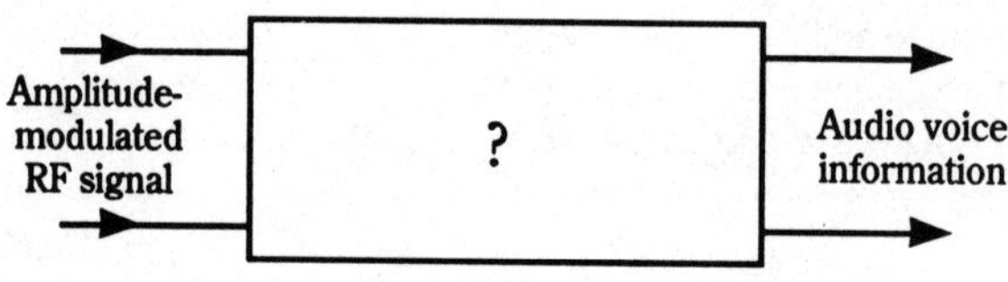

7-6 Diagram for Question 7-029.

Q7-030 The licensed operator of a marine utility station must:

A. carry his/her license on his/her person while on duty
B. post a photocopy of his/her license at the location from which the station is operated
C. post a "posting statement" at the transmitter's control point
D. carry a photocopy of his/her license while on duty
E. either choice A or D is true

Page(s) 595, 596

Q7-031 The broken line in FIG. 7-7 shows the effective:

A. voltage distribution on a $\lambda/2$ Hertz antenna
B. current distribution on a $\lambda/4$ Marconi antenna
C. current distribution on a $\lambda/2$ Hertz antenna
D. voltage distribution on a $\lambda/4$ Marconi antenna
E. impedance distribution on a $\lambda/4$ Marconi antenna

Page(s) 426

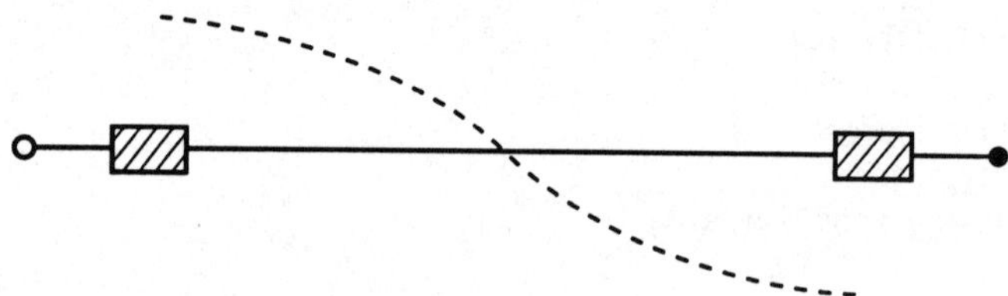

7-7 Illustration for Question 7-031.

Q7-032 How often must hand-held portable ship transmitters be tested?

A. prior to leaving port
B. once a day
C. once a week
D. once a month
E. no specific testing procedures are stated in the FCC Rules and Regulations

Page(s) 596

Q7-033 A 1-foot length of wire has a cross-sectional area of 5 circular mils and a resistance of 100 Ω. If the length is increased to 2 feet and the cross-sectional area is changed to 10 circular mils, the wire's new resistance is:

A. 100 Ω
B. 200 Ω
C. 50 Ω
D. 400 Ω
E. 25 Ω

Page(s) 22 to 25

Q7-034 On peaks of voice modulation, marine transmitters must maintain a percentage modulation value, which lies between:

A. 60% to 90%
B. 70% to 95%
C. 70% to 100%
D. 75% to 100%
E. 80% to 100%

Page(s) 588

Q7-035 In an RF transformer with tuned primary-tuned secondary circuits, the coupling factor is increased beyond its critical value. As a result of this "tight" coupling,:

A. there is maximum power transferred from the primary circuit to the secondary circuit
B. the center frequency of each circuit is increased
C. the center frequency of each circuit is lowered
D. the bandwidth is increased
E. the gain of the transformer is increased

Page(s) 170 to 173

Q7-036 Which of the following word(s) is used to signify "you are requested to wait for another call (or for additional information)"?

A. standby
B. stay on watch
C. continue to listen
D. break
E. stay alert

Page(s) 591

Q7-037 In FIG. 7-8, the percentage modulation of the AM signal is:

A. 100%
B. 80%
C. 40%
D. 50%
E. 60%

Page(s) 313, 314

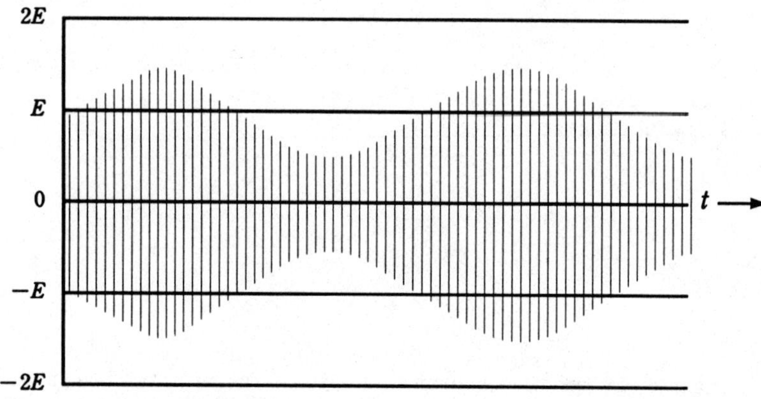

7-8 Waveform for Question 7-037.

Q7-038 Which of the following frequencies is assigned to UHF transmitters used for on-board communications?

A. 647.750 MHz
B. 467.775 MHz
C. 567.800 MHz
D. 477.825 MHz
E. 667.875 MHz

Page(s) 590

Q7-039 A series-wound dc motor is operating under normal conditions. If the mechanical load is suddenly removed:

A. the motor stops
B. there is virtually no change in the speed
C. the motor is ultimately destroyed
D. there is a sharp decrease in the speed
E. the direction of the armature's rotation is reversed

Page(s) 98

Q7-040 A microcomputer has a 12-bit address bus with 8-bits to each word. The total memory capacity of words in the microcomputer is:

A. 24
B. 8192
C. 2048
D. 4096
E. 16384

Page(s) 546, 547

Q7-041 For a ship station using G3D or G3E emission in the 156- to 162-MHz band, the frequency deviation corresponding to 100% modulation, is:

A. 10 kHz
B. 5 kHz
C. 20 kHz
D. 25 kHz
E. 75 kHz

Page(s) 548

Q7-042 A resonant circuit consists of a practical inductor and a capacitor in parallel. If a resistor is added in parallel with the circuit:

A. the impedance at resonance decreases
B. the resonant frequency is appreciably decreased
C. the value of the Q factor is raised
D. the bandwidth is lower
E. choices C and D are both true

Page(s) 158

Q7-043 Station logs that contain information about certain distress communications must be retained for a period of:

A. 1 year
B. 2 years
C. 3 years
D. 5 years
E. these logs must be retained until the FCC authorize their destruction

Page(s) 585, 586

Q7-044 The extremely low frequency (ELF) band covers the frequency range of:

A. 3 to 30 kHz
B. 300 to 3000 Hz
C. 3 to 30 Hz
D. 30 to 300 Hz
E. 30 to 300 kHz

Page(s) 443

Q7-045 All ships that are licensed to transmit telephony in the band of 1605 to 3500 kHz, must monitor the International Radiotelephone Distress frequency:

A. continuously
B. only during distress, urgency and safety signals
C. only during the silent periods
D. from 9 PM to 9 AM
E. once every hour

Page(s) 583

Q7-046 Waveguides are:

A. hollow, metal rectangular or circular tubes used to convey RF power in the SHF band
B. used as low-pass filters in the HF band
C. more economical than coaxial cables when operated at low frequencies
D. more effective over long distances
E. designed with no joins

Page(s) 452 to 454

Q7-047 A 50-MHz transmitter has a radiated carrier power of 100 W. Because of inadequate neutralization, a 49.9-MHz spurious emission with a power of 5 W is passed through a filter that provides a loss of 7 dB. The radiated power of the spurious emission is:

A. 1 W
B. 0.7 W
C. 0.5 W
D. 0.35 W
E. 1.5 W

Page(s) 303, 304

Q7-048 Which of the following bands is least affected by static interference?

A. 300 to 3000 kHz
B. 3 to 30 MHz
C. 30 to 300 kHz
D. 300 MHz to 3 GHz
E. 30 to 300 MHz

Page(s) 443

Q7-049 Excess solder is normally removed from the holes in a printed circuit board with the aid of:

A. a soldering aid
B. dykes
C. a suction syringe
D. needlenose pliers
E. a soldering brush

Page(s) 103

Q7-050 When an aircraft is descending towards a runway, the ILS Glide Path unit indicates the:

A. vertical deviation from the optimum path of descent
B. deviation from the optimum speed of descent
C. azimuth of the aircraft in relation to the axis of the runway
D. horizontal deviation from the optimum path of descent along the axis of the runway
E. vertical angle between the axis of the aircraft and the axis of the runway

Page(s) 582

Q7-051 A 1-kW 2-MHz carrier is 60% amplitude modulated by a 1-kHz test tone. If the modulation is increased to 80%, what is the percentage increase in the total sideband power?

A. 33⅓%
B. 67%
C. 25%

D. 50%
E. 78%

Page(s) 316, 317

Q7-052 Convert the decimal number, 4376_{10}, into its equivalent hexadecimal number.:

A. 1117_{16}
B. 1118_{16}
C. 1018_{16}
D. 1108_{16}
E. 1008_{16}

Page(s) 522, 523

Q7-053 The Hartley oscillator:

A. uses indirect feedback
B. is especially suitable for generating frequencies greater than 100 MHz
C. has an output waveform that is rich in harmonics
D. employs a capacitive voltage divider
E. uses mutual coupling exclusively to provide the positive feedback

Page(s) 271, 272

Q7-054 A survival craft station is operating on a frequency of 121.5 MHz. The frequency tolerance of this station is:

A. 30 ppm
B. 20 ppm
C. 20 Hz
D. 30 Hz
E. 50 ppm

Page(s) 578

Q7-055 An AM superhet receiver is tuned to a CW A1A carrier, whose frequency is 1 MHz. If the intermediate frequency is 455 kHz, the output frequency of the BFO is:

A. 1 kHz
B. 1001 kHz
C. 999 kHz
D. 454 kHz
E. either choice B or C is correct

Page(s) 359

Q7-056 Which of the following frequencies are used by a class-C Emergency Position-Indicating Radio Beacon (E.P.I.R.B)?

A. 156.75 MHz
B. 156.8 MHz
C. 156.65 MHz
D. 121.5 MHz
E. choices A and B are true

Page(s) 573, 574

Q7-057 In the circuit of FIG. 7-9, what is the voltage across the capacitor, C, after the switch, S, has been closed for a time interval of 0.5 s?

A. 3.93 V
B. 6.32 V
C. 5 V
D. 10 V
E. 0 V

Page(s) 79, 80

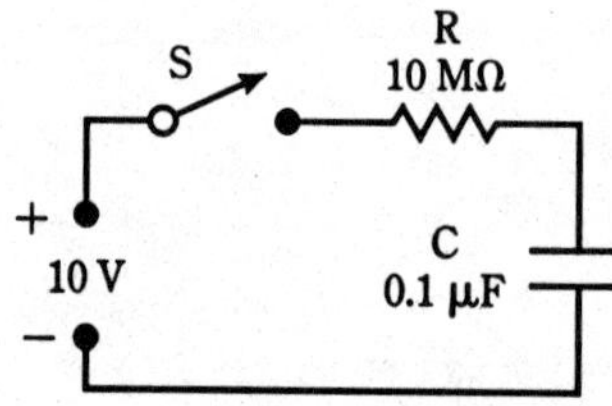

7-9 Circuit for Question 7-057.

Q7-058 What is the authorized bandwidth of a marine H3E emission?

A. 2.8 kHz
B. 8 kHz
C. 3 kHz
D. 6 kHz
E. 4 kHz

Page(s) 334

Q7-059 The Emergency Locator Transmitter (ELT) may be tested:

A. in coordination with, or under the control of an FAA representative
B. within the first five minutes of any hour
C. by using a manually activated test switch, which switches the transmitter's output to a dummy load
D. by conducting no more than three audio sweeps
E. all of the above choices are true

Page(s) 572

Q7-060 In the circuit of FIG. 7-10, calculate the value of the voltage drop across the resistor R1:

A. 6.7 V
B. 0.7 V
C. 10 V
D. 9.3 V
E. 0 V

Page(s) 198 to 200

Q7-061 For a marine 150-W FM transmitter, 100% modulation corresponds to a frequency deviation of 5 kHz. If the modulating signal is a 2-kHz test tone, the frequency swing corresponding to 80% modulation is:

A. 4 kHz

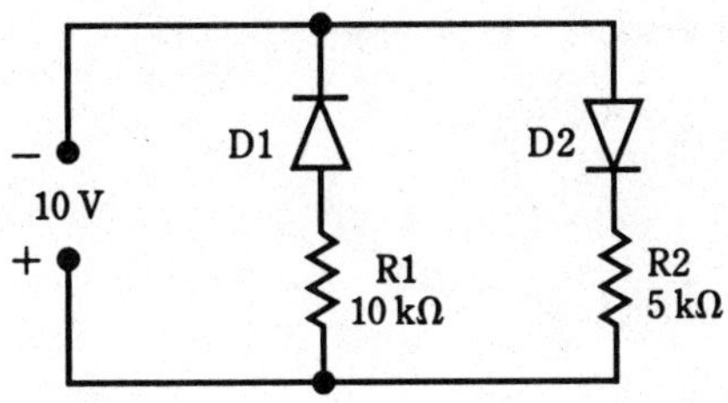

7-10 Circuit for Question 7-060.

B. 2.5 kHz
C. 2 kHz
D. 1 kHz
E. 500 Hz

Page(s) 362, 363

Q7-062 In QUES. 7-061, the value of the modulation index is:

A. 0.5
B. 1.0
C. 1.5
D. 2.0
E. 2.5

Page(s) 362, 363

Q7-063 In QUES. 7-061 and 7-062, the required bandwidth for the FM signal is:

A. 8 kHz
B. 12 kHz
C. 4 kHz
D. 16 kHz
E. 10 kHz

Page(s) 362, 363

Q7-064 The testing of the radiotelephone distress signal must be carried out:

A. on the authority of the ship's Master
B. by sending the transmission to the main antenna
C. only when in port
D. with the aid of a dummy antenna
E. only when beyond 100 miles from U.S. shores

Page(s) 570

Q7-065 The emission designation H3E, stands for:

A. single sideband, full carrier, telephony
B. single sideband, half carrier, telephony
C. single sideband, reduced carrier, telephony
D. single sideband, suppressed carrier, telephony
E. single sideband, half carrier, telegraphy

Page(s) 333

Q7-066 In a phase-modulated signal, the frequency deviation is directly proportional to the:

A. amplitude of the modulating tone
B. frequency of the modulating tone
C. carrier amplitude
D. carrier frequency
E. product of choices A and B

Page(s) 376

Q7-067 A circuit with a very low input impedance and a relatively high output impedance is the:

A. JFET amplifier
B. source follower
C. common-emitter amplifier
D. common-base amplifier
E. common-collector stage

Page(s) 237, 238

Q7-068 The international general radiotelephone calling frequency in the marine service is:

A. 2182 kHz
B. 2282 kHz
C. 2128 kHz
D. 2281 kHz
E. 500 kHz

Page(s) 557

Q7-069 The ultra high frequency (UHF) band covers the frequency range of:

A. 30 to 300 GHz
B. 3 to 30 MHz
C. 300 to 3000 MHz
D. 30 to 300 MHz
E. 3 to 30 GHz

Page(s) 443

Q7-070 The purpose of delayed AGC is to:

A. increase the sensitivity for weak signals
B. increase the sensitivity for strong signals
C. reduce the selectivity
D. increase the image-channel rejection
E. introduce a time delay before applying the AGC bias

Page(s) 354

Q7-071 In the circuit of FIG. 7-11, determine the reading of the voltmeter, V, which has a very high value of resistance:

A. 90 V
B. 100 V
C. 80 V

D. 10 V
E. 0 V

Page(s) 43 to 46

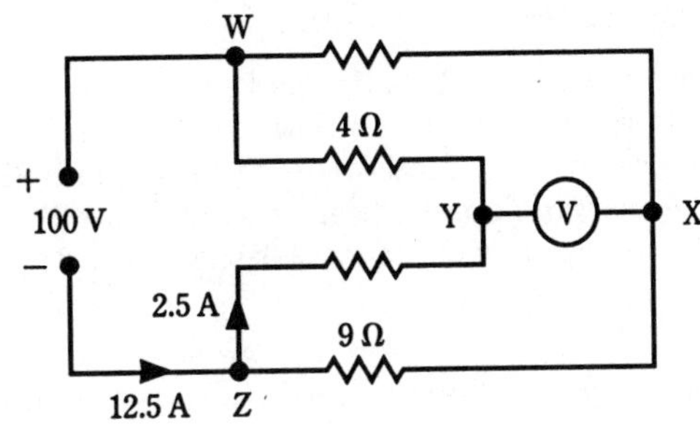

7-11 Circuit for Question 7-071.

Q7-072 What is the minimum license requirement for the operator of a bridge-to-bridge transmitter?

A. none
B. Marine Operator Permit
C. General Radiotelephone License
D. Second-Class Radiotelegraph License
E. Restricted Radiotelephone Operator Permit

Page(s) 554

Q7-073 The operating frequency of the Omega navigational system lies within the:

A. LF band
B. VLF band
C. ELF band
D. MF band
E. HF band

Page(s) 439, 443

Q7-074 The bandwidth occupied by a marine transmission contains:

A. 99% of the total radiated power
B. carrier and sidebands
C. harmonics
D. any frequency component whose power is at least 0.25% of the total radiate power
E. all of the above choice are true

Page(s) 554

Q7-075 A coil consists of 1600 turns of AWG #30 copper wire and has a self-inductance of 0.4 H. If the number of turns is increased to 2000, the new value of the self-inductance is:

A. 0.3 H
B. 0.125 H
C. 0.4 H

D. greater than 0.4 H
E. 3.5 H

Page(s) 65

Q7-076 When testing the radiotelephone auto-alarm transmission:

A. feed the main antenna with the 2182-kHz signal
B. feed the 2182-kHz signal to a dummy antenna
C. feed the dummy antenna with a signal, whose frequency is not 2182 kHz
D. feed the main antenna with a signal, whose frequency is not 2182 kHz
E. only the FCC can conduct tests on the radiotelephone auto-alarm system

Page(s) 551

Q7-077 Convert the binary number, 11011001_2, to its equivalent octal number:

A. 661_8
B. 662_8
C. 321_8
D. 631_8
E. 331_8

Page(s) 520, 521

Q7-078 The frequency tolerance of a marine transmitter operating within the band of 156 to 162 MHz, is:

A. ±10 ppm
B. ±10 Hz
C. ±20 Hz
D. ±20 ppm
E. ±5 ppm

Page(s) 335

Q7-079 How often are compulsory ship stations inspected and certified?

A. annually
B. every six months
C. every three years
D. every five years
E. inspection is only carried out when requested

Page(s) 549

Q7-080 The beam of a cathode ray tube is brought to a focus at the screen by:

A. changing the horizontal accelerating voltage
B. altering the voltage on one anode with respect to the other anode(s)
C. varying the grid to cathode voltage
D. equalizing the horizontal and vertical deflection voltages
E. reducing the beam current

Page(s) 189 to 191

Q7-081 Strong interference from one particular station can be eliminated by the use of:

A. wave traps in the antenna circuitry
B. noise limiters
C. squelch circuits
D. negative feedback
E. bypass capacitors

Page(s) 350

Q7-082 The international marine radiotelephone distress signal is the:

A. letters SOS, spoken three times
B. word mayday, spoken three times
C. word pan, spoken three times
D. word security, spoken three times
E. auto-alarm signal

Page(s) 568

Q7-083 A high signal-to-noise ratio is achieved in an FM receiver by:

A. the use of pre-emphasis in the transmitter and de-emphasis in the receiver
B. using a wide-band system, as opposed to a narrow band system
C. the presence of the limiter stage in the receiver
D. designing the RF amplifier to provide high gain with the minimum introduction of internal receiver noise
E. all of the above choices are true

Page(s) 384, 385, 388, 389

Q7-084 Radio operators who transmit in the marine bands, must:

A. listen in on the frequency before starting transmission
B. leave intervals between radiotelephone calls in regions of heavy traffic
C. keep transmissions as short as possible
D. not engage in superfluous communications
E. all of the above choices are true

Page(s) 591, 592

Q7-085 In the circuit of FIG. 7-12, the value of the total equivalent self-inductance between the points X and Y is:

A. 2.5 H
B. 5 H
C. 10 H

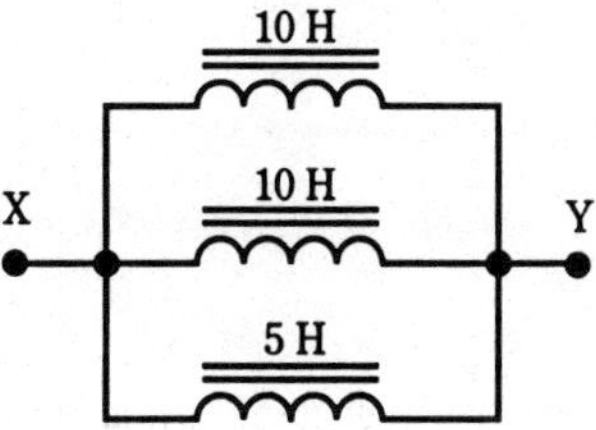

7-12 Circuit for Question 7-085.

D. 25 H
E. 4 H

Page(s) 66, 67

Q7-086 If the ownership of a vessel changes, what is the correct procedure regarding the license for the ship's main transmitter?

A. the present license may be assigned to the new owner
B. when the present license expires, the new owner must submit an application for its renewal
C. an FCC representative must conduct an inspection of the transmitter before assigning the present license to the new owner
D. the new owner must submit an application for a new license
E. the present license must be destroyed and the transmitter must be recertified by the FCC

Page(s) 560

Q7-087 A transistorized class-C RF power amplifier has a tank circuit as its collector load. The output voltage waveform from the collector consists of:

A. narrow negative pulses
B. narrow positive pulses.
C. half-cycle negative pulses
D. half-cycle positive pulses
E. entire cycles

Page(s) 249, 250

Q7-088 Which of the following provisions apply to the lighting of an antenna tower whose height exceeds 150 feet?

A. the tower lights must be visually checked once every 24 hours if not monitored by automatic means
B. details of any failure or malfunction of a tower light must be entered in the station log
C. failure of a top light must be reported immediately unless the problem is corrected within 30 minutes
D. the light and automatic lighting control devices must be inspected every three months
E. all of the above choices are true

Page(s) 612

Q7-089 The RF power to a transmitter's antenna is 12.5 kW. If the antenna's power gain is 3 dB, the effective radiated power is:

A. 37.5 kW
B. 25 kW
C. 12.5 kW
D. 6.25 kW
E. 50 kW

Page(s) 419

Q7-090 A transmitter is connected to a vertical Marconi antenna, which:

A. radiates equally well in all horizontal directions
B. radiates equally well in all vertical directions

C. has a unidirectional radiation pattern in the horizontal plane
D. requires a vertical antenna for the reception of the radiated signal
E. choices A and D are true

Page(s) 426 to 430

Q7-091 A VHF receiver is tuned to 156.8 MHz and has an IF frequency of 10.7 MHz. If the local oscillator tracks above, the frequency of the image channel is:

A. 178.2 MHz
B. 167.5 MHz
C. 146.1 MHz
D. 21.4 MHz
E. 135.4 MHz

Page(s) 346

Q7-092 It is required to increase the directional properties of a Hertz dipole, which is used for reception purposes. This can be done by:

A. increasing the dipole's length
B. adding an inductor in series with the dipole
C. adding a capacitor in series with the dipole
D. reducing the dipole's length
E. adding parasitic elements

Page(s) 422 to 424

Q7-093 In order to correct the common emitter amplifier circuit of FIG. 7-13:

A. reverse the collector battery
B. reverse both batteries
C. reverse the base battery
D. shift the ground point
E. the circuit is correct as shown

Page(s) 239, 240

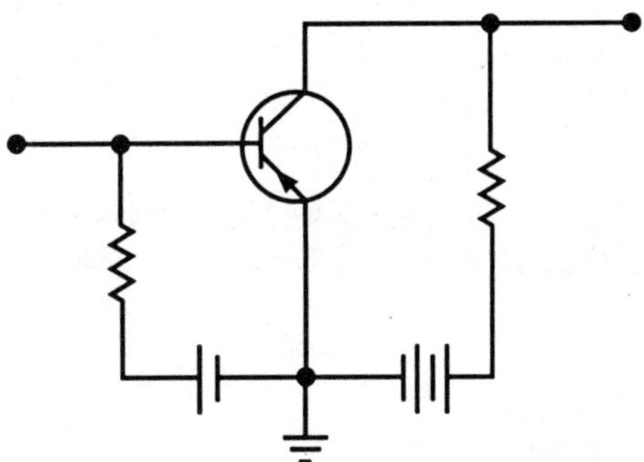

7-13 Circuit for Question 7-093.

Q7-094 Class-A operation of an amplifier stage is signified by:

A. minimum distortion
B. centering its Q point on the load line

C. low efficiency
D. continuous collector current flows throughout the cycle of the input signal
E. all of the above choices are true

Page(s) 245 to 247

Q7-095 In the circuit of FIG. 7-14, the voltage at the base relative to ground is:

A. +5 V
B. +4.3 V
C. +0.7 V
D. +20 V
E. +15 V

Page(s) 233, 234

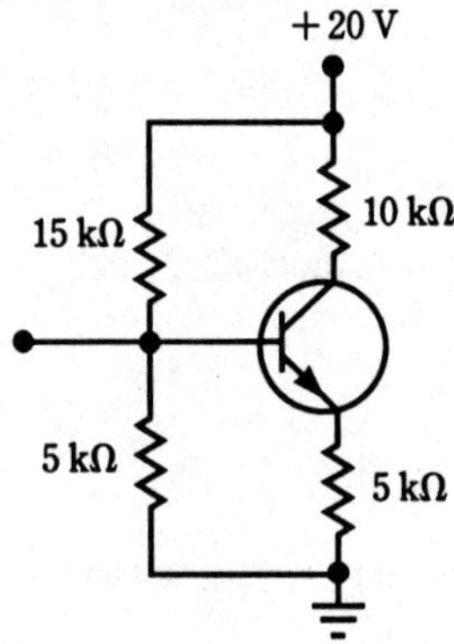

7-14 Circuit for Question 7-095.

Q7-096 Amplitude modulation created in an amplifier before the final RF stage is called:

A. indirect modulation
B. direct modulation
C. low-level modulation
D. intermediate modulation
E. high-level modulation

Page(s) 326

Q7-097 An FM broadcast receiver is tuned to 98.9 MHz and is experiencing interference from an aircraft, which is transmitting on 121.3 MHz. The most probable cause of this difficulty is:

A. crossmodulation
B. intermodulation
C. adjacent-channel interference
D. image-channel interference
E. propagation fading

Page(s) 382

Q7-098 Identify the circuit shown in FIG. 7-15:

A. audio-frequency amplifier
B. Armstrong oscillator

C. neutralized RF amplifier
D. Hartley oscillator
E. Colpitts oscillator

Page(s) 271

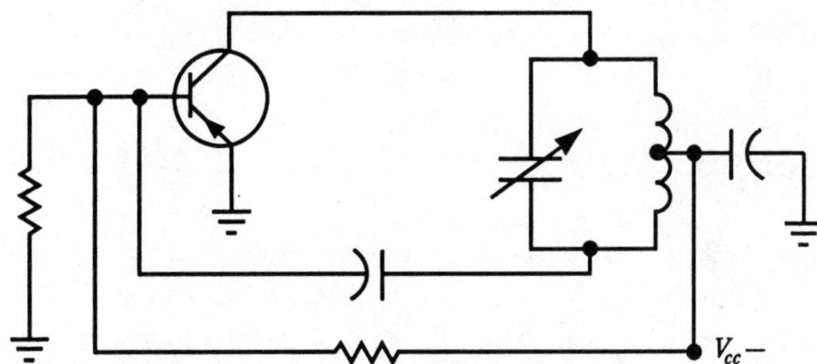

7-15 Circuit for Question 7-098.

Q7-099 The value of the standing-wave ratio (SWR) on a matched line with zero reflected power, is:

A. ∞
B. 1.2
C. 0
D. 1
E. 0.5

Page(s) 410

Q7-100 In FIG. 7-16, the ratio of the power dissipated in the parallel circuit to the power dissipated in the series circuit is:

A. 2:1
B. 1:2
C. 4:1
D. 1:4
E. 4.5:1

Page(s) 26 to 28, 36 to 38

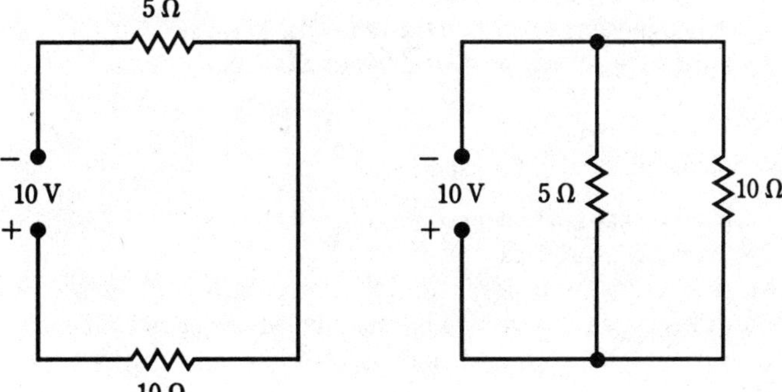

7-16 Circuit for Question 7-100.

Element 3
Test 8

Note: questions 8-001 through 8-011 refer to the schematic of FIG. 8-1.

Q8-001 In the absence of any input signal, the dc voltage across the resistor, R2, is:

A. 5 V
B. 4.3 V
C. 0.07 V
D. 10 V
E. 15 V

Page(s) 306 to 308

Q8-002 What is the function of the capacitor, C13?

A. tuning of Q3's collector load
B. C13 is part of a high-pass filter to attenuate the harmonics
C. C13 is the neutralizing capacitor
D. C13 matches the antenna load to the value of load required by the final stage
E. C13 prevents the generation of parasitic oscillations

Page(s) 306 to 308

Q8-003 What is the purpose of the capacitor, C14?

A. C14 is part of a band pass filter to accentuate the harmonics
B. C14 is the neutralizing capacitor
C. C14 is an anti-parasitic component
D. C14 matches the antenna load to the value of load required by the final stage
E. C14, in conjunction with C13, form a capacitive voltage divider to prevent positive feedback

Page(s) 306 to 308

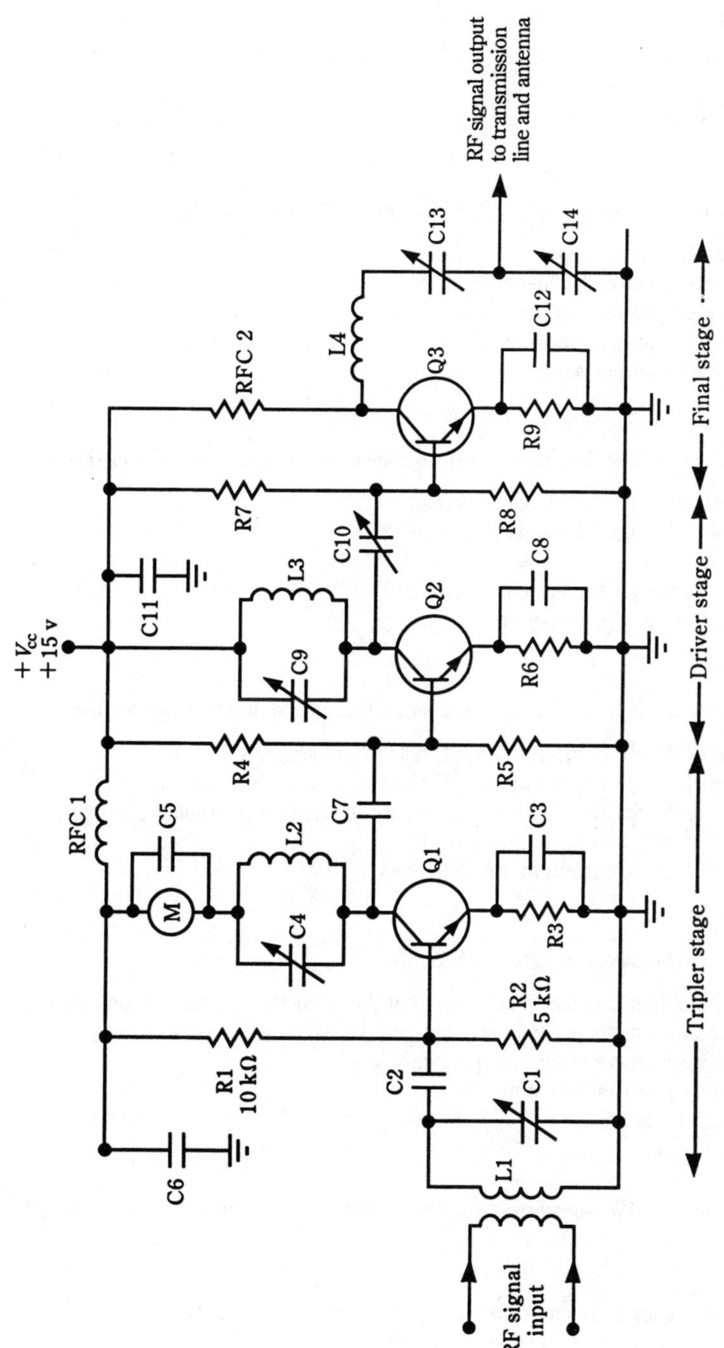

8-1 Schematic diagram for Questions 8-001 thru 8-011.

Q8-004 Which of the following events would have the least effect on the circuit's performance?

A. C13 open-circuits
B. R3 open-circuits
C. C11 open-circuits
D. C4 open-circuits
E. C14 short-circuits

Page(s) 306 to 308

Q8-005 What is the effect on the circuit's performance if C3 open-circuits?

A. parasitic oscillations increase
B. the transmitter's output frequency increases
C. the transmitter's output frequency decreases
D. the transmitter's output power increases
E. the transmitter's output power decreases

Page(s) 306 to 308

Q8-006 What is the effect on the circuit's performance if a short circuit is developed across R3?

A. the transmitter's output frequency decreases
B. the transmitter's output frequency increases
C. Q1 is cut off
D. the stability of the Q1 tripler stage is reduced
E. the transmitter's power output increases

Page(s) 306 to 308

Q8-007 As capacitor C4 is tuned through resonance at the third harmonic frequency:

A. the reading of the RF current meter, M, falls to a minimum value
B. the reading of the RF current meter, M, rises to a maximum value
C. the reading of the dc current meter, M, is zero throughout the tuning procedure
D. the reading of the dc current meter, M, dips
E. the reading of the dc current meter, M, peaks

Page(s) 306 to 308

Q8-008 If a short circuit develops across RFC2, the:

A. transmitter's output frequency increases, but the RF power output remains the same
B. transmitter's output frequency decreases, but the RF power output remains the same
C. transmitter's RF power output fails to a very low level
D. transmitter's RF power output increases
E. transistor Q3 is cut off

Page(s) 306 to 308

Q8-009 When tuning a CW transmitter, such as shown in the schematic diagram of FIG. 8-1, the first step is to:

A. connect a dummy antenna
B. switch on all stages and then transmit your call sign
C. tune all stages with the transmitter's antenna connected
D. check the output frequency of the oscillator stage
E. apply full voltage to the final stage

Page(s) 306 to 308

Q8-010 What is the purpose of the capacitor, C5?

A. to act as a capacitor shunt to extend the RF current range of the meter, M
B. to prevent current surges from damaging the meter, M
C. to bypass the RF components contained in the collector current so that these components do not affect the readings of the meter, M
D. to bypass the harmonics contained in the collector current so that only the fundamental component passed through the meter, M
E. C5 is an anti-parasitic component

Page(s) 306 to 308

Q8-011 If the harmonics radiated by the transmitter are too strong:

A. increase the amount of signal bias on the final stage
B. reduce the value of C13
C. increase the value of C14
D. adjust the value of C10 to reduce the amount of signal bias on the transistor Q3
E. either choice B or C is correct

Page(s) 306 to 308

Q8-012 If the time interval between a radar pulse being transmitted and the echo being received is 105 microseconds, what is the range of the target in nautical miles?

A. 16.98
B. 8.49
C. 19.56
D. 9.78
E. 4.89

Page(s) 483, 484

Q8-013 A 250-mV signal encounters a circuit that produces 20-dB attenuation. The output signal is:

A. 1.25 mV
B. 2.5 mV
C. 0.25 mV
D. 25 mV
E. 12.5 mV

Page(s) 145 to 147

Q8-014 If the time interval between a radar pulse being transmitted and the echo being received is 87 microseconds, what is the total distance in nautical miles from the radar set to the target and back again?

A. 16.20
B. 8.10
C. 14.07
D. 32.40
E. 7.03

Page(s) 483, 484

Q8-015 A power level of – 20 dBm is equivalent to:

A. 100 mW
B. 0.1 mW
C. 10 μW
D. 1 μW
E. 100 μW

Page(s) 145 to 147

Q8-016 A beat-frequency oscillator (BFO):

A. is a crystal oscillator contained within a TRF receiver
B. is used to detect telephony
C. produces an audio signal in the loudspeaker when the BFO's output is mixed with the local oscillator's output
D. is a crystal oscillator that substitutes for the local oscillator on fixed-frequency reception
E. is used to create an audio note in the loudspeaker during the reception of a CW telegraphy signal

Page(s) 359

Q8-017 The carrier power of a ship station's radiotelephone transmitter must:

A. not exceed 25 watts
B. not exceed 100 watts
C. be at least 10 watts
D. be at least 8 watts
E. choices A and D are true

Page(s) 615

Q8-018 All ships that are licensed to transmit telephony on one or more frequencies in the 1605- to 3500-kHz band are required to maintain a listening watch on 2182 kHz for:

A. at least three minutes, two times each hour, beginning on the hour and the half-hour
B. three minutes, twice each hour, beginning at 15 minutes and 45 minutes past each hour
C. at least three minutes, once each hour, beginning on the hour
D. at least two minutes, two times each hour, beginning on the hour and the half-hour
E. at least two minutes, two times each hour, beginning at 15 minutes and 45 minutes past each hour

Page(s) 583, 584

Q8-019 The pre-emphasis circuit in an FM transmitter is used to:

A. accentuate low audio-frequency components in order to improve their signal-to-noise ratio
B. attenuate high audio-frequency components in order to improve their signal-to-noise ratio
C. attenuate low audio-frequency components in order to improve their signal-to-noise ratio
D. accentuate high audio-frequency components in order to improve their signal-to-noise ratio
E. amplify low audio-frequency components and attenuate high audio-frequency components

Page(s) 370

Q8-020 A station in the International Fixed Services is operating within the 1605- to 30000-kHz band. The frequency tolerance of this station is:

A. 0.02%
B. 15 ppm
C. 0.0015%
D. 20 ppm
E. choices B and C are true

Page(s) 579

Q8-021 The simplified block diagram of FIG. 8-2 represents a (an):

A. low-level modulated AM transmitter
B. direct FM transmitter
C. indirect FM transmitter
D. PM transmitter
E. high-level modulated AM transmitter

Page(s) 321

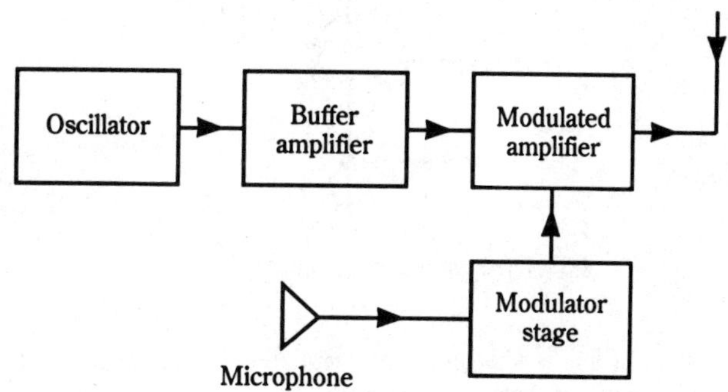

8-2 Block diagram for Question 8-021.

Q8-022 A marine VHF transmitter must be capable of:

A. producing a carrier power of at least 8 watts
B. producing a carrier power which does not exceed 25 watts
C. reducing its carrier power to 1 watt or less
D. producing a modulation percentage between 75% and 100% on modulation peaks of frequent recurrence
E. all of the above choices are true

Page(s) 615

Q8-023 The purpose of a buffer amplifier is to:

A. prevent the oscillator from being overloaded by the preceding stage
B. isolate a preceding stage from the loading effect of the following stage
C. prevent frequency instability in the oscillator stage because of the variations in the loading effect of the following stage

D. prevent RF interference from being transferred from the antenna to the oscillator stage
E. choices B and C are true

Page(s) 298

Q8-024 In FIG. 8-3, the positive feedback occurs through:

A. the drain-to-gate capacitance
B. the gate-to-source capacitance
C. the drain-to-source capacitance
D. direct feedback
E. capacitive filtering

Page(s) 278

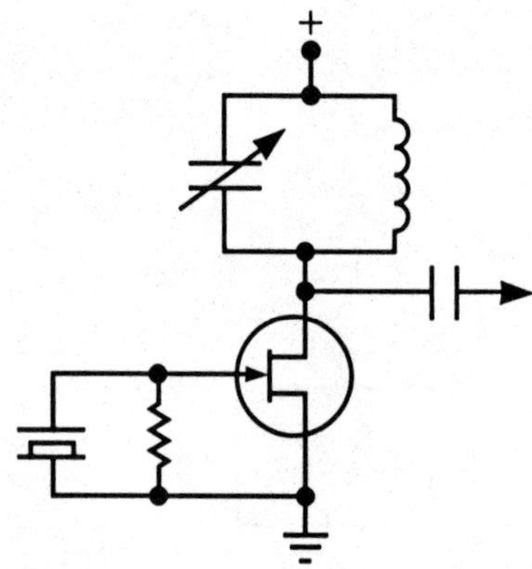

8-3 Circuit for Question 8-024.

Q8-025 A λ/4 section of line is shorted at one end and connected to an RF generator at the other end. The input impedance at the generator is:

A. theoretically infinite
B. in practice, a high value of resistance
C. equivalent to a parallel resonant LC circuit
D. the result of dividing the value of a voltage antinode by the value of a current node
E. all of the above choices are true

Page(s) 408

Q8-026 To make certain that a marine transmitter's carrier frequency is within its assigned tolerance limits:

A. zero beat the output frequency with an approved standard
B. use a frequency counter to determine the crystal oscillator's frequency
C. zero beat the output frequency with one of WWV's carriers
D. use an absorption wavemeter
E. use a grid-dip meter

Page(s) 337, 338

Q8-027 Figure 8-4 shows the display on the face of an oscilloscope. If the horizontal TIME/DIV control is set to 50 μs/div., the frequency of the sinewave voltage is:

A. 5 MHz
B. 50 MHz
C. 500 kHz
D. 50 kHz
E. 5 kHz

Page(s) 189 to 191

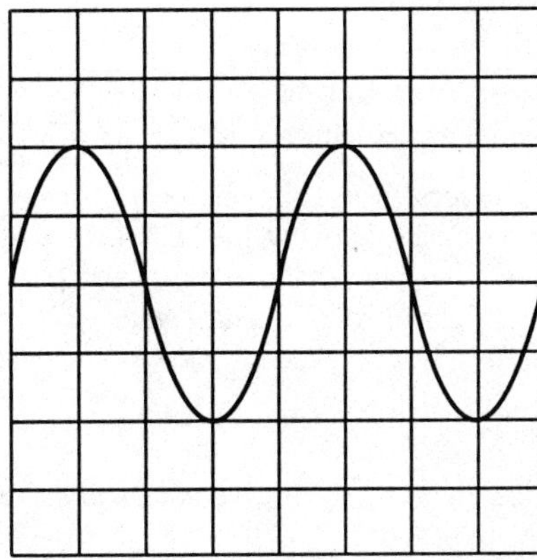

8-4 Display for Questions 8-027 and 8-028.

Q8-028 In QUES. 8-27, the vertical VOLTS/DIV control is set to 10 mV per division. The RMS value of the sine-wave voltage is:

A. 20 mV
B. 40 mV
C. 28.3 mV
D. 14.1 mV
E. 7.1 mV

Page(s) 189 to 191

Q8-029 A transmitter's output frequency is 2182 kHz. If there are three doubler stages between the oscillator and the final stage, the oscillator's frequency is:

A. 2182 kHz
B. 1091 kHz
C. 545.5 kHz
D. 272.75 kHz
E. 136.4 kHz

Page(s) 301

Q8-030 The frequency used by the Emergency Locator Transmitter is:

A. 156.8 MHz
B. 156.65 MHz
C. 121.5 MHz
D. 243 MHz
E. choices C and D are true

Page(s) 572

Q8-031 An aircraft's navigational aid measures the time interval between an interrogatory pulse and the reply from a radar beacon. The system is called:

A. Search Radar
B. Transponder Time Interval Measurement
C. Interrogatory Friend or Foe
D. Distance Measuring Equipment
E. Interrogator Transponder Range

Page(s) 509 to 511

Q8-032 The operating power of a transmitter is increased by:

A. increasing the level of reverse signal bias on the final stage
B. reducing the degree of coupling between the final stage and the antenna load
C. raising the value of the dc supply voltage to the final stage
D. reducing the amount of signal drive to the final stage
E. lowering the value of the efficiency factor

Page(s) 303

Q8-033 In the marine service, the term *safety communications* includes:

A. distress signals only
B. urgency signals only
C. safety signals only
D. urgency and safety signals only
E. distress, urgency, and safety signals

Page(s) 600

Q8-034 In FIG. 8-5, Z_f is a 150-kΩ resistor and Z_i is a 10-kΩ resistor. Assuming that the value of A is large, the gain of this operational amplifier is:

A. +15
B. −15
C. +16
D. −16
E. −15.5

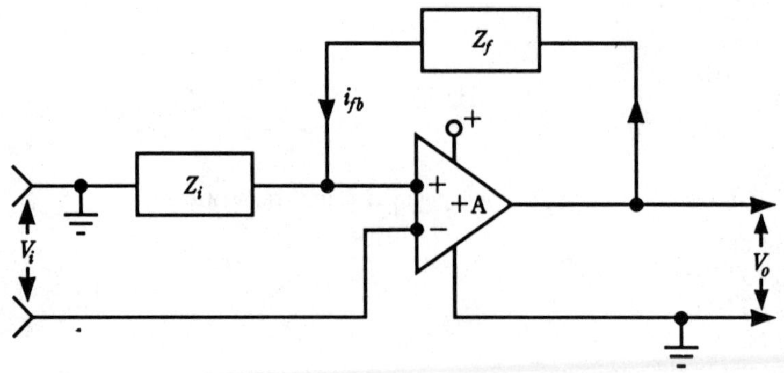

8-5 Circuit for Question 8-034.

Page(s) 286 to 288

Q8-035 The holder of a General Radiotelephone License is required:

A. when a cargo ship's station power exceeds 1500 W of peak envelope power
B. when a passenger ship carries more than six passengers and its station power exceeds a carrier of 250 W or a peak envelope power of 1500 W
C. to maintain FCC approved transmitters in the marine, aviation, and international fixed services
D. to operate a voluntary ship station that is sailing on a domestic voyage and is operating in the VHF band only
E. choices A, B, and C are true

Page(s) 580, 581

Q8-036 The disadvantage of using a squelch circuit is that:

A. noise is reduced to a minimum in the absence of an incoming signal
B. the effect of AGC is reduced for strong signals
C. very weak signals might not be received
D. receiver sensitivity is reduced for strong signals
E. receiver selectivity is reduced for strong signals

Page(s) 355

Q8-037 The cavity resonator:

A. is equivalent to an LC resonant circuit
B. produces a frequency which is independent of the cavity size
C. is confined to frequencies below 100 MHz
D. has a low Q factor for narrow-band operation
E. is confined to operation in the VHF band

Page(s) 449 to 451

Q8-038 A calling frequency is:

A. not assigned to a particular radiotelephone station
B. for example, 2182 kHz
C. one on which all stations generally listen
D. not used for the main bulk of the message traffic
E. all of the above choices are true

Page(s) 557

Q8-039 If the range of a target is 7.5 nautical miles, what is the time interval in microseconds between the radar pulse being transmitted and the target echo being received?

A. 46.3
B. 93
C. 186
D. 162
E. 81

Page(s) 483

Q8-040 An FM receiver is tuned to a carrier frequency of 157.0 MHz. If its local oscillator is generating an output whose frequency is 167.7 MHz, the frequency of the image channel is:

A. 21.4 MHz
B. 146.3 MHz
C. 135.6 MHz
D. 190.1 MHz
E. 178.4 MHz

Page(s) 382

Q8-041 If any top light or any flashing beacon of an antenna tower is extinguished or malfunctioning,.

A. the transmitter must be shut down
B. the FCC regional office must be immediately informed
C. the nearest Flight Service station must be informed if the problem cannot be corrected within 30 minutes
D. the office of the Federal Aviation Administration must be informed if the problem cannot be corrected within 30 minutes
E. either choice C or D is true

Page(s) 612

Q8-042 A six-pole alternator rotates at a speed of 1000 rpm. The value of the generated frequency is:

A. 50 Hz
B. 40 Hz
C. 60 Hz
D. 25 Hz
E. 120 Hz

Page(s) 107, 108

Q8-043 An ammeter with a resistance of 3750 Ω has a scale with 12 divisions. When 120 V is applied to the meter, the reading shows full-scale deflection. When another resistor is added in series with the meter, the reading is 7.5 divisions if the applied voltage is increased to 135 V. The value of the additional resistor is:

A. 1500 Ω
B. 7500 Ω
C. 6750 Ω
D. 3750 Ω
E. 3000 Ω

Page(s) 86, 87

Q8-044 The bridge-to-bridge radiotelephone transmitter:

A. must be capable of 8 to 25 W
B. is normally limited to a power output of 1 W
C. has a minimum power capability of 0.7 W
D. uses a G3E emission on the navigational frequency of 156.65 MHz
E. all of the above choices are true

Page(s) 554, 555

Q8-045 In FIG. 8-6, the AGC circuit has the disadvantage of:

A. increasing the sensitivity for strong signals
B. increasing the selectivity
C. reducing the image-channel rejection
D. reducing the sensitivity for weak signals
E. increasing the fluctuations in the output signal to the loudspeaker

Page(s) 354

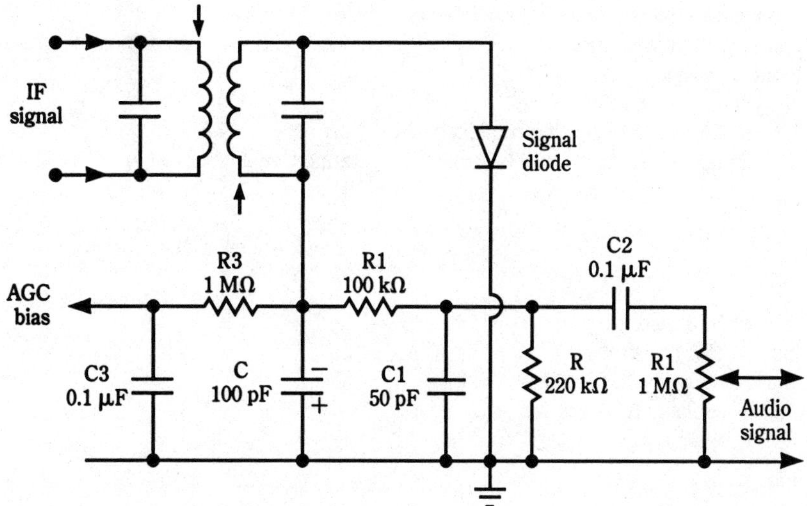

8-6 Circuit for Question 8-045.

Q8-046 What is the purpose of the electromagnets surrounding the traveling-wave tube?

A. to slow down the signal on the helix
B. to accelerate the electron beam
C. to focus the electron beam and prevent the electrons from spreading out
D. to attenuate the signal on the helix
E. to couple the signal on the helix to the output waveguide

Page(s) 467 to 469

Q8-047 The transmission of the radiotelephone auto-alarm signal is tested on a frequency that is:

A. 2182 kHz
B. 121.5 MHz
C. 500 MHz
D. not a distress frequency
E. either choice A, B, or C is correct

Page(s) 551

Q8-048 The stages that mainly determine a communications receiver's sensitivity and sensitivity are the:

A. IF amplifiers
B. mixer stage

C. detector stage
D. audio amplifiers
E. RF amplifiers

Page(s) 350

8-049 The circuitry of a marine transmitter is modified so that the operating frequency is changed. The correct procedure is to:

A. immediately inform the regional office of the FCC
B. measure the transmitter's frequency against an accepted standard and enter the results in the station log
C. apply for a new callsign
D. submit a station modification request on FCC Form 506
E. there is no correct procedure because the operating frequency must never be changed

Page(s) 549

Q8-050 Which of the following systems contains a limiter stage, a discriminator, and a de-emphasis circuit?

A. direct FM transmitter
B. indirect FM transmitter
C. single sideband AM receiver
D. double sideband AM receiver
E. FM receiver

Page(s) 383

Q8-051 Which of the following is the symbol for the bidirectional diode thyristor (diac)?

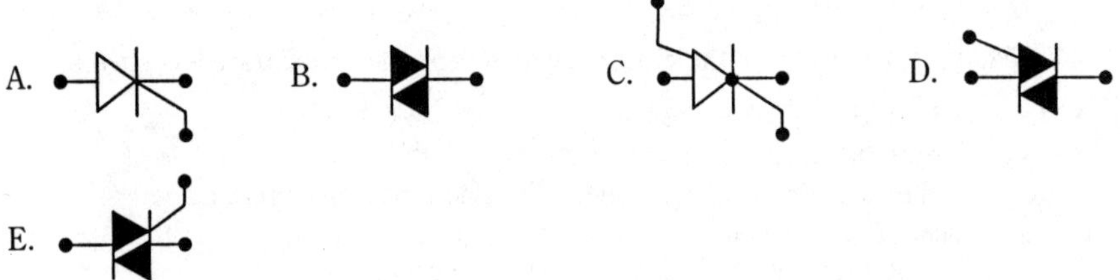

Page(s) 291 to 295

Q8-052 Referring to QUES. 8-051, which is the symbol for the bidirectional triode thyristor (triac)?

A. A
B. B
C. C
D. D
E. E

Page(s) 291 to 295

Q8-053 The circuit of FIG. 8-7 has a:

A. voltage gain of less than unity
B. low input impedance
C. low output impedance

D. high input impedance
E. poor frequency response

Page(s) 253 to 257

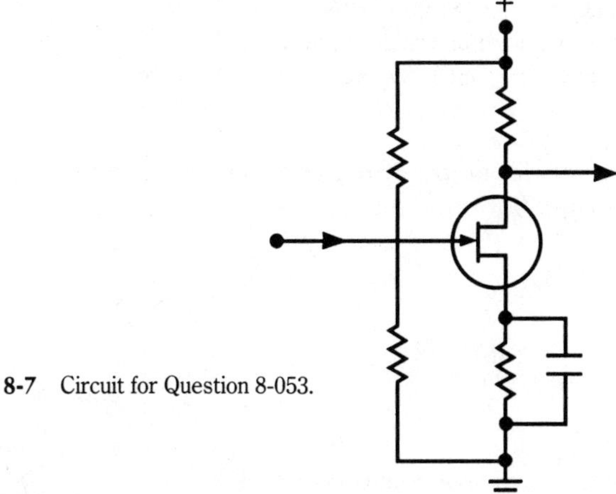

8-7 Circuit for Question 8-053.

Q8-054 A marine radiotelephone transmitter operating on 2182 kHz is to be tested while the ship is at sea. The procedure involves:

A. listening to make sure the channel is not being used
B. changing to a working frequency before initiating the test
C. transmitting the station's callsign (normally given three times) followed by the word "test"
D. a test on the international radiotelephone distress frequency is never allowed
E. choices A and C are true

Page(s) 610

Q8-055 When carrying out a soldering procedure in electronics work, it is necessary to:

A. use acid flux
B. use the least possible amount of solder
C. use an adequate but not excessive amount of heat
D. clean all parts after soldering
E. use a thermal shunt in all soldering operations for components that are not heat-sensitive

Page(s) 100 to 102

Q8-056 The supply to the primary winding of the power transformer is 100 V, 60 Hz. The secondary winding is center tapped and a voltage of 300 V is measured from one side of the secondary winding to the center tap. The transformer's turns ratio is:

A. 3:1
B. 1:3
C. 1:6
D. 6:1
E. 1:0.3

Page(s) 166 to 168

Q8-057 The load on a shunt-wound motor is temporarily removed. What occurs if the field winding then open-circuits?

A. the motor stops
B. there is a sharp decrease in the speed
C. there is virtually no change in the speed
D. the direction of the armature rotation reverses
E. the armature speeds up and could ultimately be destroyed

Page(s) 99

Q8-058 When compared with the peak envelope power, the carrier of an aeronautical J3E emission must be suppressed by at least:

A. 10 dB
B. 20 dB
C. 30 dB
D. 40 dB
E. 50 dB

Page(s) 605

Q8-059 What, if anything, is wrong with the circuit of FIG. 8-8?

A. replace the pnp transistor with an equivalent npn transistor
B. reverse the collector battery
C. remove R1
D. interchange the emitter and the collector
E. the circuit is correct as shown

Page(s) 232, 233

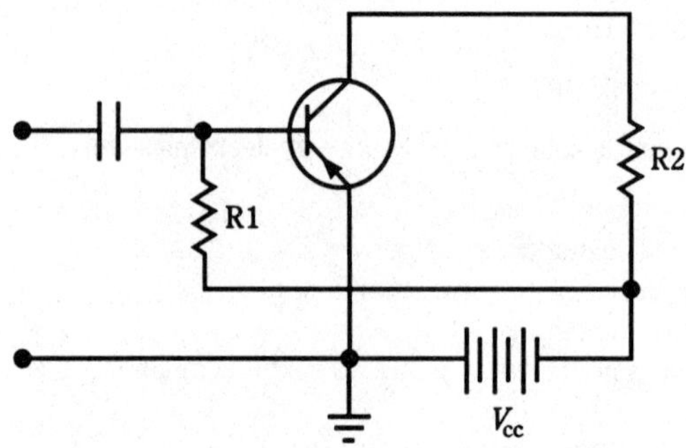

8-8 Circuit for Question 8-059.

Q8-060 Which of the following emission designators has the greatest necessary bandwidth?

A. 2K80J3E
B. 2K66H3N
C. 16K0F3E
D. 300HJ2B
E. 6K00A3E

Page(s) 334

Q8-061 The signal radiated from the antenna of a marine MF transmitter is:

A. horizontally polarized
B. elliptically polarized
C. vertically polarized
D. circularly polarized
E. either choice A or C is true

Page(s) 437

Q8-062 It is required to increase the bandwidth of a series LCR circuit without altering the resonant frequency. This result can be achieved by:

A. lowering the value of L
B. increasing the value of C
C. raising the ratio, $L{:}C$, without altering the value of the product, $L \times C$
D. lowering the value of Q
E. lowering the value of the resistance

Page(s) 149 to 154

Q8-063 Under which of the following circumstances may an operator use the information in an intercepted communication for his personal benefit?

A. when the communication has been broadcast
B. when the communication has been transmitted by an amateur
C. when the communication has been transmitted for the use of the general public
D. when a communication relates to a ship in distress
E. all of the above choices are true

Page(s) 563

Q8-064 When installing electrolytic capacitors, precautions should be taken to ensure that the:

A. correct polarity is observed
B. value of the capacitance does not exceed a certain critical value
C. voltage rating is not more than the value of the applied voltage
D. capacitor is not used in dc circuits
E. temperature of the surrounding air is maintained at a constant level

Page(s) 74

Q8-065 Which of the following frequencies can be assigned to a VOR station?

A. 111.05 MHz
B. 115.05 MHz
C. 118.10 MHz
D. 121.50 MHz
E. 119.05 MHz

Page(s) 620

Q8-066 The percentage of modulation for an AM transmitter is increased from 0 to 80%. The percentage increase in the antenna current is:

A. 15%
B. 18%
C. 19.5%
D. 17.5%
E. 16%

Page(s) 330, 331

Q8-067 When an operator receives a notice of violation, he/she must forward a written response within:

A. 3 days
B. 5 days
C. 10 days
D. 15 days
E. 30 days

Page(s) 618, 619

Q8-068 A conductor is cutting a magnetic field. The value of the voltage induced in the inductor depends on the:

A. length of the conductor
B. velocity of the conductor
C. angle at which the conductor is cutting the flux lines
D. flux density
E. all of the above are true

Page(s) 61

Q8-069 An audio-amplifier uses a pnp transistor in a common-emitter configuration. If the collector-base junction is forward-biased, the:

A. stage will behave as a conventional linear amplifier
B. emitter-base circuit would operate in the cut-off mode
C. transistor could be ruined
D. transistor is operating in the saturation mode
E. choices C and D are true

Page(s) 239, 240

Q8-070 In the combinatorial logic circuit of FIG. 8-9, all of the inputs are in the "low" state so that the output is also "low." Which single input can be changed from "low" to "high" in order to produce a "high" output?

A. A
B. B
C. C
D. D
E. E

Page(s) 543

Q8-071 When an AM transmitter uses high level modulation, the audio signal is introduced into the:

A. oscillator stage (direct method)
B. phase modulator (indirect method)

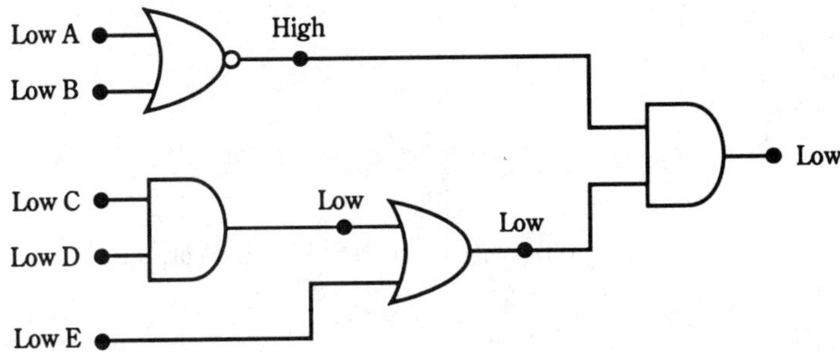

8-9 Logic circuit for Question 8-070.

C. intermediate RF amplifier
D. buffer stage
E. RF final stage

Page(s) 326

Q8-072 A transmitter uses a 3-MHz crystal with a temperature coefficient of +10 Hz/MHz/°C. If the crystal oscillator is followed by three doubler stages, what is the transmitter's output frequency if the temperature falls by 20°C?

A. 24 MHz
B. 24.0016 MHz
C. 23.9984 MHz
D. 24.0048 MHz
E. 23.9952 MHz

Page(s) 276

Q8-073 A sine-wave signal is applied to a transistorized class-A amplifier. For how many degrees of the signal cycle does the collector current flow?

A. 360°
B. 270°
C. 180°
D. 120°
E. 90°

Page(s) 245 to 247

Q8-074 If a radio operator services and maintains more than one radio station:

A. the operator's license is posted at the primary control point and a photocopy of the license is carried on his/her person
B. the operator must obtain a verification card from the regional FCC office
C. a photocopy of his/her license must be posted at the control point of each transmitter
D. the operator's license must be enclosed with the details of all the transmitters that the operator is servicing
E. the operator does not post his/her license, but carries it on his/her person at all times

Page(s) 598

Q8-075 A marine VHF transmitter with F3E emission must be capable of reducing its operating power to:

A. 0.1 W or less
B. 1 W or less
C. 5 W or less
D. 8 W or less
E. 25 W or less

Page(s) 615

Q8-076 The gauge number of a wire must be adequate for the current flowing through the wire, otherwise:

A. the insulation on the wire might melt
B. there might be too much power loss in the wire
C. the voltage drop across the wire might be excessive
D. if the wire were too thin, its resistance would be too high
E. all of the above choices are true

Page(s) 25

Q8-077 A message concerning the safety of navigation is preceded by the word:

A. warning
B. care
C. safety
D. security
E. pan

Page(s) 600

Q8-078 If the RF final stage of a marine transmitter is 100% modulated by a pure tone, the ratio of the power output of the (audio) modulator stage to the dc power input to the modulated stage is:

A. 1:1
B. 1:2
C. 2:1
D. 1:$\sqrt{2}$
E. 1:3

Page(s) 326

Q8-079 A 60-W electric light bulb is rated at 120 V. What is the value of the current that flows through the filament of the light bulb?

A. 2 A
B. 0.5 A
C. 4 A
D. 1 A
E. 1.5 A

Page(s) 12 to 14

Q8-080 In FIG. 8-10, the symbol is that of a:

A. npn junction transistor
B. junction field effect transistor
C. DE MOSFET

D. pnp junction transistor
E. E MOSFET

Page(s) 225

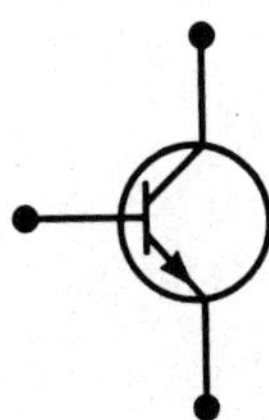

8-10 Symbol for Question 8-080.

Q8-081 Which of the following actions should be taken when communications are difficult or when signals are weak?

A. increase the power of the transmitter
B. switch to the calling frequency
C. increase the percentage of modulation
D. use the phonetic alphabet
E. shout into the microphone as loudly as possible

Page(s) 339, 340

Q8-082 Portable hand-held ship transmitters when at sea:

A. require their own individual licenses
B. are operated under the authorization of the ship station license
C. must each be operated by a General Radiotelephone licensee
D. must each be operated by the holder of a Marine Operator Permit
E. must each be operated by the holder of a Restricted Radiotelephone Permit

Page(s) 596

Q8-083 The display of FIG. 8-11 indicates the input to the spectrum analyzer is a:

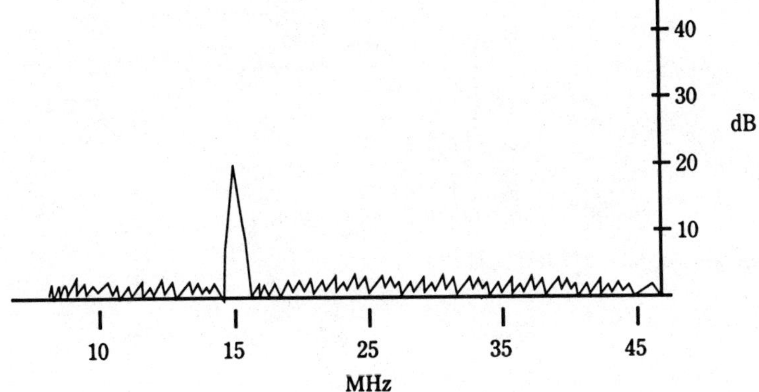

8-11 Display for Question 8-083.

A. 15-MHz sine-wave signal
B. 15-MHz positive sawtooth signal
C. 15-MHz square-wave signal
D. 15-MHz triangular signal
E. 15-MHz negative sawtooth signal

Page(s) 317, 318

Q8-084 What is the maximum authorized power for hand-held portable units on board a ship?

A. 1 watt
B. 3 watts
C. 5 watts
D. 8 watts
E. 25 watts

Page(s) 596

Q8-085 An operator may signify a separation between portions of a message by using the word:

A. break
B. separate
C. pause
D. split
E. divide

Page(s) 591

Q8-086 Which of the following logic gates corresponds to the truth table of FIG. 8-12?

A. P Q R
B. P Q R
C. P Q R
D. P Q R
E. P Q R

P	*Q*	*R*
Low	Low	High
Low	High	High
High	Low	High
High	High	Low

8-12 Truth table for 8-086.

Page(s) 533 to 535

Q8-087 When compared with a voltmeter, a logic probe:

A. has less loading-up effect
B. has a direct readout
C. is smaller in size
D. is less accurate
E. choices B and C are true

Page(s) 599

Q8-088 An on-board mobile unit is used to establish communications with:

A. other units of the same station for operational communications
B. on-board stations of another ship during the transfer of 250 or more barrels of oil
C. other units of the same station in the immediate vicinity of the ship while the ship is docking
D. on-board units of other ships owned by the same licensee
E. choices A, B, and C are true

Page(s) 590

Q8-089 When a marine transmitter uses frequency or phase modulation, the peak modulation must be maintained between:

A. 60% to 90%
B. 65% to 100%
C. 70% to 100%
D. 75% to 100%
E. 80% to 100%

Page(s) 588

Q8-090 What is the authorized bandwidth of a marine J3E emission?

A. 4 kHz
B. 3 kHz
C. 6 kHz
D. 8 kHz
E. 2.8 kHz

Page(s) 334

Q8-091 A transmitter on an aircraft has an assigned frequency of 156.4 MHz and a frequency tolerance of ± 10 ppm. What is the value of the maximum permitted frequency deviation?

A. 1.564 kHz
B. 156.4 Hz
C. 15.64 kHz
D. 15.64 Hz
E. 1.564 Hz

Page(s) 297

Q8-092 A class-B Emergency Position-Indicating Radio Beacon (E.P.I.R.B) is tested:

A. by switching to a dummy antenna
B. in coordination with the U.S. Coast Guard
C. during the first five minutes of each hour with the test not lasting more than one second
D. without the radiation exceeding 25 μV/m at a distance of 150 feet
E. all of the above choices are true

Page(s) 573, 574

Q8-093 Which of the following details are contained in the log of a ship's radiotelephone station?

A. summary of all distress, urgency, and safety traffic
B. details of all installation, service, and maintenance work carried out
C. signature of the operator at the beginning and end of a watch period

D. name of the vessel and its callsign
E. all of the above choices are true

Page(s) 585, 586

Q8-094 In the circuit of FIG. 8-13 a voltmeter is used to determine the total power delivered by the voltage source. One procedure is to measure the voltage between:

A. the points W and Z. Then, multiply this reading by 150000 and divide the product by 2000
B. the points Y and Z. Square this voltage and divide the result by 2000
C. the points W and Y. Divide this voltage by 150000, then multiply the result by the value of the voltage measured between points Y and Z
D. the points W and X. Divide this voltage by 150000, then multiply this result by the voltage measured between points W and Z
E. the points W and X. Divide this voltage by 150000, then multiply the result by the voltage measured between points W and Y

Page(s) 31 to 33

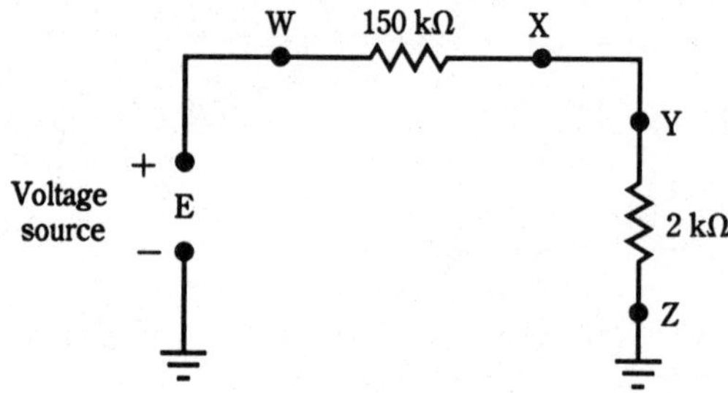

8-13 Circuit for Question 8-094.

Q8-095 The antenna system of a marine radar set uses a parabolic reflector in order to:

A. widen the beam and increase the surface coverage
B. match the impedance of the waveguide horn and free space
C. eliminate the requirement for separate transmitter and receiver antenna systems
D. lower the field gain and thereby broaden the antenna system's response
E. provide a unidirectional narrow beam

Page(s) 493

Q8-096 The property of conductance is measured in:

A. farads per meter
B. siemens
C. henrys per meter
D. ohms
E. coulombs

Page(s) 17, 18

Q8-097 The oscillator of an FM transmitter operates at one twelfth of the output frequency. If 100% modulation corresponds to a frequency deviation of 5 kHz and the transmitter is 60% modulated by a 1-kHz test tone, calculate the value of the frequency deviation at the oscillator stage:

A. 3 kHz
B. 250 Hz
C. 1 kHz
D. 417 Hz
E. 125 Hz

Page(s) 367

Q8-098 An FM broadcast receiver is experiencing image-channel interference from an aviation transmitter that is operating on a frequency of 121.5 MHz. The frequency of the receiver's local oscillator is:

A. 101.1 MHz
B. 132.2 MHz
C. 110.8 MHz
D. 142.9 MHz
E. 90.4 MHz

Page(s) 382

Q8-099 A room temperature of 86° F is equivalent to:

A. 30° C
B. 54° C
C. 48° C
D. 27° C
E. 35° C

Page(s) 623

Q8-100 The output stage of an FM transmitter has a frequency deviation of 18 kHz, while the modulating tone has a frequency of 300 Hz. The value of the modulation index is:

A. 6
B. 60
C. 10
D. 167
E. 3.3

Page(s) 362

Element 3
Test 9

Q9-001 Which of the following signals has the highest priority?

A. distress
B. urgency
C. safety
D. security
E. emergency

Page(s) 599, 600

Q9-002 Why is it impossible to use a waveguide at low radio frequencies?

A. high dielectric loss
B. severe attenuation
C. excessive skin effect
D. excessive radiation
E. the size of the waveguide

Page(s) 452 to 454

Q9-003 Which of the following systems contains a variable frequency oscillator and a varactor diode modulator?

A. direct FM transmitter
B. indirect FM transmitter
C. AM transmitter
D. SSB transmitter
E. FM receiver

Page(s) 367

Q9-004 Which of the following logic circuits has an operation that corresponds to two or more switches (or relays) in parallel?

A. AND gate
B. NAND gate
C. OR gate
D. NOR gate
E. EX-OR gate

Page(s) 527 to 529

Q9-005 FIG. 9-1A represents the top and bottom views of a printed circuit board. Which of the schematics in FIG. 9-1B best corresponds to the circuit shown?

A. a
B. b
C. c
D. d
E. e

Page(s) 43 to 46

Q9-006 Express a frequency tolerance of $\pm 0.01\%$ in parts per million (ppm).

A. ± 1000 ppm
B. ± 100 ppm
C. ± 10 ppm
D. ± 1 ppm
E. ± 10000 ppm

Page(s) 297

Q9-007 When establishing the initial contact between two marine stations, the call signal is limited to:

A. 15 seconds and then not repeated for 1 minute if there is no reply
B. 30 seconds and then not repeated for 2 minutes if there is no reply
C. 45 seconds and then not repeated for 3 seconds if there is no reply
D. 1 minute and then not repeated for 5 minutes if there is no reply
E. 90 seconds and then not repeated for 5 minutes if there is no reply

Page(s) 557

Q9-008 Zener diodes are used:

A. to provide practically constant dc output voltages with variations in the load currents
B. to provide practically constant dc output voltages with variations in the line voltages
D. to act as voltage reference levels
D. with breakdown voltages which extend from 2 V to 200 V
E. all of the above choices are true

Page(s) 215, 216

Q9-009 What is the normal power output of a bridge-to-bridge transmitter?

A. 0.5 W
B. 1 W
C. 5 W

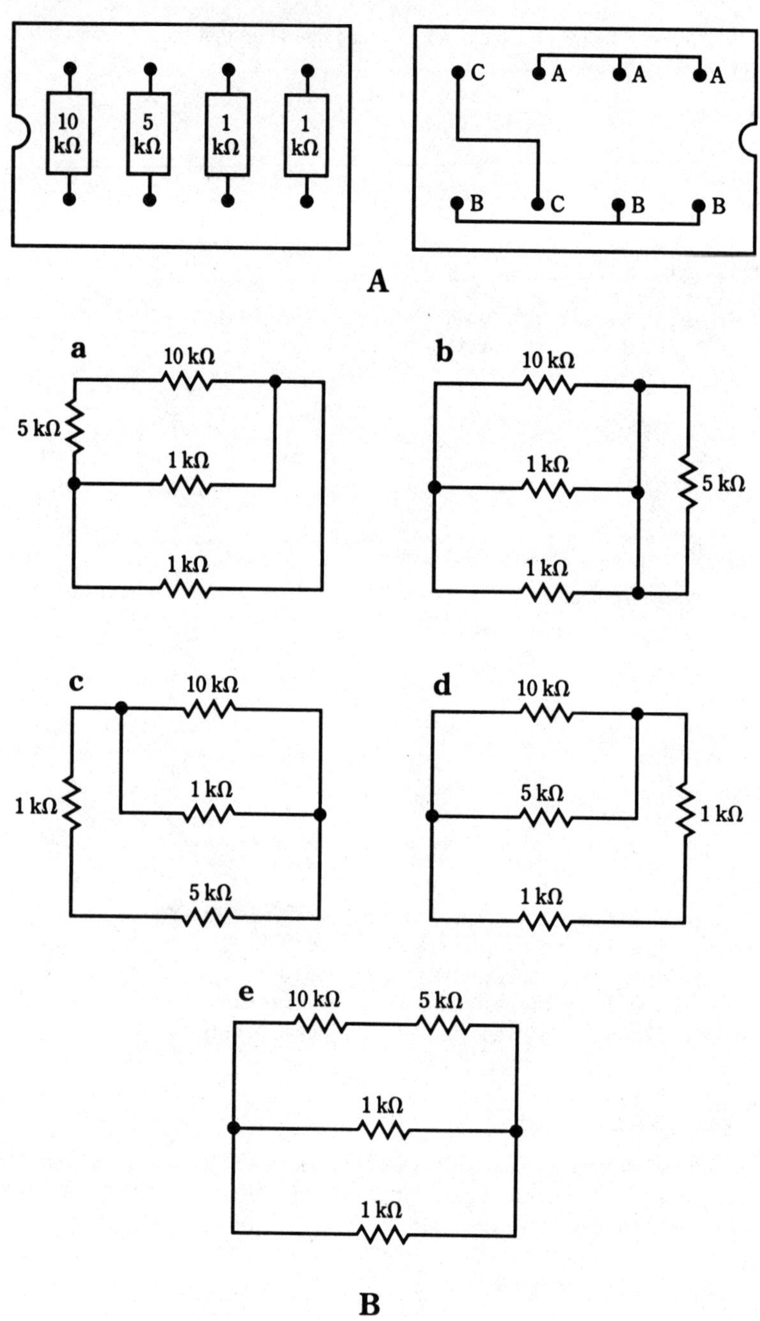

9-1 Circuit for Question 9-005.

D. 8 W
E. 25 W

Page(s) 554, 555

Q9-010 Parasitic oscillations can occur in a (an):

A. transmitter
B. receiver
C. RF amplifier
D. RF oscillator
E. all of the above choices are true

Page(s) 282, 283

Q9-011 What substance in its crystalline form can be used in oscillators?

A. silicon
B. germanium
C. carbon
D. quartz
E. sapphire

Page(s) 274

Q9-012 The radiotelephone auto-alarm receiver is used to:

A. activate automatic alarms in the radio room, bridge, and radio operator's quarters
B. alert the radio operator on watch that a distress signal or other important safety information is about to be transmitted
C. test the auto-alarm system
D. receive signals on 500 kHz
E. choices A and B are true

Page(s) 551

Q9-013 The limiter stage of an FM receiver:

A. feeds directly into the discriminator circuit
B. is an IF amplifier with a low gain
C. operates from a low dc voltage supply
D. is used to improve the signal-to-noise ratio in the output from the final audio stage
E. all of the above choices are true

Page(s) 384, 385

Q9-014 If a communications receiver is attempting to intercept a very weak signal:

A. the squelch circuit should be turned off
B. delayed AGC should be used
C. the AGC bias level must be increased
D. the squelch circuit should be switched on
E. choices B and D are true

Page(s) 355

Q9-015 The application for a ship's station license renewal must be signed by the:

A. ship's Master
B. ship's owner
C. ship's radio officer
D. General Radiotelephone operator
E. applicant

Page(s) 549

Q9-016 Calculate the maximum value of voltage that can be applied across a 15-kΩ 2-W resistor without exceeding its power rating:

A. 150 V
B. 300 V
C. 122 V
D. 200 V
E. 173 V

Page(s) 18

Q9-017 At an ac source the readings are: voltmeter 12 V, ammeter 9 A, wattmeter 90 W. The value of the power factor is:

A. 1.0
B. 0.9
C. 0.75
D. 0.83
E. 0.95

Page(s) 189

Q9-018 The mixer stage of an AM superhet receiver:

A. provides high gain for the input RF signal
B. provides high gain for the local oscillator signal
C. acts as a nonlinear device
D. produces the sum and difference frequencies of the local oscillator signal and the incoming RF signal
E. choices C and D are correct

Page(s) 348, 349

Q9-019 A temperature of 40° C (Celsius or Centigrade) is equivalent to:

A. 92°F
B. 104°F
C. −11°F
D. 72°F
E. 8°F

Page(s) 623

Q9-020 The intermediate-frequency amplifier of a communications receiver contains an RF transformer with tuned primary-tuned secondary circuits. If the bandwidth is too high so that the selectivity is inadequate:

A. increase the coupling factor to beyond its critical value
B. increase the value of the intermediate frequency
C. decrease the value of the intermediate frequency

D. decrease the coupling factor to below its critical value
E. reduce the amount of the signal input to the amplifier

Page(s) 170

Q9-021 Which of the following is used as a high-power microwave oscillator?

A. reflex klystron
B. traveling-wave tube
C. thyraton
D. magnetron
E. klystron

Page(s) 458 to 461

Q9-022 Features of a transmitter's buffer stage include:

A. reduction of harmonics
B. high gain
C. harmonic generation
D. low input impedance
E. improvement in frequency stability of the oscillator

Page(s) 298

Q9-023 The amplitude of an FM modulating test tone is maintained at a constant level, but its frequency is lowered. As a result:

A. the value of the modulation index is reduced
B. there are a greater number of significant sidebands
C. the amplitude of the carrier is reduced
D. the percentage of modulation is increased
E. the frequency separation between adjacent sidebands is increased

Page(s) 362, 363

Q9-024 The speed of a series-wound dc motor is primarily controlled by the:

A. value of the applied dc voltage
B. value of the armature current
C. value of the field current
D. mechanical load
E. mechanical torque

Page(s) 98

Q9-025 Which of the following wire gauges has the greatest current capacity with the smallest power loss?

A. #14
B. #10
C. #20
D. #12
E. #4

Page(s) 25

Q9-026 In the event of an antenna tower's light failure, which of the following details must be entered in the station log?

A. nature of failure
B. date and time the failure was observed
C. date, time, and nature of the adjustments, repairs, or replacements made
D. identification of the air-traffic communications station notification of the failure together with the date and time of the notification
E. all of the above must be entered

Page(s) 612

Q9-027 Which of the following contains a de-emphasis circuit?

A. FM receiver
B. VHF AM transmitter
C. double sideband AM receiver
D. single sideband AM receiver
E. FM transmitter

Page(s) 388, 389

Q9-028 In the circuit of FIG. 9-2, the voltage across the resistor, R, is:

A. 15 V
B. 6 V
C. 0.7 V
D. 9 V
E. 21 V

Page(s) 266, 267

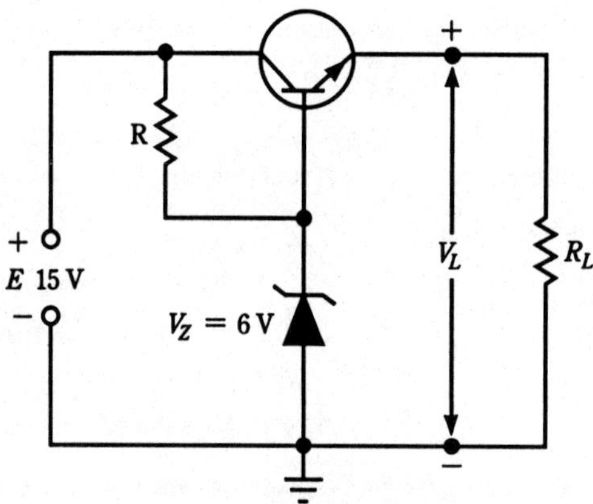

9-2 Circuit for Questions 9-028 and 9-029.

Q9-029 In the circuit of FIG. 9-2, the output voltage, V_L, across the load, R_L, is:

A. 6 V
D. 0.7 V
C. 5.3 V
D. 15 V
E. 9 V

Page(s) 266, 267

Q9-030 A radiotelephone ship station should send a test transmission:

A. every day if the station is sharing a channel
B. provided the authorized power is less than 1 kW
C. every day provided the station is not sharing a channel
D. unless normal use is sufficient to indicate that the radio equipment is operating correctly
E. Under no circumstances may test transmissions be sent more than once a week

Page(s) 610

Q9-031 With the simplex mode:

A. the two stations operate on different frequencies
B. simultaneous communication in both directions is possible
C. the two stations operate on the same frequency
D. only telegraphy can be used
E. it is only possible to operate a one-way communications system

Page(s) 605

Q9-032 A parallel LCR circuit is used as the load of an RF amplifier. Initially, the tuning capacitor is set so that the circuit's resonant frequency is below that of the input signal. If the capacitance is then reduced so that the circuit's resonant frequency equals the input signal frequency and afterwards exceeds it, the output voltage across the load:

A. increases from a low value to a maximum value and afterwards falls back to a low value
B. increases from a low value to a maximum value at resonance and afterwards stays at the same level
C. decreases from a high value to a minimum value at resonance, and afterwards stays at the same level
D. does not change as the capacitance is reduced
E. decreases from the high value to the minimum value and afterwards rises back to the high value

Page(s) 159

Q9-033 Which of the following has the lowest impedance at the frequency of 100 MHz?

A. A six-inch length of AWG #22 copper wire
B. A six-inch length of aluminum wire whose cross-sectional area is one circular mil
C. A thin sheet of copper that is six inches long and two inches wide
D. A 0.01-μF paper capacitor
E. A six-inch length of silver wire whose cross-sectional area is one circular mil

Page(s) 155

Q9-034 Which of the following has the second priority of communications?

A. distress signals
B. safety signals
C. urgency signals
D. navigational signals
E. radio direction-finding communications

Page(s) 599, 600

Q9-035 In a multistage receiver, the RF amplifier's are normally shielded in order to:

A. avoid undesired coupling between the various stages
B. prevent the radiation of spurious emissions from the antenna
C. prevent the generation of parasitic oscillations in the various stages
D. introduce negative feedback that will stabilize the operation of the amplifiers
E. provide positive feedback which will increase the receiver's sensitivity

Page(s) 341 to 343

Q9-036 In the circuit of FIG. 9-3, the value of the true power dissipated in the resistor is:

A. 6 W
B. 5.6 W
C. 9.2 W
D. 11 W
E. 5 W

Page(s) 126, 127

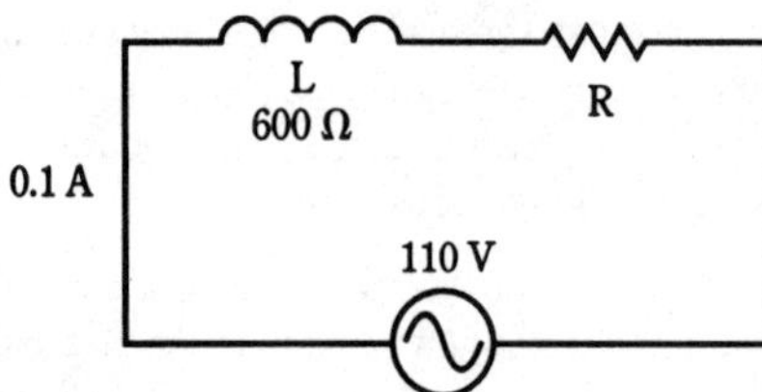

9-3 Circuit for Question 9-036.

Q9-037 The limiter stage of an FM receiver:

A. prevents any amplitude modulation of the IF signal, as a result of noise, from being passed through the discriminator
B. prevents any frequency or phase modulated noise from affecting the discriminator
C. limits the amount of frequency deviation in the IF signal
D. limits the overall bandwidth of the IF stages
E. both choices A and B are true

Page(s) 384, 385

Q9-038 If a radio operator leaves a transmitter unattended:

A. the transmitter can be left, but it must be operated in the unattended automatic mode
B. a note of the operator's whereabouts must be included in the station log
C. the transmitter must be inaccessible to unauthorized persons
D. all power must be removed from the transmitter
E. either choice A or C is true

Page(s) 618

Q9-039 A 100-MHz FM carrier is 100% modulated by a single tone. The ratio of the peak envelope power to the unmodulated carrier power is:

A. 4:1
B. 2:1
C. $\sqrt{2}$:1
D. 3:1
E. 1:1

Page(s) 361, 362

Q9-040 A compulsory cargo ship of 300 gross tons and upward, but less than 1600 gross tons has a radiotelephone installation, which on A3E or H3E emission must be capable of a daytime minimum range of:

A. 25 nautical miles
B. 50 nautical miles
C. 100 nautical miles
D. 150 nautical miles
E. 200 nautical miles

Page(s) 616

Q9-041 A transmitter is operating on a frequency of 122.5 MHz with an assigned power of 100 W. There is a strong fourth harmonic (490 MHz) component whose radiated power is 5 W. If the 490-MHz component is fed through a filter with a 7-dB loss, what is the new value of the harmonic's radiated power?

A. 0.7 W
B. 3.5 W
C. 0.2 W
D. 1 W
E. 4.3 W

Page(s) 303, 304

Q9-042 A 70-Ω line is matched to a 70-Ω resistive load. The length of the line must be any:

A. odd multiple of one quarter wavelength
B. even multiple of one quarter wavelength
C. even multiple of one half wavelength
D. multiple of one wavelength
E. desired length

Page(s) 400 to 403

Q9-043 A radio operator may carry a photocopy of his/her FCC General Radiotelephone License on his/her person when:

A. the license is posted at the control point of the primary transmitter
B. when the operator is employed at a number of work stations
C. the original license has been lost
D. the original license has been forwarded for renewal
E. choices A and B are true

Page(s) 598

Q9-044 Hand-held portable ship transmitters may:

A. be used to communicate from the shore
B. only be used for bridge-to-bridge communications
C. increase their power outputs to over 8 W under emergency conditions
D. communicate with other ships not associated with their own ship
E. none of the above choices is true

Page(s) 596

Q9-045 The standard phonetic alphabet words that correspond to the letters G, H, I, are:

A. Gold, Harry, Ink
B. Golf, Hotel, India
C. Good, Hotel, India
D. Golf, Hat, Ink
E. Good, Harry, India

Page(s) 595

Q9-046 Figure 9-4 shows the block diagram of an AM superhet receiver that is tuned to 1 MHz. If this receiver is experiencing image-channel interference, the frequency of the interfering station is:

A. 1910 kHz
B. 90 kHz
C. 1.91 MHz
D. 1455 kHz
E. choices A and C are both true

Page(s) 346

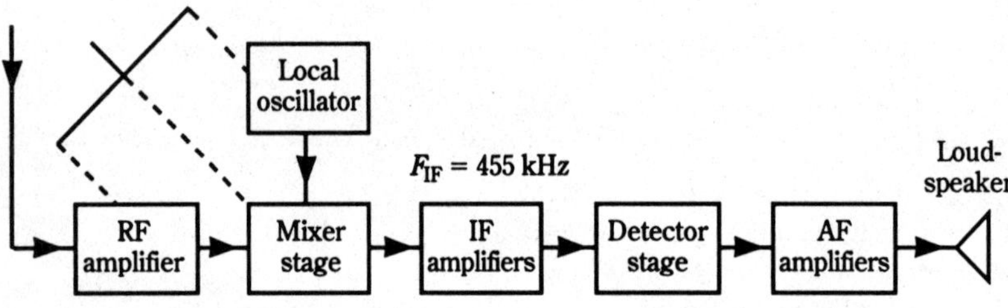

9-4 Block diagram for Question 9-046.

Q9-047 Figure 9-5 illustrates a frequency-multiplier (tripler) stage. What happens if the capacitor, C, open-circuits?

A. the transistor is cut off
B. the transistor is driven into saturation
C. the RF power output increases
D. the RF power output decreases
E. the capacitor only determines the circuit's dc conditions; therefore, there is no appreciable change in the RF power output

Page(s) 249, 250

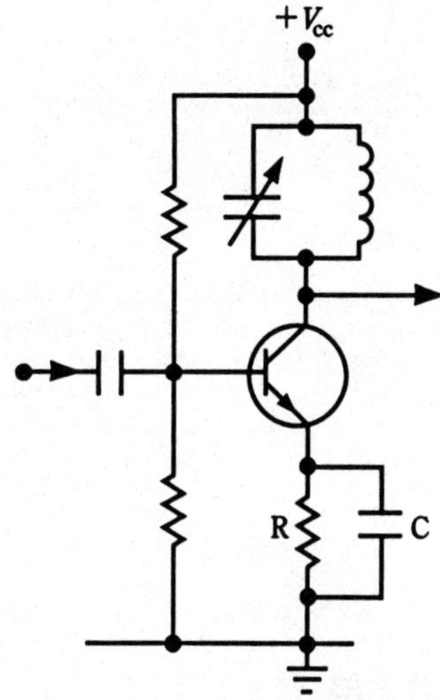

9-5 Circuit for Question 9-047.

Q9-048 If the cosine of the phase angle is multiplied by the product of the effective source voltage and the effective source current, the result is the:

A. true power
B. reactive power
C. apparent power
D. impedance
E. energy consumed

Page(s) 124

Q9-049 A quarter-wave section of line is terminated by a short circuit and is connected to a RF source at the other end. The input impedance to the line at the source is:

A. inductive
B. capacitive
C. a low resistance
D. equivalent to a parallel resonant LC circuit
E. theoretically zero

Page(s) 408

Q9-050 If an operator wishes the whole or part of the communication to be repeated, he/she uses the word(s):

A. repeat
B. words twice
C. say again
D. retransmit
E. message twice

Page(s) 591

Q9-051 Frequency multiplier stages are operated in:

A. class A
B. class AB
C. class B
D. class C
E. class D

Page(s) 250

Q9-052 In the circuit of FIG. 9-6, the value of the voltage drop across the resistor R3 is:

A. 4.3 V
B. 5.7 V
C. 0.4 V
D. 0.7 V
E. 5 V

Page(s) 198 to 200

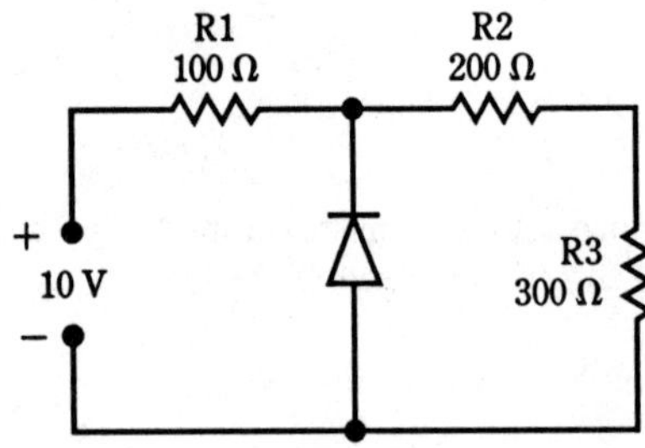

9-6 Circuit for Question 9-052.

Q9-053 The letters "SSSC" stand for:

A. suppressed sideband, single carrier
B. suppressed sideband, suppressed carrier
C. single sideband, single carrier
D. single sideband, suppressed carrier
E. suppressed sideband, single channel

Page(s) 332

Q9-054 A coil contains 500 turns of AWG #26 copper wire and has an air core. If a ferrite core is inserted into the coil, the value of the self-inductance is:

A. decreased
B. unchanged
C. multiplied by the relative permittivity of the ferrite material
D. increased
E. choices C and D are true

Page(s) 65

Q9-055 Convert the octal number, 673_8 into its equivalent decimal number:

A. 443_{10}
B. 453_{10}

C. 513_{10}
D. 429_{10}
E. 449_{10}

Page(s) 520

Q9-056 When initiating a call to another ship, the first step is:

A. transmit on the working frequency
B. transmit on the calling frequency
C. switch to maximum power
D. monitor the working frequency before transmitting
E. test the transmitter for correct operation

Page(s) 591

Q9-057 A common base amplifier has a:

A. high input impedance
B. 180° phase difference between its input and output signals
C. low output impedance
D. low input impedance
E. high current gain

Page(s) 237, 238

Q9-058 The durable nameplate mounted on a marine transmitter indicates:

A. assigned frequency
B. operating power
C. frequency tolerance
D. model number
E. type of emission

Page(s) 589

Q9-059 The type of two-way communications that allows for simultaneous transmission and reception, is:

A. diplex
B. simplex
C. duplex
D. uniplex
E. biplex

Page(s) 326, 327

Q9-060 A Hertz antenna is operating on a frequency of 2182 kHz and consists of a horizontal wire that is slung between two towers. The frequency of its third harmonic is:

A. 6546 kHz
B. 727 kHz
C. 4364 kHz
D. 6.546 MHz
E. choices A and D are true

Page(s) 411 to 419

Q9-061 Station logs that contain information about communications under FCC investigation, must be retained for a period of:

A. 1 year
B. 2 years
C. 3 years
D. 5 years
E. these logs must be retained until the FCC authorize their destruction

Page(s) 585, 586

Q9-062 Two 3-W 6-V lamps are connected in parallel with a 6-V battery, whose internal resistance is 1.2 Ω. The amount of current drawn from the battery is:

A. 1 A
B. 0.5 A
C. 0.83 A
D. 2 A
E. 0.67 A

Page(s) 50 to 54

Q9-063 When a class-C RF amplifier is collector AM modulated, its average dc level collector current does not change. This indicates:

A. a normal condition
B. either positive or negative carrier shift
C. excessive drive to the base
D. insufficient drive to the base
E. insufficient audio modulation

Page(s) 326

Q9-064 While at sea, each U.S. cargo ship which is equipped with a radiotelephone station for compliance with Part II of Title III of the Communications Act, shall:

A. maintain a continuous watch on 2182 kHz in the radio operator's room
B. maintain a continuous watch on 156.8 MHz in the room from which the vessel is steered
C. use a watch receiver with a loudspeaker and a radiotelephone auto alarm to maintain a continuous watch on 2182 kHz
D. use the radiotelephone auto alarm to maintain a continuous watch on 156.8 MHz
E. choices B and D are true

Page(s) 583, 584

Q9-065 A 0.001-μF capacitor is connected across a sine-wave voltage source, whose angular frequency, $\omega = 2\pi f = 1000$ rad/s. The reactance of this capacitor is:

A. 159 kΩ
B. 628 kΩ
C. 1 MΩ
D. 1 kΩ
E. 1590 kΩ

Page(s) 119 to 121

Q9-066 Which of the following frequencies are most affected by the phenomenon of knife-edge diffraction?

A. frequencies in the VLF and LF bands
B. 300 to 3000 kHz
C. 3 to 30 MHz
D. frequencies in the UHF band
E. 30 to 300 MHz

Page(s) 440

Q9-067 The radio license of a compulsory ship is valid for:

A. 3 years
B. 5 years
C. 10 years
D. 15 years
E. the lifetime of the transmitter

Page(s) 583

Q9-068 The effective value of a sine-wave voltage is equal to the:

A. peak value $\times \sqrt{2}$
B. peak value $\times$ 1.414
C. average value $\div$ 1.11
D. peak value $\div$ 0.707
E. peak value $\div \sqrt{2}$

Page(s) 109, 110

Q9-069 A marine transmitter is operating on a frequency of 156.8 MHz. Express the tolerance of this transmitter in hertz:

A. 3136 Hz
B. 1568 Hz
C. 6272 Hz
D. 784.5 Hz
E. 4704 Hz

Page(s) 579

Q9-070 A 12.6-V 55-A.h battery continuously supplies 325 W to a transmitter and 50 W to a receiver. For how many hours can the battery supply full power to both the transmitter and the receiver?

A. 1.8
B. 375
C. 29.76
D. 55
E. 12.6

Page(s) 51

Q9-071 The carrier of an AM transmitter is the:

A. transmitter's output signal when the modulation is zero
B. transmitter's output signal when the modulation is present

C. output signal from the crystal oscillator
D. RMS value of the AM signal
E. transmitter's output signal when the modulation percentage is 50%

Page(s) 312 to 315

Q9-072 The frequency of an airport's aviation transmitter is determined:

A. when the transmitter is originally installed
B. when any change or adjustment is made in the transmitter that might affect its operating frequency
C. upon receipt of an FCC notice of off-frequency operation
D. when there is reason to believe that the operating frequency has shifted beyond its tolerance
E. all of the above choices are true

Page(s) 577

Q9-073 Express 3.00 PM Pacific Standard Time (PST) in terms of Universal Time Coordinated (UTC).

A. 0700 hrs
B. 1100 hrs
C. 1500 hrs
D. 0300 hrs
E. 2300 hrs

Page(s) 442

Q9-074 A class-C Emergency Position-Indicating Radio Beacon (E.P.I.R.B) can be tested:

A. in coordination with the U.S. Coast Guard
B. by switching to a dummy antenna
C. without the radiation exceeding 25 μV/m at a distance of 150 feet
D. during the first five minutes of each hour with the testing not lasting more than 10 seconds
E. choices A and D are true

Page(s) 573, 574

Q9-075 In the circuit of FIG. 9-7, $R_1 = R_2$, $R_3 = R_4$ and the two transistors are identical. If the switch S1 is closed but the switch S2 is open, both of the lamps L1 and L2 are lit. If both S1 and S2 are closed:

A. both lamps are lit
B. neither lamp is lit
C. only L1 is lit
D. only L2 is lit
E. the two lamps are lit alternately

Page(s) 232, 233, 235, 236

Q9-076 The battery of an Emergency Locator Transmitter must be changed after:

A. one year
B. the transmitter has been used in an emergency situation
C. six months

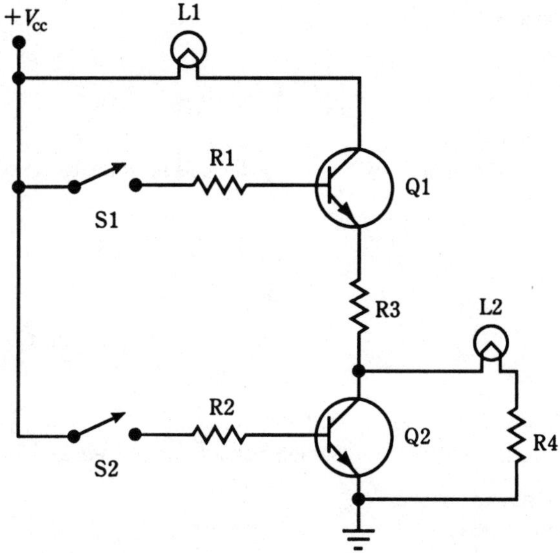

9-7 Circuit for Question 9-075.

D. the date specified by the manufacturer when 50% of its useful life has expired
E. choices B and D are true

Page(s) 572, 573

Q9-077 A 100-Ω 10-W resistor and a 10-Ω 10-W resistor are connected in parallel. If the wattage rating of either resistor is not to be exceeded, the maximum power dissipated in the circuit is:

A. 10 W
B. 20 W
C. 15 W
D. 5 W
E. 11 W

Page(s) 36 to 38

Q9-078 The operating position of a radio station is:

A. at the location of the transmitter
B. at the location of the receiver
C. either at the location of the transmitter or at the location of the receiver
D. at the control point
E. on the bridge

Page(s) 564

Q9-079 Which of the following operating frequencies is used for the modern loran navigational system?

A. loran A: 1950 kHz
B. loran B: 900 kHz

C. loran C: 100 kHz
D. loran D: 10.2 kHz
E. loran E: 3.7 kHz

Page(s) 439

Q9-080 In a marine J3E emission, by how many decibels must the carrier be suppressed below the peak envelope power?

A. 30 dB
B. 40 dB
C. 50 dB
D. 60 dB
E. 70 dB

Page(s) 334

Q9-081 On a compulsory ship, radiotelegraph installations are required for cargo vessels of:

A. 300 gross tons and upward
B. 500 gross tons and upward
C. 800 gross tons and upward
D. 1000 gross tons and upward
E. 1600 gross tons and upward

Page(s) 562

Q9-082 A vertical steel tower radiates a signal whose fundamental frequency is 450 kHz. The frequency of its seventh harmonic is:

A. 3150 kHz
B. 3.15 MHz
C. 3150 Hz
D. 3150 MHz
E. choices A and B are true

Page(s) 426 to 430

Q9-083 For how long is an FCC General Radiotelephone License valid?

A. three years
B. five years
C. four years
D. ten years
E. for the lifetime of the licensee

Page(s) 583

Q9-084 When calibrating a secondary frequency standard against the primary standard, WWV, which of the following steps is wrong or not necessary?

A. allow a ½ hour to 1 hour warming-up period for the secondary standard
B. tune the receiver to WWV
C. beat the WWV signal with one of the crystal's harmonics and obtain the zero beat
D. calibrate the receiver's tuning with WWV
E. if necessary, adjust the value of the trimmer capacitor across the crystal in order to achieve the zero beat

Page(s) 337, 338

Q9-085 From measurements it is determined that the input power to a transmission line is 100 W and the associated reflected power is 1 W. If the transmission line is 50 ft long and has a distributed attenuation of 6 dB/100 ft, the output power to the Marconi antenna is:

A. 49.5 W
B. 50 W
C. 99 W
D. 47 W
E. 48.5 W

Page(s) 426 to 430

Q9-086 The correct procedure for a distress call is:

A. the word *mayday* (spoken three times) the words *this is*, followed by the call sign of the station in distress (spoken three times)
B. the words *this is* (spoken three times) and the word *mayday* (spoken three times)
C. the letters SOS (spoken three times) the letters DE, followed by the callsign of the station in distress (spoken three times)
D. the word *mayday*, the words *this is*, followed by the callsign and name of ship (spoken three times)
E. the word *mayday* (spoken three times), the words *this is*, followed by the callsign (spoken three times) and name of the ship in distress

Page(s) 568

Q9-087 Calculate the maximum value of current that can flow through a 10-kΩ ½-W resistor without exceeding its power rating:

A. 5 mA
B. 7.1 mA
C. 20 mA
D. 50 mA
E. 14.1 mA

Page(s) 18

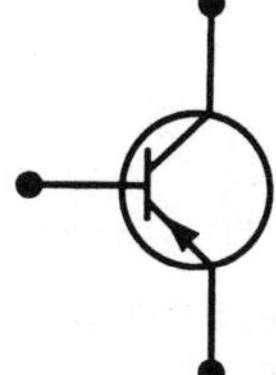

9-8 Symbol for Question 9-088.

Q9-088 In FIG. 9-8 the symbol is that of a:

A. junction field-effect transistor
B. pnp junction transistor
C. E MOSFET

D. E MOSFET
E. npn junction transistor

Page(s) 253 to 255

Q9-089 Express a speed of 10 statute miles per hour in terms of knots:

A. 1.5
B. 11.5
C. 15.0
D. 8.7
E. 1.15

Page(s) 402, 403

Q9-090 The broken line in FIG. 9-9 shows the effective:

A. voltage distribution on a λ/4 Marconi antenna
B. current distribution on a λ/2 Hertz antenna
C. current distribution on a λ/4 Marconi antenna
D. voltage distribution on a λ/2 Hertz antenna
E. radiated power distribution on a λ/4 Marconi antenna

Page(s) 426

9-9 Illustration for Question 9-090.

Q9-091 A transmission line is 200 ft long and its input RF power is 500 W. The line has an attenuation of 3 dB/100 ft and feeds an antenna whose power gain is 9 dB. The effective radiated power is:

A. 125 W
B. 250 W
C. 750 W
D. 1000 W
E. 1500 W

Page(s) 418, 419

Q9-092 When testing the Emergency Locator Transmitter (ELT):

A. the operator uses a manually activated test switch that switches the transmitter's output to a dummy load
B. the test can be done in coordination with an FCC representative
C. an operational test is conducted within the first ten minutes of any hour
D. the test must not be longer than five audio sweeps
E. no test can be carried out in the absence of a manually activated test switch

Page(s) 572 to 574

Q9-093 In an n-channel FET oscillator circuit, electron current would flow:

A. from V_{DD} to the drain
B. from the drain to the source
C. from gate to ground through the resistor that provides signal bias
D. from ground to gate through the resistor that provides signal bias
E. from the drain to the gate

Page(s) 272, 273

Q9-094 A 110-V 60-Hz sine-wave voltage is applied across a 5-H inductor. If the frequency is increased to 120 Hz, the new value of the inductance is:

A. 5 H
B. 10 H
C. 2.5 H
D. 20 H
E. 1.25 H

Page(s) 116 to 119

Q9-095 The time constant of a series RC circuit is found by:

A. dividing the value of the capacitance by the value of the resistance
B. dividing the value of the resistance by the value of the capacitance
C. multiplying the value of the capacitance by the value of the resistance
D. multiplying the value of the capacitance by the square of the value of the resistance
E. multiplying the square of the value of the capacitance by the value of the resistance

Page(s) 79, 80

Q9-096 In the circuit of FIG. 9-10, what is the value of R_L that will allow maximum power transfer to the load?

A. 10 Ω
B. 20 Ω
C. 30 Ω
D. 15 Ω
E. 150 Ω

Page(s) 50 to 55

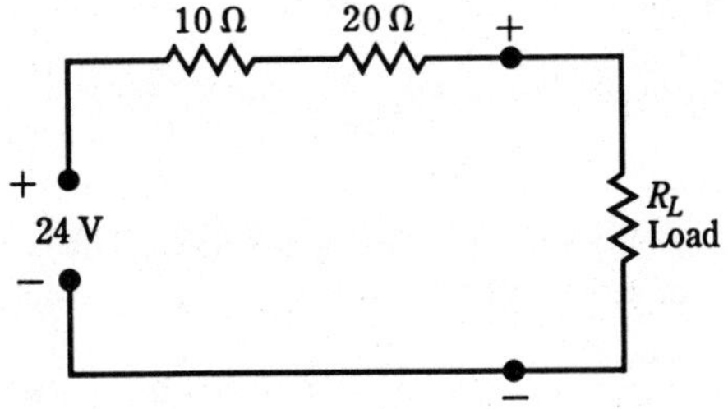

9-10 Circuit for Question 9-096.

Q9-097 To correct the circuit of FIG. 9-11:

A. reverse diode D1
B. reverse diode D2

C. reverse both diodes, D1 and D2
D. change the polarity of the output dc voltage
E. no correction is necessary

Page(s) 208 to 210

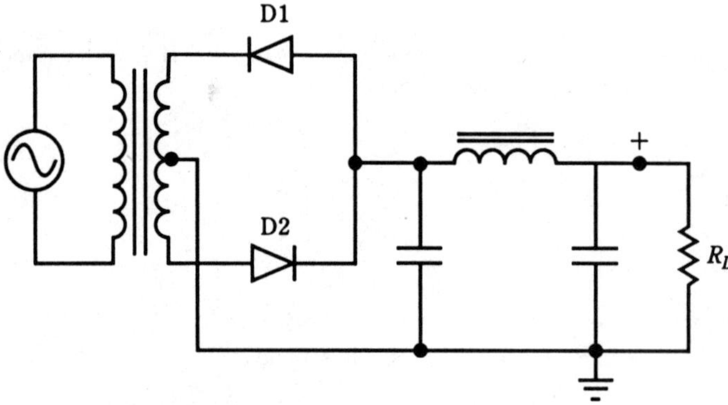

9-11 Circuit for Question 9-097.

Q9-098 Express the hexadecimal number D_{16} or the binary number 1101_2 as a decimal number to the base 10:

A. 11_{10}
B. 12_{10}
C. 14_{10}
D. 8_{10}
E. 13_{10}

Page(s) 522, 523

Q9-099 A varactor diode is used:

A. to provide amplitude modulation (AM) of an RF carrier
B. to provide pulse modulation (PM) of an RF carrier
C. for frequency division in the microwave region
D. as an alternative to the tunnel diode
E. to provide frequency modulation (FM) of an RF carrier

Page(s) 219, 220

Q9-100 If a licensee receives a Notification of Suspension and does not apply for a hearing, the suspension order becomes effective within:

A. 3 days
B. 7 days
C. 10 days
D. 15 days
E. 30 days

Page(s) 608

Part II

Ship Radar Endorsement Practice Tests

Element 8
Test 1

Q1-01 A radar set with a peak pulse power output of 500 kW, has a pulse repetition rate (frequency) of 400 per second. What is the value of the pulse repetition time?

A. 25 ms
B. 4.0 ms
C. 400 μs
D. 2500 μs
E. 0.0004 s

Page(s) 479

Q1-02 If in QUES. 1-01, the pulse width is 0.5 μs, what is the average pulse power?

A. 100 W
B. 250 W
C. 400 W
D. 500 W
E. 800 W

Page(s) 479

Q1-03 The antenna system of a marine radar set uses a parabolic reflector in order to:

A. widen the beam and increase the surface coverage
B. match the impedances of the waveguide horn and free space
C. eliminate the requirement for separate transmitter and receiver antenna systems
D. lower the field gain and thereby broaden the antenna system's response
E. provided a unidirectional narrow beam

Page(s) 493

Q1-04 Which of the following may be the cause of the appearance of the bright flashing pie sections on the P.P.I. display?

A. defective crystal in the AFC circuit
B. defective crystal diode in the mixer stage
C. defective STC circuit
D. defective magnetron or weak magnetron magnet
E. defective duplexer

Page(s) 499, 500

Q1-05 If the range of a target is 7.5 nautical miles, what is the time interval in microseconds between the radar pulse being transmitted and the target echo being received?

A. 46.3
B. 93
C. 186
D. 162
E. 81

Page(s) 483

Q1-06 In order to be responsible for installation, maintenance, and servicing of a ship radar station, the operator must possess a:

A. ship radar endorsement to a First-Class Radiotelegraph License
B. ship radar endorsement to a General Radiotelephone License
C. Second-Class Radiotelegraph License
D. First-Class Radiotelegraph License
E. choices A and B are true

Page(s) 507, 508

Q1-07 Who of the following has the necessary qualifications to replace receiver fuses and tubes in a marine radar set?

A. only General Radiotelephone Licensees
B. only those with a minimum of a Marine Operator's Permit
C. only those with a minimum of a Second Class Radiotelegraph License
D. anyone holding a Radar Endorsement to his license
E. anyone who is regarded as sufficiently competent to carry out these tasks

Page(s) 507, 508

Q1-08 Which of the following may not cause damage to a silicon crystal diode?

A. the applications of very high frequency voltages in the SHF band
B. excessive current
C. mechanical pressure
D. static charges
E. a defective duplexer

Page(s) 486 to 488

Q1-09 In the receiver of a marine SHF radar set, a ratio detector might be used as:

A. the first detector stage and as an alternative to the crystal mixer
B. the second detector stage

C. part of the STC system
D. part of the AFC system
E. none of the above is true. A ratio detector could serve no useful purpose in a radar receiver

Page(s) 484, 485

Q1-10 The Doppler effect is used in CW radar to determine the:

A. target range
B. bearing of the range
C. target size
D. target speed
E. target's elevation

Page(s) 503, 504

Q1-13 If the interior dimensions of a rectangular waveguide are 1.25 inches by 3 inches, the waveguide's cut-off wavelength in inches, is:

A. 6.0
B. 2.5
C. 1.5
D. 3.0
E. 1.25

Page(s) 452 to 454

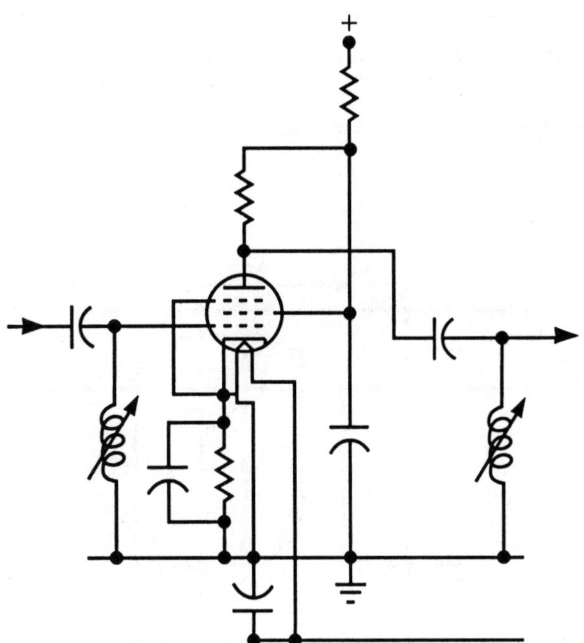

10-1 Circuit for Question 1-12.

Q1-12 In an SHF pulsed radar set, the circuit of FIG. 10-1 could represent a (an):

A. compensated video amplifier
B. pulse limiter stage
C. IF amplifier stage
D. modulator stage
E. second detector stage

Page(s) 484, 485

Q1-13 Who of the following are allowed to operate a ship radar station?

A. those who possess a First-Class or Second-Class Radiotelegraph License
B. those who possess a General Radiotelephone License
C. those who possess a Ship Radar Endorsement
D. the Master of the ship or his designee
E. the station licensee or his designee

Page(s) 494

Q1-14 Which of the following frequency ranges is generally regarded as applicable to the operation of klystrons?

A. 600 MHz to 3 GHz
B. 3000 MHz to 60 GHz
C. 3 GHz to 30 GHz
D. 300 MHz to 60 GHz
E. 600 MHz to 30 GHz

Page(s) 507, 508

Q1-15 The circuit of FIG. 10-2 represents a (an):

A. echo box
B. directional coupler for measuring the reflected power
C. SWR indicator
D. duplexer
E. dual stub matching device

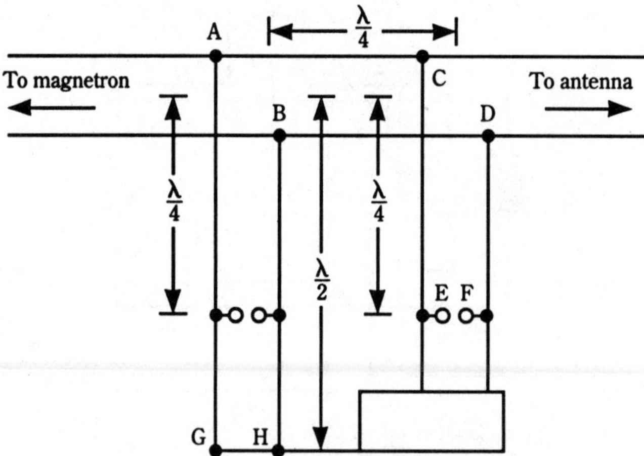

10-2 Circuit for Question 1-15.

Page(s) 496 to 498

Q1-16 The pulse frequency of a radar set is reduced but the peak power, the pulse duration and the radio frequency remain the same. As a result the:

A. definition of the targets on the PPI display will be improved
B. average power will be increased
C. value of the duty cycle will increased
D. maximum range available may be increased
E. bandwidth of the signal in the IF stages will be increased

Page(s) 479, 480

Q1-17 Pulsed radar sets are primarily used to find the:

A. size and speed of a target
B. speed and course of a target
C. target's range and bearing
D. target's range and speed
E. direction and size of a target

Page(s) 474, 475

Q1-18 If the time interval between a radar pulse being transmitted and the echo being received, is 105 microseconds, what is the range of the target in nautical miles?

A. 16.98
B. 8.49
C. 19.56
D. 9.78
E. 4.89

Page(s) 483

Q1-19 A marine radar set might cause interference problems in:

A. loran C equipment
B. communications receivers
C. the auto-alarm system
D. the direction-finding equipment
E. all of the above choices are true

Page(s) 502, 503

Q1-20 Marine radar transmitters are allowed to operate on:

A. 2460 to 2650 MHz
B. 6900 to 7100 MHz
C. 7300 to 7500 MHz
D. 8900 to 9100 MHz
E. 9300 to 9500 MHz

Page(s) 480

Q1-21 Which of the waveforms shown is associated with the current that flows through the deflection coils of a PPI display?

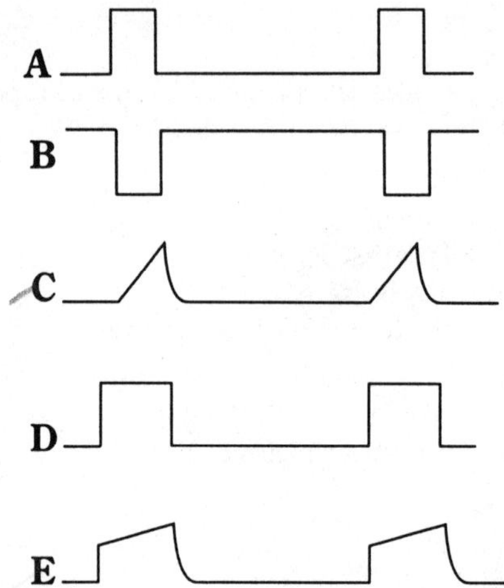

Page(s) 499, 500

Q1-22 The circuit of FIG. 10-3 represents a:

A. modulator unit
B. complete synchronizer unit
C. tuned-line oscillator
D. blocking oscillator
E. duplexer unit

Page(s) 475

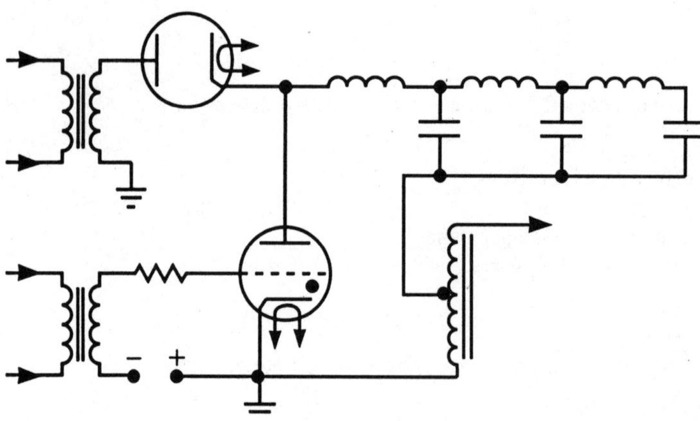

10-3 Circuit for Question 1-22.

Q1-23 On a PPI display, the heading flash is achieved by the use of a (an):

A. electronic synchronizer included in the sweep generator circuit
B. electronic generator that feeds a negative pulse to the PPI grid
C. mechanical switch associated with the rotating antenna

D. electronic timer that is calibrated to synchronize with the rotating antenna
E. crystal oscillator, followed by the shaping circuit for the intensifier pulse

Page(s) 499, 500

Q1-24 In a pulsed radar set, the duty cycle is equal to:

A $\dfrac{1}{\text{pulse frequency} \times \text{pulse width}}$

B $\dfrac{\text{peak power}}{\text{average power}}$

C $\dfrac{\text{pulse repetition time}}{\text{pulse duration}}$

D $\dfrac{\text{pulse width}}{\text{pulse frequency}}$

Page(s) 479

Q1-25 In an SHF marine radar set, the pulse frequency is 500 per second and the pulse duration is 0.5 μs. What is the bandwidth required by the IF stages of the receiver?

A. 10 MHz
B. 5 MHz
C. 4 MHz
D. 2 MHz
E. 1 kHz

Page(s) 489

Q1-26 The purpose of the polystyrene window placed across the end of the waveguide, is:

A. as an alternative to the horn radiator
B. to match the waveguide impedance to the impedance of free space
C. to form the E-M energy into a narrow beam
D. to act as a resonant iris and raise the value of the SWR
E. choices A and B are true

Page(s) 495

Q1-27 Which of the following can occur if a magnetron's magnet becomes too weak?

A. the magnetron current meter will indicate an increase
B. internal arcing in the tube of the modulator unit
C. the magnetron's undercurrent relay will drop out
D. internal arcing in the magnetron
E. the curvature of the paths taken by the electrons will increase

Page(s) 461, 462

Q1-28 In a marine radar set, the pulse duration is 0.5 μs. What is the maximum range separation in yards between two targets that cannot be distinguished on the display?

A. 246
B. 328
C. 164
D. 82
E. 41

Page(s) 479, 480

Q1-29 In the modulator unit of a pulsed radar set, the artificial discharge transmission line is used to:

A. provide the calibration pulses that create the range-marker circles
B. determine the duration of the transmitted pulse
C. determine the duty cycle
D. determine the pulse repetition rate
E. match the load of the magnetron to the load required by the thyratron

Page(s) 479

Q1-30 Which of the following can be found in the modulator unit of a marine radar set?

A. thyratron
B. magnetron
C. multicavity klystron
D. rotary spark gap
E. choices A and D are true

Page(s) 479

Q1-31 In a marine radar set, the magnetron frequency starts to drift upwards from 3003 MHz when the reflex klystron's output is 2973 MHz. If the receiver's IF is 30 MHz, the:

A. potential of the klystron's repeller plate will change from zero to positive
B. potential of the repeller plate will change from zero to negative
C. potential of the repeller plate will be more negative
D. potential of the repeller plate will be less negative
E. potential of the repeller plate will be less positive

Page(s) 484, 485

Q1-32 The reflex klystron of a SHF pulsed radar receiver may be mechanically tuned by:

A. screwing a brass plug into the wall of the cavity
B. changing the pressure on the cavity's flexible wall
C. varying the depth to which an iron dust slug is inserted into the cavity wall
D. adjusting the capacitance between the repeller and the cavity
E. choices A and B are true

Page(s) 466, 467

Q1-33 In an SHF radar system, the end of the waveguide horn is positioned at the parabolic reflector's:

A. centroid
B. center
C. focus
D. apex
E. vertex

Page(s) 493, 494

Q1-34 The peak power output of a pulsed radar set is multiplied by a factor of 16. Assuming that all other parameters remain the same, the maximum range obtainable will be multiplied by:

A. 2
B. 4
C. 8
D. 16
E. 32

Page(s) 479

Q1-35 The operating frequency of a marine radar set is 3 GHz. The value of the receiver's IF would typically be:

A. 455 kHz
B. 10 MHz
C. 4.5 MHz
D. 12.75 MHz
E. 30 MHz

Page(s) 484

Q1-36 If the time interval between a radar pulse being transmitted and the echo being received is 87 microseconds, what is the total distance in nautical miles from the radar set to the target and back again?

A. 16.20
B. 8.10
C. 14.07
D. 32.40
E. 7.03

Page(s) 483

Q1-37 The common number of IF stages in the superheterodyne receiver of a marine radar set is:

A. 1
B. 2
C. 3
D. 4
E. more than 5

Page(s) 489

Q1-38 The pulse frequency of a radar set is 400. If the value of the duty cycle is 2×10^{-4} and the average power of the transmitted pulse is 200 watts, what is the pulse width in microseconds?

A. 0.1
B. 0.2
C. 0.25
D. 0.5
E. 1.0

Page(s) 479

Q1-39 In QUES. 1-38, what is the peak power of the transmitted pulse?

A. 1.0 MW
B. 500 kW
C. 250 kW
D. 200 kW
E. 100 kW

Page(s) 479

Q1-40 The block diagram of FIG. 10-4 is that of the pulsed radar receiver. Block A represents the:

A. signal discriminator
B. local oscillator
C. signal crystal mixer
D. microwave pre-amplifier
E. AFC crystal detector stage

Page(s) 484, 485

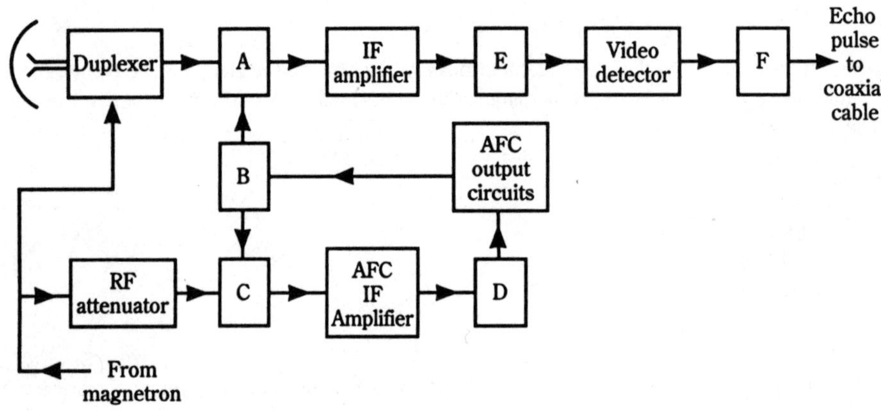

10-4 Block diagram for Questions 1-40 thru 1-45.

Q1-41 In the block diagram of FIG. 10-4, block B represents the:

A. signal crystal mixer
B. detector stage
C. signal discriminator
D. reflex klystron stage
E. AFC crystal detector stage

Page(s) 484, 485

Q1-42 In the block diagram of FIG. 10-4, block C represents the:

A. signal crystal mixer
B. AFC crystal detector stage
C. AFC discriminator

D. second detector stage
E. local oscillator

Page(s) 484, 485

Q1-43 In the block diagram of FIG. 10-4, block D represents the:

A. local oscillator
B. AFC discriminator
D. signal second detector stage
D. AFC crystal detector stage
E. reflex klystron stage

Page(s) 484, 485

Q1-44 In the block diagram of FIG. 10-4, block E represents the:

A. signal discriminator stage
B. crystal mixer stage
C. second detector stage
D. signal-limiter stage
E. AFC crystal detector stage

Page(s) 484, 485

Q1-45 In the block diagram of FIG. 10-4, block E represents a (an):

A. high-gain video amplifier
B. compensated video power amplifier
C. pulse-shaping amplifier
D. emitter follower
E. noise limiter

Page(s) 484, 485

Q1-46 It is required to produce range marker circles on a PPI display with a separation of ½ nautical mile in range between adjacent circles. The frequency of the range-marker oscillator is:

A. 186.2 kHz
B. 161.7 kHz
C. 93.1 kHz
D. 323.4 kHz
E. 213.8 kHz

Page(s) 499, 500

Q1-47 In a pulsed radar set, the STC circuit is used to:

A. counteract the effects of frequency drift in either the magnetron or the reflex klystron
B. reduce interference from the effects of sea return
C. improve the target bearing resolution
D. increase the receiver sensitivity for the echoes from targets at maximum range
E. vary the pulse frequency in order to control the maximum target range

Page(s) 500

Q1-48 Which of the following waveforms best represents a magnetron's output to the waveguide?

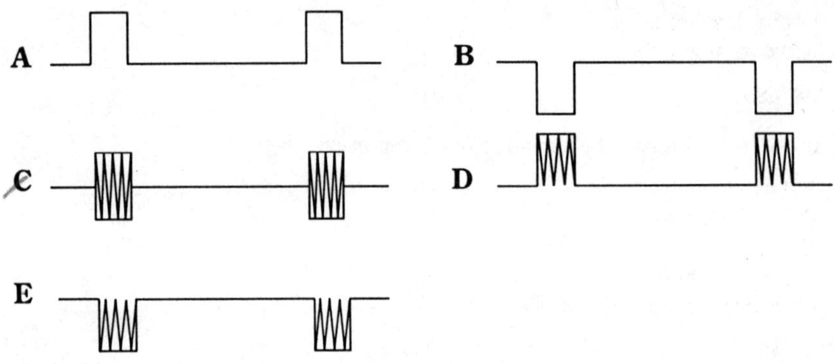

Page(s) 476

Q1-49 In an SHF pulsed radar set, the mixer (first detector) stage of the receiver normally uses a:

A. PN junction diode
B. low transit-time triode
C. silicon crystal diode
D. npn transistor
E. thermionic diode

Page(s) 486 to 488

Q1-50 The bright circle of light at the center of a PPI display is caused by:

A. a defective TR box
B. a defective STC control
C. the normal "seq return"
D. interference from other radar sets
E. the transmitted pulse and is a normal condition.

Page(s) 500

Element 8
Test 2

Q2-01 Under what conditions can a Ship Radar station be operated by unlicensed personnel?

A. the radar equipment is entirely operated by external controls
B. whenever the holder of a Ship Radar Endorsement is on board
C. whenever the holder of a General Radiotelephone License is on board
D. the radar equipment uses a nontunable pulsed magnetron
E. choices B and D are true

Page(s) 507, 508

Q2-02 It is possible to increase the maximum range of a radar equipment by:

A. lowering the pulse frequency
B. raising the peak power of the transmitter
C. narrowing the beam width
D. increasing the pulse duration
E. all the above choices are true

Page(s) 478

Q2-03 A marine radar set is operating on 9.35 GHz. The wavelength of its transmission in free space is:

A. 3.21 cm
B. 1.60 cm
C. 6.42 cm
D. 0.16 cm
E. 6.10 cm

Page(s) 480

Q2-04 In a pulsed radar set, the magnetron frequency is drifting downward. If the local oscillator klystron's frequency is below that of the magnetron:

A. the AFC circuit action will make the klystron's repeller positive
B. the drift in the value of the IF will exceed the drift in the magnetron's frequency
C. the klystron's repeller will be made less negative because of the AFC action
D. the klystron's repeller will be made more negative
E. the klystron must be manually returned to the new magnetron frequency

Page(s) 485

Q2-05 The sweep, noise, and range markers are present on a PPI display, but no targets can be observed. This could be caused by a defective:

A. duplexer
B. reflex klystron
C. crystal mixer
D. magnetron
E. second detector diode

Page(s) 499, 500

Q2-06 Which of the following factors is mainly concerned in the design of an antenna system for a pulsed radar set?

A. duty cycle
B. pulse frequency
C. radio frequency
D. pulse length
E. average power

Page(s) 479, 480

Q2-07 The block diagram of FIG. 11-1 represents part of a marine SHF pulsed radar set. Block 1 could represent a:

A. magnetron oscillator
B. reflex klystron oscillator
C. duplexer unit
D. preamplifier
E. blocking oscillator

Page(s) 476

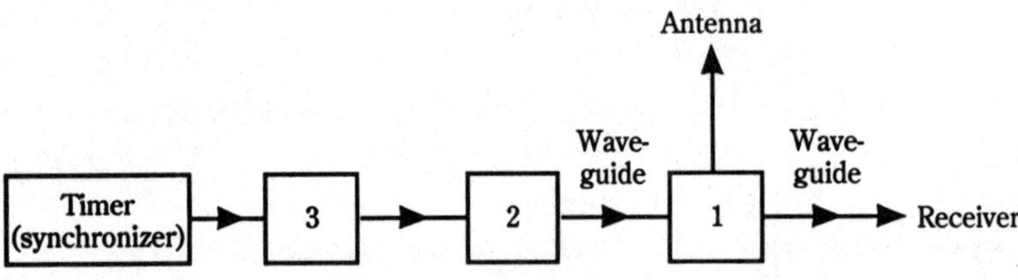

11-1 Block diagram for Questions 2-07 thru 2-210.

Q2-08 In the block diagram of FIG. 11-1, block 2 could represent a:

A. magnetron oscillator
B. reflex klystron oscillator
C. blocking oscillator
D. duplexer unit
E. thyratron modulator

Page(s) 476

Q2-09 In the block diagram of FIG. 11-1, block 3 could represent a:

A. magnetron oscillator
B. reflex klystron oscillator
C. symmetrical square-wave generator
D. rotary-spark gas modulator
E. sawtooth generator

Page(s) 476

Q2-10 In the block diagram of FIG. 11-1, the timer or synchronizer unit contains a:

A. sawtooth generator
B. klystron multi-cavity amplifier
C. blocking oscillator
D. crystal oscillator
E. RC phase shift oscillator

Page(s) 476

Q2-11 In an SHF pulsed radar set, the signal mixer stage of the receiver might use a:

A. pentagrid converter tube
B. silicon crystal diode
C. thermionic diode
D. junction transistor
E. PN junction diode

Page(s) 486 to 488

Q2-12 The time interval between a radar pulse being transmitted and the target echo being received is 49.4 μs. What is the range of the target?

A. 1600 yds
B. 8 nautical miles
C. 4000 yds
D. 4 nautical miles
E. 0.8 nautical mile

12.3 / 49.4

Page(s) 483

Q2-13 The repetition rate of a pulsed radar system indicates the:

A. frequency of the range-marker oscillator
B. speed at which the antenna is rotating, measured in revolutions per minute
C. reciprocal of the duty cycle
D. frequency with which the pulses are transmitted
E. number of target echoes received in one second

Page(s) 479

Q2-14 Which of the following frequency ranges is generally regarded as applicable to the operation of magnetrons?

A. 600 MHz to 3 GHz
B. 3000 MHz to 60 GHz
C. 3 GHz to 30 GHz
D. 300 MHz to 60 GHz
E. 600 MHz to 30 GHz

Page(s) 457

Q2-15 When carrying out maintenance on ship radar equipment, which of the following entries must be made in the station record?

A. date and place of initial installation
B. nature and date of any complaint
C. details of all component failures
D. responsible operator's name and date of his Ship Radar Endorsement
E. all of the above choices are true

Page(s) 508

Q2-16 With regard to the display of a marine radar set, the letters "PPI" stand for:

A. polar plan indicator
B. plan position indicator
C. polar picture indicator
D. position polar indicator
E. position plan indicator

Page(s) 499

Q2-17 Which of the following maintenance procedures may be carried out by unlicensed personnel?

A. fine tuning of the magnetron frequency
B. replacement of receiver tubes and fuses
C. adjusting the resonant frequency of the reflex klystron
D. optimizing the value of the waveguide system's SWR
E. optimizing the performance of the duplexer

Page(s) 507, 508

Q2-18 The purpose of an echo box in a marine radar set is to:

A. act as a dummy antenna in order to test out the transmitter under loaded conditions and in radar silence
B. act as part of the duplexer system
C. provide the echo attenuation required by the STC system
D. provide an artificial target for test purposes
E. provide a boost to the echo signal prior to its reaching the crystal mixer stage

Page(s) 492

Q2-19 A choke joint may be used to:

A. prevent vibration in the rotating antenna system from being translated to the magnetron assembly

B. join together two waveguide sections with little loss of EM energy
C. permit the easy removal of a waveguide section for maintenance purposes
D. allow rotation between one circular waveguide section and another
E. all of the above choices are true

Page(s) 455, 456

Q2-20 The magnetron's anode is:

A. normally made of aluminum
B. grounded
C. operated with a high positive dc potential
D. operated with a low negative dc potential
E. heavily insulated from the chassis

Page(s) 458, 459

Q2-21 In a marine radar set, which of the following precautions should be observed with regard to the magnetron?

A. the magnet must not be subjected to extreme heat
B. the magnet must not be subjected to mechanical shock
C. all ferromagnetic materials, such as tools, must be kept away from the magnet
D. the magnetron must never be operated without the magnet in position
E. all of the above choices are true

Page(s) 461, 462

Q2-22 The wide bandwidth that is required by the IF stages of a pulsed radar set can be achieved by:

A. RC coupling between stages
B. damping resistors across the tuned circuits
C. doubled tuned circuits with the degree of coupling greater than the critical (transitional) value
D. staggered tuning
E. choices B, C, and D are true

Page(s) 489

Q2-23 In an SHF pulsed radar set, the magnetron is used as a (an):

A. magnetic amplifier
B. microwave pre-amplifier
C. local oscillator
D. transmitter oscillator
E. oscillator in the calibrator circuit

Page(s) 457

Q2-24 Entries are made in the maintenance log of a Ship Radar station, by:

A. an operator with a First-Class Radiotelegraph License
B. an operator with a General Radiotelephone License
C. an operator with a Ship Radar Endorsement to a Second-Class Radiotelegraph License
D. the Master or his designee

E. an unlicensed person under the supervision of the operator responsible for service and maintenance

Page(s) 507, 508

Q2-25 In a radar set, a blocking oscillator can be used to:

A. produce a trigger pulse for the transmitter
B. act as the local oscillator stage
C. act as the frequency converter stage
D. provide the sweep voltage for the PPI tube
E. amplify the echo pulse output from the second detector stage

Page(s) 475

Q2-26 The intensity of the echoes (target definition) on a PPI display is determined by the:

A. radio frequency
B. pulse frequency
C. duty cycle
D. antenna rotation rate
E. choices B and D are true

Page(s) 499, 500

Q2-27 Which of the following is the main factor in the determination of a radar set's bearing resolution?

A. rotation speed of the antenna
B. pulse frequency
C. beam width
D. pulse duration
E. transmitter's peak power

Page(s) 479, 480

Q2-28 The interior of a rectangular waveguide may be silver-plated in order to:

A. improve the SWR value
B. reduce the possibility of interior arcing
C. reduce the eddy current loss
D. prevent the rotation of the EM wave's plane of polarization
E. choices A and B are true

Page(s) 452

Q2-29 If, in a magnetron, the two sides of each resonant cavity mouth carry instantaneous RF potentials of opposite polarity, the manner of operation is called the:

A. $\frac{\pi}{4}$ mode
B. $\frac{\pi}{2}$ mode
C. π mode
D. $\frac{3\pi}{2}$ mode
E. 2π mode

Page(s) 458, 459

Q2-30 The aquadag coating on the inside of a PPI tube is used:

A. to focus the beam of primary electrons
B. as a second anode
C. to prevent the build-up of secondary emission at the screen
D. to shield the electron beam from unidirectional magnetic fields
E. choices B and C are true

Page(s) 499

Q2-31 The effect of sea return is to:

A. limit the detection of targets far from the ship
B. reduce the maximum target range available
C. lower the receiver sensitivity for distant targets
D. create interference for the echoes from targets close to the ship
E. create errors in range for targets close to the ship

Page(s) 500

Q2-32 The operating frequency of a marine radar set is 9.4 GHz. The value of the receiver's IF would typically be:

A. 455 kHz
B. 10.7 MHz
C. 4.5 MHz
D. 9.4 MHz
E. 60.0 MHz

Page(s) 484

Q2-33 The pulse duration of a radar set is reduced. If the parameters of peak power, pulse repetition rate, and radio frequency remain the same, the:

A. duty cycle will increase
B. target discrimination will be worse
C. bandwidth of the signal in the IF stages will be greater
D. average power will increase
E. maximum target range available will increase

Page(s) 479, 480

Q2-34 To which part of the PPI tube's circuitry may the echo pulse be applied?

A. vertical deflection coils
B. cathode
C. rotating deflection coil
D. focusing coil
E. horizontal deflecting coils

Page(s) 499, 500

Q2-35 The surface of a radar set's parabolic reflector is coated with a thin layer of soot and dirt. As a result:

A. the indicated range of a target will be in error
B. the Doppler effect will be increased

C. a correction must be applied to the indicated bearing of the target
D. the radar beam will be badly scattered
E. none of the above is true

Page(s) 495

Q2-36 In a pulsed radar set, the function of the duplexer is to:

A. aid in calibrating the display unit
B. allow the transmitter and the receiver to operate from a common antenna system
C. protect the receiver from the transmitter pulse
D. prevent frequency drift in the klystron
E. choices B and C are true

Page(s) 496 to 498

Q2-37 The pulse frequency is equal to:

A. the reciprocal of the pulse repetition rate
B. pulse width × peak power/average power
C. duty cycle/pulse width
D. peak power/(pulse width × average power)
E. choices A and C are true

Page(s) 479 to 481

Q2-38 Which of the following stages can be included in the AFC circuitry of a pulsed radar receiver?

A. SHF amplifier
B. crystal mixer
C. AM diode detector
D. discriminator
E. choices B and D are true

Page(s) 485

Q2-39 The basic action of a magnetron can be compared with that of a:

A. cathode ray tube
B. beam power tube
C. diode
D. thyratron
E. phasitron tube

Page(s) 458

Q2-40 The pulse frequency of a marine radar set is 500 per second. If 750 microseconds is the required recovery time, what is the maximum range of the set in nautical miles?

A. 101
B. 50.53
C. 203
D. 144
E. 72

Page(s) 479, 480

Q2-41 In a navigational radar set, the time interval between the pulse being transmitted and a target echo being displayed, is of the order of:

A. milliseconds
B. microseconds
C. nanoseconds
D. picoseconds
E. 10^{-8} seconds

Page(s) 483

Q2-42 The resonant cavities of a magnetron are strapped in order to:

A. stabilize the degree of positive feedback and hence control the peak power output
B. provide a coarse tuning control to set up the magnetron's frequency
C. provide critical coupling between the cavities and thereby obtain the required bandwidth
D. concentrate the manner of operation in the π mode
E. provide an impedance match between the cavities and the waveguide

Page(s) 458, 459

Q2-43 Which of the following can be used to eliminate radar interference in communication receivers?

A. ratio detectors
B. crystal filters in the IF stages
C. wave traps
D. squelch circuits
E. none of the above choices is true. There is no adequate means of eliminating radar interference in communication receivers

Page(s) 502, 503

Q2-44 The tubes of a radar receiver, as well as fuses, may be replaced:

A. only by the holder of a Ship Radar Endorsement
B. only by the holder of a First Class Radiotelegraph License
C. only by the Master or his designee
D. only by the holder of a General Radiotelephone License
E. by an unlicensed person under the supervision of the responsible licensed operator

Page(s) 507

Q2-45 Marine radar transmitters are allowed to operate on a frequency range of:

A. 2300 to 2500 MHz
B. 2900 to 3100 MHz
C. 3460 to 3650 MHz
D. 5300 to 5500 MHz
E. 8900 to 9100 MHz

Page(s) 480

Q2-46 In a radar set, the peak power of a 0.2-microsecond pulse output is 250 kW. If the pulse frequency is 500, what is the value of the duty cycle?

A. 0.0001
B. 0.0002

C. 0.00025
D. 0.0005
E. 0.002

Page(s) 479 to 481

Q2-47 A pulsed radar set with a peak power output of 600 kW has a pulse repetition time of 2000 μs. What is the value of the pulse frequency (repetition rate)?

A. 500
B. 400
C. 200
D. 150
E. 100

Page(s) 479 to 481

Q2-48 If in QUES. 2-47, the average power output is 150 W, what is the value of the pulse width (duration) in microseconds?

A. 0.1
B. 0.2
C. 0.25
D. 0.5
E. 1.0

Page(s) 479 to 481

Q2-49 Which of the waveforms shown, best represents the modulator unit's pulse output which is applied to the magnetron?

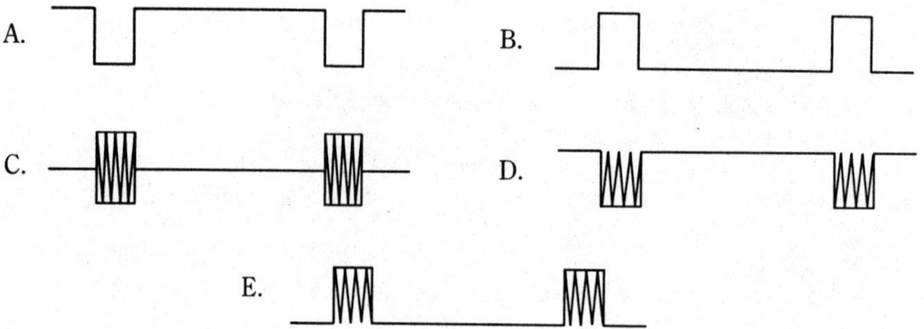

Page(s) 476

Q2-50 In an SHF pulsed radar set, a reflex klystron can be used as a:

A. local oscillator
B. single mixer stage
C. microwave preamplifier
D. transmitter oscillator
E. duplexer stage

Page(s) 484, 485

Part III
Answers and Solutions

Element 3 Practice Tests

Note: references to TAB Book #4055 are shown in parentheses. As examples, (4-7) and (14) respectively indicate section 4-7 and chapter 14. The Appendix is shown as (App.).

Test 1

Q1-001 B (4-7)

Q1-002 C (9-3)

Q1-003 E (14)

Q1-004 D (1-7) For each resistor, there is a certain maximum current above which the power rating of the resistor is exceeded.

For the 5000-Ω resistor:

$$I_{max} = \sqrt{\frac{P}{R}} = \sqrt{\frac{20 \text{ W}}{5000 \ \Omega}} = 63.24 \text{ mA}$$

For the 1000-Ω resistor,

$$I_{max} = \sqrt{\frac{5 \text{ W}}{1000 \ \Omega}} = 70.7 \text{ mA}$$

It follows that the current must not exceed 63.24 mA and that the highest value of applied voltage is 63.24 mA × (5000 Ω + 1000 Ω) = 379 V.

Q1-005 A (1-7) From the solution of QUES. 1-004, the maximum allowed current is 63.24 mA; therefore, the voltage drop across the 5000-Ω resistor is 63.24 mA × 5 kΩ = 316 V.

Q1-006 E (4-1)

Q1-007 E (10-4) Refer to (TAB. 2-3). A loss of 7 dB is equivalent to a power ratio of 1/5, whereas a gain of 3 dB is the same as a power ratio of 2. Therefore, the effective radiated power is $1000 \times 2 \times 1/5 = 400$ W.

Q1-008 B (App.) The resistors are connected in series. By using the voltage division rule, the voltage at F is $+9\ \text{V} \times 220\ \Omega / (220\ \Omega + 470\ \Omega + 100\ \Omega) = +9 \times 220/790 = +2.5$ V.

Q1-009 A (7-11)

Q1-010 E (8-3) Frequency deviation at the output stage, $f_d = 3 \times 3 \times 2 \times 1$ kHz $=$ 18 kHz.

Q1-011 D (5-1) The amount of the deviation is $156.8 \times 10^6 \times 1/10^6$ Hz $= 156.8$ Hz.

Q1-012 B (6-5) Refer to (TAB. 6-2).

Q1-013 C (2-10) *Power gain* $= 100$ mW/1 mW $= 100$. Gain in dB, $N = 10 \log 100 = 10 \times 2 = +20$ dB.

Q1-014 D (14)

Q1-015 A (10-2) Refer to (TAB. 2-3). The power ratio corresponding to -7 dB is 1/5. Therefore, the reflected power is $(1/5) \times 5 = 1$ W and the load power is $5 - 1 = 4$ W (EQ. 10-14).

Q1-016 B (1-17)

Q1-017 D (8-3) The product factor of the multiplier stages is $2 \times 2 \times 3 = 12$. Therefore, the output carrier frequency is $12 \times 8 = 96$ MHz.

Q1-018 E (14)

Q1-019 A (4-3)

Q1-020 A (7-5)

Q1-021 E (9-1) The receiver is tuned to $121.1 - (2 \times 10.7) = 99.7$ MHz.

Q1-022 A (11-8)

Q1-023 C (2-7) *True power* $= I^2R$ watts

Q1-024 B (14)

Q1-025 E (6-5) Refer to (TAB. 6-3).

Q1-026 E (14)

Q1-027 D (1-24)

Q1-028 D (2-1) Period of the sine wave, $T = (1/5) \times (1/50) = 1/250$ s. Frequency, $f = 1/T = 1/(1/250) = 250$ Hz.

Q1-029 D (14)

Q1-030 A (8-1) If the effect of pre-emphasis is neglected, the deviation is independent of the value of the modulating frequency. The frequency deviation therefore remains at 3 kHz.

Q1-031 E (3-5)

Q1-032 C (4-4)

Q1-033 A (10-2) Total attenuation of the transmission line = 200 ft × 6 dB/100 ft = 12 dB. Refer to (TAB. 2-3). Because a loss of 3 dB (−3 dB) is equal to a power ratio of 1/2, an attenuation of 12 dB = 4 × 3 dB is the same as a power ratio of $(1/2)^4$ = 1/16. Therefore, the output power is 100 × (1/16) = 6.25 W. Alternatively, referring to Section 2-26, output power = 100 W × Antilog (−12/10) = 6.31 W.

Q1-034 D (14)

Q1-035 C (5-4)

Q1-036 E (14)

Q1-037 A (2-9) Because the values of the frequency and the components are known, the power factor can be calculated.

Q1-038 D (1-21) After one time constant, the capacitor has discharged to 36.8% of its initial voltage.

Q1-039 B (14)

Q1-040 C (13-3) Octal number, $673_8 = \underbrace{100}_{6}\,\underbrace{111}_{7}\,\underbrace{011}_{3} = 110111011_2$

Q1-041 D (4-6)

Q1-042 E (14)

Q1-043 B (10-6)

Q1-044 E (14)

Q1-045 C (2-11) The self-capacitance of the resistor is in parallel with the resistance and therefore at high frequencies, the value of this resistance is reduced.

Q1-046 E (6-5) In the order of the choices, the necessary bandwidths are 160 Hz, 280 Hz, 300 Hz, 160 Hz, and 1.4 kHz.

Q1-047 D (14)

Q1-048 A (13-5) Refer to FIG. 13-7B.

Q1-049 A (14)

Q1-050 E (4-3)

Q1-051 E (4-3)

Q1-052 E (14)

Q1-053 C (2-14) *True power* = $E \times I \times$ *power factor* = 220 V × 0.3 A × 0.6 = 39.6 W.

Q1-054 E (14)

Q1-055 E (10-7) Refer to FIG. 10-31.

Q1-056 B (14)

Q1-057 E (5-4)

Q1-058 A (14)

Q1-059 D (1-21) Under steady-state conditions in a dc circuit the inductor behaves as a short circuit and the capacitor as an open circuit. Total resistance = 20 + 10 = 30 Ω. Total conductance = 1/(30 Ω) = 0.033 S.

Q1-060 E (14)

Q1-061 B (13-11) Assign 0 and 1 logic states to waveforms of the input and output elements. The following truth table emerges:

INPUTS		OUTPUTS
A	B	*f*(A,B)
0	0	0
0	1	0
1	0	0
1	1	1

Refer to FIG. 13-9. The truth table corresponds to that of an AND gate.

Q1-062 C (1-5) The nominal resistance value is 1 (Brown), 0 (Black) with a zero multiplier (Black) or 10 Ω. Because gold indicates a 5% tolerance, the upper limit is 10 (1 + 5/100) = 10.5 Ω

Q1-063 C (2-12) Turns ratio, $N_p/N_s = \sqrt{400/10} = \sqrt{400} = 20{:}1$. Note that the audio transformer is "step-down."

Q1-064 A (14)

Q1-065 E (7-1)

Q1-066 A (3-1) The diode, D1, is reverse biased and therefore does not conduct (to a first approximation). Using the second approximation, the voltage drop across the diode D2 is 0.7 V and the remaining 12 − 0.7 = 11.3 V is divided between the 10-Ω and 5-Ω resistors. Using the voltage division rule (SEC. 1-7), the IR drop across the 5-Ω resistor is 11.3 V × 5 Ω/(5 Ω + 10 Ω) = 3.8 V and the output voltage, V_o = 3.8 + 0.7 = 4.5 V.

Q1-067 A (14)

Q1-068 C (6-3)

Q1-069 E (14)

Q1-070 D (1-19) The time constant is L/R seconds.

Q1-071 B (4-11) The gain of the inverting amplifier is $-R_f/R_i = 150/10 = -15$.

Q1-072 E (14)

Q1-073 C (14)

Q1-074 E (10-9)

Q1-075 E (14)

Q1-076 E (6-3)

Q1-077 B (14)

Q1-078 C (4-10)

Q1-079 D (14)

Q1-080 E (11-3)

Q1-081 D (14)

Q1-082 E (6-2) The frequency of the lower sideband is $f_c - f_m$ = 1000 kHz − 200 Hz = 999.8 kHz. The frequency of the upper sideband is $f_c + f_m$ 1000 kHz + 200 Hz = 1000.2 kHz. The AM signal contains the carrier and both sidebands; the required combination of frequencies is therefore 999.8, 1000, and 1000.2 kHz.

Q1-083 B (4-10)

Q1-084 A (14)

Q1-085 C (14)

Q1-086 E (10-10) The very high frequency (VHF) band covers the frequency range of 30 to 300 MHz (choice D). This range can also be expressed as 30,000 to 300,000 kHz (choice A). Choices A and D are both true.

Q1-087 E (14)

Q1-088 C (13-11) Assign 0 and 1 logic states to the waveforms of the input and output elements. The following truth table emerges:

INPUTS A	B	OUTPUT f(A,B)
0	0	0
0	1	1
1	0	1
1	1	1

Refer to FIG. 13-7. The truth table corresponds to that of an OR gate.

Q1-089 C (8-2)

Q1-090 C (14)

Q1-091 E (1-4) Conductance, $G = I/E = 1/R = 1/(2000\ \Omega) = 0.5 \times 10^{-3} S = 500\ \mu S$.

Q1-092 A (10-10) From EQ. 10-35, $UTC = EST + 5$ hrs = 1500 + 0500 = 2000 hrs.

Q1-093 A (14)

Q1-094 B (14)

Q1-095 B (9-2)

Q1-096 E (6-2)

Q1-097 C (2-6) In FIG. 1-12, i leads e by 90°; therefore, the circuit is entirely capacitive.

Q1-098 D (14)

Q1-099 B (8-3) Frequency deviation for 50% modulation = (50/100) × 5 = 2.5 kHz. Neglecting the effect of pre-emphasis, the frequency deviation is the same at both frequencies.

Q1-100 D (14)

Test 2

Q2-001 D (4-10)

Q2-002 E (9-2)

Q2-003 A (10-10) The operating frequency of loran C is 100 kHz, which lies within the low frequency (LF) band of 30 to 300 kHz.

Q2-004 C (10-10)

Q2-005 D (3-7)

Q2-006 D (3-7)

Q2-007 B (3-2) Let the primary voltage be 100 V and let a 100 Ω load be connected across the secondary winding. The secondary voltage is then 5 × 100 = 500 V and the secondary current is 500 V/100 Ω = 5 A. The secondary power is 500 V × 5 A = 2500 W; therefore the primary power is also 2500 W (assuming no losses in the transformer). Primary current is 2500 W/100 V = 25 A. The secondary current (5 A) is 20% of the primary current (25 A)

Q2-008 E (8-5)

Q2-009 D (14)

Q2-010 C (13-10)

Q2-011 D (14)

Q2-012 E (10-10)

Q2-013 C (1-8) Insert the ground points so that the circuit can be redrawn as in FIG. 2-2B. The two voltage sources are in series-aiding so that the total voltage in the circuit is 35 + 15 = 50 V with the electron flow in the CCW direction. This current, I = 50 V/(30 kΩ + 70 kΩ) = 0.5 mA so that the voltage drop across the 70-kΩ resistor is 0.5 mA × 70 kΩ = 35 V with its polarity, as shown. Because this voltage drop and the 15-V source are series-opposing, the potential at the point A, with respect to ground, is + 35 − 15 = + 20 V

Q2-014 B (14)

Q2-015 D (7-6) Refer to FIG. 7-8.

Q2-016 B (2-11) Because $X_L = X_C$ = 100 Ω, the series circuit is resonant and the total impedance, $Z = R$ = 100 Ω. The current is 100 V/100 Ω = 1 A and the voltage across the inductor = 1 A × 100 Ω = 100 V.

Note: There is 100 V each across the resistor, the inductor, and the capacitor. The voltages across the inductor and the capacitor are 180° out of phase and therefore cancel. The voltage across the resistor then balances the source voltage.

Q2-017 E (14)

Q2-018 A (1-5) The nominal resistance value is 1 (Brown), 0 (Black), 00 (Red), or 1000 Ω = 1 kΩ. Silver indicates a 10% tolerance.

Q2-019 D (11-5)

Q2-020 E (14)

Q2-021 E (6-6)

Q2-022 D (1-1) The atom becomes negatively charged and is a negative ion.

Q2-023 B (14)

Q2-024 D (14)

Q2-025 E (7-12)

Q2-026 D (14)

Q2-027 D (14)

Q2-028 D (5-3)

Q2-029 E (10-7) Choices A and B are true.

Q2-030 A (14)

Q2-031 D (1-13) Resistors R2 and R3 are in series so that their total equivalent resistance is 28 + 26 = 54 Ω. Resistors R5 and R6 are in parallel; therefore, $R_5//R_6 = 12 \times 24/(12 + 24) = 8\ \Omega$. R_4 is in series with $R_5//R_6$ and the total resistance of this branch is 10 + 8 = 18 Ω. Equivalent resistance of $R_{2,3,4,5,6} = 18 \times 54/(18 + 54) = 13.5\ \Omega$. Resistance presented to the source, $R_T = 13.5 + 12 + 10 = 35.5\ \Omega$. Total current, $I_T = 142\ \text{V}/35.5\ \Omega = 4\ \text{A}$. By the current division rule (CDR), $I_1 = 4\ \text{A} \times 54\ \Omega/(18\ \Omega + 54\ \Omega) = 3\ \text{A}$. Repeating the current division rule, $I_3 = 3\ \text{A} \times 24\ \Omega/ (12\ \Omega + 24\ \Omega) = 2\ \text{A}$. Therefore, the reading of M3 is 2 A.

Q2-032 A (4-10)

Q2-033 E (14)

Q2-034 D (App.) The maximum range for VHF communications is normally 20 miles so that choice E is eliminated. Midnight is the start of a silent period so that communication on 2182 kHz is not permitted. The marine band lies between 1605 kHz and 3500 kHz; consequently, choices A and B are not possible. The correct answer is choice D.

Q2-035 E (14)

Q2-036 E (14)

Q2-037 D (1-19) Because the relative permeability of soft iron is much greater than that of air, the self-inductance is increased.

Q2-038 A (5-2) Maximum permitted deviation $= 156.4 \times 10^6 \times 0.002/100$ Hz = 3136 Hz = 3.136 kHz.

Q2-039 A (14)

Q2-040 A (6-5) Refer to (TAB. 6-2).

Q2-041 D (9-3) Refer to FIG. 9-5.

Q2-042 D (4-7) Refer to FIG. 4-30A.

Q2-043 D (14)

Q2-044 D (2-10) Gain in decibels, $N = 10 \log(0.1\ \text{W}/10\ \text{W}) = 10 \log 0.01 = -20$ dB. Therefore, the amount of attenuation is 20 dB.

Q2-045 D (1-20)

Q2-046 C (14)

Q2-047 E (6-5) Refer to (TAB. 6-2).

Q2-048 A (6-6) Only WWV radiates a continuous 20-MHz carrier.

Q2-049 C (13-13) If N is the required minimum number of address lines, $2^N = 4096$. Because $4096 = 64^2$ and $2^6 = 65$, $(2^6)^2 = 2^{12} = 4096$. Therefore, $N = 12$.

Q2-050 E (14)

Q2-051 A (1-20) The capacitance of C_3 and C_4 in series is $C_{3,4} = 2/2 = 1\ \mu F$. The capacitor C_2 is in parallel with $C_{3,4}$ for an equivalent capacitance of $2 + 1 = 3\ \mu F$, which is in series with C_1. Total equivalent capacitance between the points X and Y is $2 \times 3/(2 + 3) = 1.2\ \mu F$.

Q2-052 A (8-4)

Q2-053 D (14)

Q2-054 C (4-6)

Q2-055 D (8-1)

Q2-056 E (14)

Q2-057 C (6-3)

Q2-058 A (10-7) Refer to FIG. 10-30A.

Q2-059 E (14)

Q2-060 E (3-3) The modulation index $m = f_d/f_m$ and the maximum value of the instantaneous frequency, f_d, is directly proportional to the tone's amplitude.

Q2-061 E (14)

Q2-062 E (2-8) Net reactance, $X = X_L - X_C = 52 - 40 = 12\ \Omega$. Therefore, $R = X = 12\ \Omega$. Phase angle, $\phi = +45°$. The circuit is inductive so that I lags E.

Q2-063 D (14)

Q2-064 E (4-3)

Q2-065 E (14)

Q2-066 E (6-3)

Q2-067 C (14)

Q2-068 E (1-22) The high resistor acts as a "multiplier" to extend the voltage range.

Q2-069 E (4-3) The positive half cycle of the input signal will increase the instantaneous forward bias applied to the emitter-base junction; as a result, the emitter, base, and collector currents all increase.

Q2-070 D (14)

Q2-071 D (2-7) Impedance, $Z = E_{RMS}/I_{RMS}$ and therefore is measured in ohms.

Q2-072 C (14)

Q2-073 B (1-24)

Q2-074 A (14)

Q2-075 E (10-4) Refer to FIG. 10-19. Choices A and D are both true.

Q2-076 B (9-1) The frequency of the second IF must be 200 kHz or less. For choice A, the first IF is 156.7 − 146 = 10.7 MHz and the second IF is 10.7 − 10.114 MHz = 586 kHz, which is too high. With Choice B, the first IF is 156.7 − 146.664 = 10.036 MHz and the second IF is 10.144 − 10.036 MHz = 108 kHz.

Q2-077 C (14)

Q2-078 B (14) Refer to (TAB. 14-3).

Q2-079 D (14)

Q2-080 E (6-1)

Q2-081 A (14)

Q2-082 E (13-4) Binary number, $11100101111_2 = \underbrace{0111}_{7}\ \underbrace{0010}_{2}\ \underbrace{1111}_{F(15)} = 72F_{16}$.

Q2-083 A (APP) VOR stations operate in the band of 112.050 to 117.950 MHz with a channel spacing of 50 kHz. These stations can also be assigned frequencies in the 108- to 112-MHz band.

Q2-084 D (10-3) To prevent the production of standing waves on the outer conductor, it is normally grounded at the input end and the output end. Sometimes the outer conductor is also grounded at certain intervals along the length.

Q2-085 C (7-8)

Q2-086 B (14)

Q2-087 E (7-3)

Q2-088 E (8-2)

Q2-089 B (7-2) Intermediate frequency = 167.7 − 157.0 = 10.7 MHz. *Image-channel frequency* = 167.7 + 10.7 = 178.4 MHz.

Q2-090 E (1-3) Original resistance = 36 × 12 = 432 Ω. *New resistance* = 432/(1/3) = 1296 Ω.

Q2-091 B (9-3)

Q2-092 B (10-2) Refer to EQ. 10-10.

Q2-093 D (13-2) $11_{10} = 8_{10} + 2_{10} + 1_{10} = 1 \times 2^3 + 0 \times 2^2 = 1 \times 2^1 + 1 \times 2^0 = 1011_2$.

Q2-094 D (4-1)

Q2-095 A (8-1) Because the frequencies of the sidebands are $f_c \pm f_m$, $f_c \pm 2f_m$, $f_c \pm 3f_m$ and so on, each sideband is separated from its neighbor by the value of the modulating frequency, f_m.

Q2-096 D (2-1) One cycle corresponds to an angle of 360° or 2π radians. The angle for three quarters of a cycle is $\frac{3}{4} \times 2\pi = 3\pi/2$ radians or $\frac{3}{4} \times 360° = 270°$.

Q2-097 E (10-2) Because 1 statute mile = 0.87 nautical mile, 2.3 statute miles = 2.3 × 0.87 = 2.0 nautical miles, rounded off.

Q2-098 A (APP) Because of their lower dielectric hysteresis loss, waveguides are preferred over coaxial cables at microwave frequencies.

Q2-099 D (10-10) From EQ. 10-34, $UTC = CST + 6$ hrs $= 1500 + 0600 = 2100$ hrs.

Q2-100 A (14) The aircraft would not use the distress frequency of 121.5 MHz.

Test 3

Q3-001 A (14)

Q3-002 A (1-23) The percentage of regulation for a dc generator is equal to $[(E_{NL} - E_{FL})/E_{FL}] \times 100\%$.

Q3-003 A (2-6) In FIG. 3-1, *e* leads *i* by 90°; therefore the circuit is entirely inductive.

Q3-004 C (6-6) *Error in the frequency monitor* $= +10$ Hz $- (-8$ Hz$) + 18$ Hz $= 18$ Hz high.

Q3-005 A (14)

Q3-006 D (3-2)

Q3-007 C (10-2) Wavelength, $\lambda = c/f = 3 \times 10^8$ m/s/$(500 \times 10^6$ Hz$) = 0.6$ m $= 60$ cm.

Q3-008 E (11-5)

Q3-009 E (7-9)

Q3-010 C (8-3) Product factor of the multiplier stages = 98.1 MHz/4905 kHz = 20. *Oscillator's frequency swing* $= \pm 5$ kHz/20 $= \pm 250$ Hz.

Q3-011 E (5-3)

Q3-012 A (13-6) Refer to FIG. 13-9C.

Q3-013 E (9-2)

Q3-014 D (App.) The complementary inputs to the AND gate are Q and $\overline{Q}$. The output is $Q.\overline{Q} = 0$, irrespective of whether $Q = 0$ or $Q = 1$.

Q3-015 A (4-10)

Q3-016 A (14)

Q3-017 A (2-12) Secondary voltage, $E_s = 110 \times 2400/400 = 660$ V. Secondary current, $I_s = 600$ V/33 kΩ $= 20$ mA.

Q3-018 C (14)

Q3-019 A (1-21) Under steady-state conditions in this dc circuit, the inductor behaves as a short circuit and the capacitor as an open circuit. *Power* $= V \times A = V^2/R_2 = A^2 \times R_2$.

Q3-020 C (14)

Q3-021 B (7-7)

Q3-022 E (14)

Q3-023 C (5-4) Oscillator frequency $= 16$ MHz$/(2 \times 2 \times 2) = 2$ MHz. Maximum permitted deviation at the oscillator is $2 \times 10^6 \times 0.002/100 = 40$ Hz.

Q3-024 D (14)

Q3-025 E (6-5) Refer to (TAB. 6-3). The frequency band for J3E emissions is 1605 to 27500 kHz. Both 10 MHz and 20 MHz fall within this band.

Q3-026 E (4-7) The circuit is that of a source follower, which has a very high input impedance and a low output impedance.

Q3-027 D (14)

Q3-028 C (5-5) *Power ratio* = 500/0.5 = 1000. *Amount of attenuation* = 10 log 1000 = 30 dB.

Q3-029 D (1-20) A capacitor can open circuit, short circuit, or partially short circuit.

Q3-030 A (10-10) If the frequency is increased, the amount of bending in the ionosphere is less and the skip distance increases.

Q3-031 E (14)

Q3-032 B (8-1)

Q3-033 E (14)

Q3-034 C (1-19) Because $L = N^2 A \mu / l$ H, L is directly proportional to N^2.

Q3-035 A (2-11) The amount frequency, $f_r = 1/(2\pi \sqrt{LC})$ Hz and is therefore inversely proportional to the square root of the capacitance. Consequently the capacitance must be reduced to one quarter of its original value. The required ratio is 1:4.

Q3-036 B (14)

Q3-037 D (6-5) The bandwidth is halved and its new value is therefore 10 kHz/2 = 5 kHz.

Q3-038 D (14)

Q3-039 C (8-3) The high modulating frequencies are accentuated by the pre-emphasis circuit.

Q3-040 D (14)

Q3-041 D (4-4)

Q3-042 A (14)

Q3-043 B (7-5)

Q3-044 D (14)

Q3-045 E (1-19) The two 10-H inductors are in parallel so that their equivalent inductance is 10/2 = 5 H. This equivalent inductance is in series with the right-hand 5-H inductor so that one branch between the points P and Q has a total inductance of 5 + 5 = 10 H. The other branch contains only the bottom 5-H inductor so that the total equivalent inductance of this series-parallel circuit is $\frac{5 \times 10}{5 + 10} = \frac{50}{15} = 3.3$ H, rounded off.

Q3-046 E (14)

Q3-047 A (2-10) Power level, P = 10 log (0.1 mW/1 mW) = 10 log 0.1 = −10 dBm.

Q3-048 E (14)

Q3-049 E (4-6)

Q3-050 E (6-3) Because the frequencies of CB channels lie between 26.965 MHz and 27.405 MHz, the TV channels are experiencing harmonic interference.

Q3-051 A (14)

Q3-052 B (14) For a PM wave, the frequency deviation is directly proportional to the product of the tone amplitude and the modulating frequency. The frequency deviation is therefore multiplied by $2 \times 2 = 4$.

Q3-053 C (8-3)

Q3-054 B (10-10) From EQ. 10-33, $UTC = MST + 7$ hrs $= 0900 + 0700 = 1600$ hrs.

Q3-055 E (14)

Q3-056 E (6-3)

Q3-057 B (13-2) From EQ. 13-1, $1101_2 = (1 \times 2^3) + (1 \times 2^2) + (0 \times 2^1) + (1 \times 2^0) = 8 + 4 + 0 + 1 = 13_{10}$.

Q3-058 E (14)

Q3-059 E (8-3) Because the RF power in an FM signal is independent of the modulation, the total power remains at 100 W.

Q3-060 E (14)

Q3-061 A (7-1)

Q3-062 D (2-8) Capacitive reactance, $X_C = ½ \pi FC = 1/(2 \times \pi \times 60 \times 0.002 \times 10^{-6})\Omega = 1.33\ \text{M}\Omega$. Impedance, $Z = \sqrt{R^4 + X_{C2}}\ \sqrt{1^2 + 1.33^2}\ \text{M}\Omega = 1.66\ \text{M}\Omega$

Q3-063 E (14)

Q3-064 E (4-5)

Q3-065 E (14)

Q3-066 B (11-3)

Q3-067 E (14)

Q3-068 C (6-2) The strong second harmonic has a frequency of $2 \times 1.5 = 3$ kHz. Bandwidth, $BW = 2 \times$ (highest modulating frequency) $= 6$ kHz. Note that the assigned bandwidth of a marine double-sideband AM transmitter is 8 kHz, which means the highest audio frequency transmitted is only 4 kHz. This is adequate for voice communication, but it would be insufficient for the transmission of music.

Q3-069 B (9-3) Refer to FIG. 9-3. The diagram is that of a de-emphasis circuit with its time constant of 75 μS.

Q3-070 E (3-2)

Q3-071 B (9-2)

Q3-072 E (14)

Q3-073 A (7-2)

Q3-074 B (1-10) The voltage, V_L, across the relay coil is $0.1\ \text{A} \times 600\ \Omega = 60$ V. Voltage drop across the protection resistor is 110 V = 60 V = 50 V. *Required resistance* = 50 V/0.1 A = 500 Ω.

Q3-075 A (1-10) Power dissipated, $P_D = I_L V_D = 0.1\text{ A} \times 50\text{ W}$

Q3-076 E (14)

Q3-077 C (10-10)

Q3-078 C (4-3)

Q3-079 E (14)

Q3-080 A (2-2) Peak value, $E_{peak} = E_{RMS} \times 1.414 = 20 \times 1.414 = 28.3$ V, rounded off.

Q3-081 D (14)

Q3-082 D (10-10)

Q3-083 E (14)

Q3-084 C (13-12) The two "highs" applied to the NAND gate cause point A to be "low". The "high" and "low" inputs to the first OR gate cause point B to be "high". Point C is also "high" because of the "low" and "high" inputs to the second OR gate.

Q3-085 A (4-1) In the top view of the microchip pin 1 is identified by the dot (e). Counting counterclockwise from pin 1, pin 9 is identified by "a."

Q3-086 A (2-15) To synthesize an approximation to a symmetrical square wave, the fundamental and all odd harmonic components are required.

Q3-087 C (4-1)

Q3-088 E (10-7) Frequency of the fifth harmonic, $f = 5 \times 520$ kHz = 2600 kHz = 2.6 MHz. Choices C and D are true.

Q3-089 D (14)

Q3-090 B (10-6)

Q3-091 D (2-13) The circuit can be redrawn as in FIG. 2-71 and represents a two-section m-derived low-pass filter (refer to FIG. 2-66)

Q3-092 D (4-3) The circuit shows a common emitter configuration; consequently, there is a 180° phase reversal between the input and output signals.

Q3-093 D (4-3)

Q3-094 C (10-4) The resonant frequency is inversely proportional to the antenna's length (EQ. 10-18). Consequently, if the length is increased, the resonant frequency decreases.

Q3-095 D (10-3) Standing waves are the result of a mismatch between the line and the load.

Q3-096 D (14)

Q3-097 B (10-2) *Range* = 62 μs/12.368 μs/n.m = [illegible]5.0 nautical miles, rounded off.

Q3-098 E (3-5)

Q3-099 E (14)

Q3-100 D (2-8) Reactance of the capacitor, $X_C = 1/2\pi Fc = 1/(1000 \times 0.001 \times 10^{-6}) = 10^6 = 1\text{ M}\Omega$. Impedance of the circuit, $Z = \sqrt{R^2 + X_C^2} = \sqrt{1^2 + 1^2} = \sqrt{2}\text{ M}\Omega$.

Test 4

Q4-001 B (11-6).

Q4-002 D (App.) Diode D1 is conducting and its voltage drop is assumed to be 0.7 V. By the voltage division rule, the voltage drop across R1 is 0.7 V × 5 Ω /(5 Ω + 10 Ω) = 0.23 V.

Q4-003 D (14)

Q4-004 E (2-16)

Q4-005 E (6-5) Refer to (TAB. 6-1).

Q4-006 A (4-6)

Q4-007 E (14)

Q4-008 A (7-3)

Q4-009 D (14)

Q4-010 E (3-20)

Q4-011 C (14)

Q4-012 E (8-3)

Q4-013 C (14)

Q4-014 E (5-4)

Q4-015 A (1-21) The time constant of the circuit is $RC = 5 \times 10^3 \times 10 \times 10^{-6}$ s = 50 ms. After one time constant the capacitor is charged to 0.632 × 12 = 7.56 V.

Q4-016 D (9-1) The product factor of the transmitter's frequency multiplier stages is doubled and therefore the frequency deviation is doubled.

Q4-017 C (14)

Q4-018 D (13-4) Hexadecimal number, $A6B_{16} = \underbrace{A(10)}_{1010}\ \underbrace{6}_{0110}\ \underbrace{B(11)}_{1011} = 101001101011_2$ ($= 2667_{10}$).

Q4-019 B (1-24)

Q4-020 B (2-3) The effective value of the phasor sum is:
$\sqrt{3^2 + 4^2} = \sqrt{9 + 16} = \sqrt{25} = 5$ V.

Q4-021 D (10-4) Refer to FIG. 10-15C.

Q4-022 B (9-2)

Q4-023 B (6-5) Refer to (TAB. 6-3).

Q4-024 D (14)

Q4-025 E (10-7) Refer to FIG. 10-30B.

Q4-026 B (8-1) If pre-emphasis is neglected, the frequency deviation is solely determined by the tone's amplitude.

Q4-027 E (14)

Q4-028 C (10-10)

Q4-029 E (8-3)

Q4-030 E (14)

Q4-031 A (1-24)

Q4-032 A (14)

Q4-033 E (14)

Q4-034 C (10-4) From EQ. 10-18, the resonant frequency, f = 468/[length of Hertz antenna (ft)] MHz. If the length is shortened, the resonant frequency increases.

Q4-035 D (4-6)

Q4-036 A (6-3)

Q3-037 E (14)

Q4-038 A (8-3)

Q4-039 E (1-14)

Q4-040 E (2-7) True power $E_{RMS} \times I_{RMS} \times \text{Cos.}\phi$ watts (EQ. 2-27). Because the cosine of a phase angle is less than unity, the value of the true power decreases.

Q4-041 D (14)

Q4-042 B (13-6) Refer to FIG. 13-9B.

Q4-043 B (14)

Q4-044 D (1-20) The two capacitors in series have a total equivalent capacitance of 0.1/2 = 0.05 μF; the total charge stored is therefore 0.05 μF × 120 V = 6 μC. When the third capacitor is connected in parallel, the total capacitance is 0.05 + 0.1 = 0.15 μF. The voltage across the third capacitor is 6 μC/0.15 μF = 40 V.

Q4-045 E (14)

Q4-046 B (14)

Q4-047 B (1-14)

Q4-048 A (14)

Q4-049 E (14)

Q4-050 E (4-3)

Q4-051 E (11-3)

Q4-052 D (14)

Q4-053 D (8-5)

Q4-054 C (2-13)

Q4-055 E (5-5) *Dc power input to the final stage* = 1220 V × 320 mA = 390.4 W. Efficiency factor, F = 250 W/390.4 W = 0.64 or 64%. Note that the efficiency factor can either be expressed as a decimal fraction or as a percentage.

Q4-056 E (1-16) Each nickel-cadmium cell has an operating voltage of 1.25 V. *Total EMF* *available* = 12 × 1.25 = 15 V. Note: the equivalent internal resistance of the series arrangement is still very low.

Q4-057 C (2-12)

Q4-058 E (14)

Q4-059 B (6-2) Total sideband power, $P_{S8} = 0.5 \times 12 \times 500 = 250/2 = 125$ W.

Q4-060 E (4-11) The circuit is that of an inverting comparator. Because $V_i > V_{ref}$, the circuit is driven into negative saturation so that $V_o = -12$ V.

Q4-061 A (14) The tolerance in hertz is ± 243 × 50 = ± 12150 Hz = 0.01215 MHz. The upper frequency limit is 243.01215 MHz and the lower frequency limit is 242.98785 MHz.

Q4-062 D (10-1)

Q4-063 A (10-2) Refer to (TAB. 14-4).

Q4-064 D (14) Because $V = I \times Z_o$ (EQ. 10-1), the voltage is equal to the line current and the surge impedance.

Q4-065 B (14)

Q4-066 A (8-4)

Q4-067 A (9-3)

Q4-068 E (14)

Q4-069 E (1-21) The time constant of the circuit is $RC = 20 \times 10^3 \times 5 \times 10^{-6}$s = 100 ms. Because 500 ms is equivalent to five time constants, the capacitor is assumed to be fully charged to 12 V.

Q4-070 D (10-10) The low-frequency (LF) band covers the frequency range of 30 to 300 kHz.

Q4-071 C (14)

Q4-072 B (4-10)

Q4-073 E (14)

Q4-074 B (2-11) Resonant frequency, $f_r = 1/(2\pi\sqrt{LC}) = 1/(2 \times \pi \times \sqrt{5 \times 10^{-6} \times 5 \times 10^{-12}})$ Hz = $10^9/(2 \times \pi \times 5)$ Hz = 31.8 MHz.

Q4-075 A (14)

Q4-076 C (2-10) Power ratio = $10^{10/10} = 10^1 = 10$.

Q4-077 C (5-2) Maximum permitted deviation = $2182 \times 10^3 \times 10/10^6$ Hz = 21.82 Hz.

Q4-078 E (14) The international bridge-to-bridge frequency is 156.65 MHz, which is designated as Channel 13.

Q4-079 E (3-4) The zener diode provides a reference level of 3 V so that the voltage across the resistor, R_1, is 12 − 3 = 9 V.

Q4-080 C (3-4) The zener diode provides a reference level so that the total voltage across R2 and R3 in series is 3 V. By the VDR (SEC. 1-7), the voltage across R2 is 3 V × 5 kΩ/(5 kΩ + 10 kΩ) = 1 V.

Q4-081 E (10-7) The shorter is the antenna, the higher is its resonant frequency (choice D). By adding a capacitor in series, the electrical length of the antenna is lowered (choice A).

Q4-082 C (1-11) Total resistance of the series circuit, $R_S = R + R = 2R\ \Omega$. Power dissipated in the series circuit, $P_S = E^2/R_S = E^2/2R$ W. Total resistance of the parallel circuit, $R_P = R \times R/(R + R) = R/2\ \Omega$. Power dissipated in the parallel circuit, $P_P = E^2/P_P = E^2/(R/2) = 2E^2/R$ W. Required ration, $P_P/R_S = (ZE^2/R)/E^2/2R) = 4{:}1$.

Q4-083 D (5-2) *Percentage tolerance* $= \pm 10/10^4 = \pm 1 \times 10^{-3} = \pm 0.001\%$.

Q4-084 A (14)

Q4-085 E (14)

Q4-086 E (14)

Q4-087 A (2-7) Although the apparent power is 10 V × 1 A = 10 VA, the inductor and the capacitor are assumed to be ideal components with no resistive losses. Consequently, the true power in the circuit is zero (0 W)

Q4-088 E (14)

Q4-089 E (7-5) The required bandwidth is equal to twice the value of the highest audio frequency, 2 × 4 kHz = 8 kHz.

Q4-090 B (1-4) Choose some convenient numbers to solve the question. Original conditions: $E = 10$ V, $R = 1\ \Omega$. Power dissipated, $P = (10\text{ V})^2/1\ \Omega = 100$ W. New conditions: $P = 100$ W, $E = 2 \times 10 = 20$ V. Resistance, $R = E^2/P = (20\text{ V})^2/100\text{ W} = 4\ \Omega$. The resistance has to be quadrupled or multiplied by 4.

Q4-091 A (4-10)

Q4-092 A (13-12) One method of obtaining answer is to try out each choice in turn and find out which one works! Alternatively we can observe that for the output to be "high," one of the OR gate inputs must be "high." For the lower input to be "high," both E and F must be "high" (choice A). For the upper input to be "high," both A and B must be "high" (choice C), and, in addition, both C and D must be "low" (which is not satisfied by choice C). Consequently, the only possible answer is choice A.

Q4-093 E (7-7) The very weak signal will not be able to overcome the delay bias on the AGC diode.

Q4-094 D (4-8) Refer to FIG. 4-38B.

Q4-095 E (4-8) Refer to FIG. 4-41B.

Q4-096 E (14)

Q4-097 B (7-2) The carrier frequency of the wanted signal is 1570 − 2 × 455 = 660 kHz.

Q4-098 C (4-3)

Q4-099 D (10-1) The RF value of the surge impedance is equal to $\sqrt{L/C}\ 0°\ \Omega$.

Q4-100 D (1-24)

Test 5

Q5-001 C (App.) The capacitor has lost 100 − 14 = 86% of its initial voltage. This corresponds approximately to two time constants (86.5%).

Q5-002 D (2-15) The harmonic analysis of the symmetrical square wave contains a fundamental sine wave (at the same frequency as the square wave) together with all odd harmonic components.

Q5-003 B (13-3) Using the repeated division method, 5693/8 = 711, remainder 5; 711/8, remainder 7; 88/8 = 11, remainder 0; 11/8 = 1, remainder 3; 1/8 = 0, remainder 1. Therefore, 5693_{10} = 13075 g.

Q5-004 E (10-10) In a vacuum (free space) the velocity of a radio wave is constant and equal to the velocity of light.

Q5-005 E (9-2)

Q5-006 A (14)

Q5-007 E (4-1)

Q5-008 A (14)

Q5-009 A (2-13)

Q5-010 D (14)

Q5-011 B (6-2) Modulated values of the carrier frequency are ignored. *Percentage of variance* = [(25.00025 − 25)/25] × 100% = 0.001%.

Q5-012 E (14)

Q5-013 A (6-3)

Q5-014 E (13-7) Refer to FIG. 13-11B.

Q5-015 B (14)

Q5-016 E (4-11) The circuit is that of a noninverting comparator, which is driven into positive saturation. Therefore, V_o is approximately +14 V.

Q5-017 C (2-11) As a result of its larger surface area, multistrand wire suffers less from skin effect than a single conductor.

Q5-018 C (1-3) Energy consumed, $W = P \times t$ = 242 W × 31 hr = 7502 W.h = 7.5 kWh, rounded off.

Q5-019 C (4-6)

Q5-020 E (14)

Q5-021 B (10-10) From EQ. 10-32, UTC = *PST* + 8 hrs = 1800 + 0800 = 2600 (−2400) = 0200 hrs.

Q5-022 C (14)

Q5-023 C (3-3) Refer to FIG. 3-15A. Reverse both diodes D2 and D4.

Q5-024 A (5-5) By the direct method, *operating power* = $(3\text{ A})^2 \times 15\ \Omega$ = 115 W. DC power input to the final stage = 600 V × 0.3 A = 180 W. Efficiency factor, F = 145 W/180 W = 0.75.

Q5-025 A (14)

Q5-026 B (8-1)

Q5-027 B (14) In order to be grounds for suspension, the act or treaty must be one which the FCC is authorized to administer.

Q5-028 E (6-3)

Q5-029 C (9-3)

Q5-030 E (4-10)

Q5-031 D (2-10) *Power ratio* $= \frac{1 \text{ mW}}{100 \text{ mW}} = 0.01$. Gain in decibels, $N = 10 \log 0.01 = 10 \times (-2) = -20$ dB. Therefore, the loss provided by the attenuation is 20 dB.

Q5-032 E (14)

Q5-033 C (10-10) The very low frequency (VLF) band covers the range of frequencies from 3 to 30 kHz.

Q5-034 E (14)

Q5-035 C (7-9)

Q5-036 A (14)

Q5-037 B (2-14) When the grid is made more negative, with respect to the cathode, the beam current is reduced; this in turn lowers the beam intensity.

Q5-038 A (2-10) *Power ratio* $= 10^{-40/10} = 0.0001$. *Power output* $= 0.0001 \times 1$ mW $= 10^{-4}$ mW $= 0.1$ μW.

Q5-039 D (4-5) Because the emitter is grounded, the bias in the absence of a signal is 0.7 V.

Q5-040 E (14)

Q5-041 A (5-4) *Percentage of variance* $= [(50.01 - 50/50] \times 100\%$ (EQ. 5-3) $= 0.02\%$.

Q5-042 B (2-5) For maximum power transfer to the load, $R_L = 10 + 20 = 30\ \Omega$. *Maximum load power* $= (30 \text{ V})^2/(4 \times 30\ \Omega) = 7.5$ W.

Q5-043 C (4-3) R_E acts as the load of an emitter-follower circuit so that output 1 is in phase with the base input signal. Because the collector current is only slightly less than the emitter current, output 2 is virtually the same size as output 1, but this output from the collector is 180° out of phase with the base input signal. We, therefore, have two equal outputs, which are 180° out of phase and the circuit is called a ***phase inverter***, which is capable of providing the required voltages for the push-pull arrangement of Section 4-5.

Q5-044 A (14)

Q5-045 D (9-1)

Q5-046 A (14)

Q5-047 E (6-5) Refer to (TAB. 6-1).

Q5-048 E (14)

Q5-049 C (10-10)

Q5-050 E (14)

Q5-051 C (7-5)

Q5-052 E (14)

Q5-053 C (11-1)

Q5-054 C (14)

Q5-055 C (4-3) The base battery is providing reverse bias instead of the required forward bias.

Q5-056 C (8-5)

Q5-057 D (14)

Q5-058 C (2-1) The frequency of the fifth harmonic is 5 × 520 = 2600 kHz = 2.6 MHz.

Q5-059 B (6-4) Using the suggested values in SEC. 6-4, the antenna current (I_A), when 50% modulated is $I_A = \sqrt{112.5\text{ W}/100\ \Omega} = 1.061$ A. For 80% modulation, $I_A = \sqrt{132\text{ W}/100\ \Omega} = 1.149$ A. Percentage increase = [(1.149 - 1.061)/1.061] × 100 = 8.3%, rounded off.

Q5-060 E (14)

Q5-061 A (1-20) The two capacitors in parallel have a total equivalent capacitance of 2 × 0.1 = 0.2 μF and the total charge stored is 0.2 μF × 120 V = 24 μC. When the third capacitor is connected, the total capacitance is 3 × 0.1 = 0.3 μF; the voltage across the third capacitor is 24 μC/0.3 μF = 80 V.

Q5-062 D (14)

Q5-063 D (3-4)

Q5-064 D (10-7) Gain in decibels, N = 10 log (0.5 W/500 W) = 10 log 0.001 = 10 × (−3) = −30 dB. Attenuation of the second harmonic component is 30 dB.

Q5-065 D (14)

Q5-066 A (1-22)

Q5-067 A (14)

Q5-068 C (4-2) Under normal conditions the value of V_{EE} is less than that of V_{cc}.

Q5-069 D (14)

Q5-070 C (13-12) The high and low inputs to the top AND gate cause point A to be "low." The two high inputs to the bottom AND gate cause point B to be "high." Point C is "low" because of the low and high inputs to the NOR gate.

Q5-071 C (8-5)

Q5-072 C (14)

Q5-073 E (10-5) The addition of parasitic elements to a dipole increases its directional characteristics and raises its power gain. Choices A and C are both true.

Q5-074 B (14)

Q5-075 B (5-4) Oscillator frequency = 16/(2 × 2 × 2) = 2 MHz. *Maximum permitted frequency deviation* = 2 × 10^6 × 200/10^6 = 400 Hz.

Q5-076 E (1-4) Choose some convenient numbers to solve the question. Original conditions: $E = 10$ V, $R = 2\ \Omega$. Power dissipated, $P = (10\ \text{V})^2/2\ \Omega = 50$ W. New conditions: $P = 50$ W, $R = 2/2 = 1\ \Omega$. EMF, $E = \sqrt{150\ \text{W} \times 1\ \Omega} = \sqrt{50} = 7.07$ V. The voltage is multiplied by a factor of 7.07 V/10 V = 0.707.

Q5-077 B (1-20)

Q5-078 B (14)

Q5-079 B (4-1) In the bottom view pin 1 is identified by "e." Counting clockwise from pin 1, pin 10 is indicated by "b."

Q5-080 B (11-6)

Q5-081 D (14)

Q5-082 A (8-1)

Q5-083 E (14)

Q5-084 A (8-3) In a narrow-band system the information is contained in a small number of strong significant sidebands. This results in a greater propagation range than that possessed by a wideband system.

Q5-085 C (10-4) If the antenna is too short, it behaves as a capacitive load and can therefore be brought to resonance by adding an inductor in series.

Q5-086 D (7-1)

Q5-087 D (1-15) Percentage regulation = [(660 − 600)/600)] × 100% = 10%.

Q5-088 B (14)

Q5-089 D (1-11) The maximum voltage that can be safely applied across the 100-Ω resistor is $\sqrt{100\ \Omega \times 10\ \text{W}} = 31.6$ V. The maximum voltage that can be easily safely applied across the 50-Ω resistor is $\sqrt{50\ \Omega \times 10\ \text{W}} = 22.36$ V. Consequently, the applied voltage must not exceed 22.36 V. Total resistance, $R_T = 100 \times 50/(100 + 50) = 33.33\ \Omega$. Maximum power, $P_{max} = E^2/R_T = (22.36\ \text{V})^2/33.33\ \Omega = 15$ W.

Q5-090 B (5-5) By the direct method, operating power = $I^2_A R_A = (3.2\ \text{A})^2 \times 15\ \Omega = 150$ W. Note that by the indirect method, *operating power* = $E \times I \times F$ = 500 V × 0.4 A × 0.7 = 140 W.

Q5-091 D (10-2) Line current, $I = \sqrt{P/Z_o} = \sqrt{200\ \text{W}/100\ \Omega} = \sqrt{2} = 1.4$ A, rounded off.

Q5-092 D (14)

Q5-093 C (1-1) The current is the result of an electron flow.

Q5-094 A (10-2) Because 1 nautical mile = 1.15 statute miles (EQ. 10-7), 1.74 nautical miles = 1.74 × 1.15 = 2.0 statute miles, rounded off.

Q5-095 A (7-2) *Carrier frequency* = 2675 − 455 = 2220 kHz.

Q5-096 E (8-3)

Q5-097 E (7-3)

Q5-098 B (8-5)

Q5-099 B (10-10)

Q5-100 E (14)

Test 6

Q6-001 A (10-2) Refer to (TAB. 2-2). A 20-dB loss is equivalent to a power ratio of 0.01 or 1/100. The power reaching the antenna is $0.01 \times 1000 = 10$ W.

Q6-002 E (14)

Q6-003 C (11-4)

Q6-004 D (14)

Q6-005 B (App.) The number of cycles in 790° is 790°/360° = 2.19.

Q6-006 C (10-3) The value of the load power, $P_L = P_i - P_r = 25 - 5 = 20$ W (EQ. 10-14). Therefore, a value of 20 W is entered in the transmitter's log.

Q6-007 E (14)

Q6-008 E (6-2) A power ratio of $20 = 2 \times 10$. From (TAB. 2-3), a power ratio of 2 is equal to 3 dB, and a power ratio of 10 is the same as 10 dB. Therefore, a power ratio of 20 can be expressed as $3 + 10 = 13$ dB quieting.

Q6-009 D (8-1)

Q6-010 D (1-21) Refer to (TAB. 1-7).

Q6-011 E (1-2) Because watts = joules per second, 1 joule = 1 watt-second. Large units of energy or work are the watt-hour (1 Wh = 3600 J) and the kilowatt-hour (1 kWh = 1000 Wh = 3,600,000 J).

Q6-012 E (9-3) Refer to FIG. 9-3.

Q6-013 B (5-4) *Output frequency* = $2 \times 2 \times 2 \times 2 = 16$ MHz. The maximum permitted deviation of the output frequency is $16 \times 10^6 \times 0.002/100$ Hz = 320 Hz.

Q6-014 C (4-10) The output frequency is $3 \times 1 = 3$ MHz.

Q6-015 E (14)

Q6-016 C (10-10)

Q6-017 A (14)

Q6-018 E (2-7) Because the values of the frequency and R_2 are unknown, the power factor cannot be calculated.

Q6-019 D (14)

Q6-020 A (10-10) From EQ. 10-32, PST = UTC − 8 hrs = 11 PM − 8 hrs = 3:00 PM. Note that this time is the same as 4:00 PM MST, 5:00 PM CST, and 6:00 PM EST.

Q6-021 A (14)

Q6-022 C (2-12)

Q6-023 E (4-10)

Q6-024 E (14)

Q6-025 B (5-5) Attenuation of 40 dB is equivalent to a power ratio of Antilog $(-40 \text{ dB}/10) = 10^{-4} = 0.0001$. The second harmonic power $= 1 \text{ kW} \times 0.0001 = 1000 \times 0.0001 \text{ W} = 0.1 \text{ W}$.

Q6-026 E (14)

Q6-027 E (10-10) The medium frequency (MF) band covers the frequency range of 300 to 3000 kHz (choice D). This range can also be expressed as 300 kHz to 3 MHz (choice C). Both choices C and D are true.

Q6-028 D (14)

Q6-029 C (9-3)

Q6-030 A (14)

Q6-031 B (13-11) Figure 6-4 illustrates a NOR gate. When the input waveform is in its "0" state, the output is "1." However, when the input waveform is in its "1" state, the output is "0." Consequently, the output waveform is inverted when compared with the input waveform.

Q6-032 A (14)

Q6-033 E (10-8)

Q6-034 E (5-5)

Q6-035 A (4-6)

Q6-036 D (4-6)

Q6-037 C (10-7) Refer to FIG. 10-30B.

Q6-038 B (14)

Q6-039 C (2-11)

Q6-040 C (8-3) Refer to FIG. 8-6A.

Q6-041 E (14)

Q6-042 E (8-3)

Q6-043 D (7-5)

Q6-044 C (14)

Q6-045 C (10-5)

Q6-046 C (1-20) Because $C = \varepsilon A/d$ F, the capacitance is directly proportional to the area of one side of one plate.

Q6-047 E (14)

Q6-048 E (6-5)

Q6-049 A (8-1) There is a total of $2 \times 8 = 16$ significant sidebands. The bandwidth is therefore $16 \times 2 = 32$ kHz.

Q6-050 E (4-4)

Q6-051 D (14)

Q6-052 A (3-4) The zener diode provides a reference level so that the total voltage across

R2 and R3 in series is 3 V. By the VDR (Section 1-7), the voltage across R2 is 3 V × 10 Ω/(10 Ω + 20 Ω) = 1 V.

Q6-053 C (14)

Q6-054 A (13-2) From EQ. 13-1, $11010_2 = (1 \times 2^4 + (1 \times 2^3) + (0 \times 2^2) + (1 \times 2^1) + (0 \times 2^0) = 16 + 8 + 0 + 2 + 0 = 26_{10}$.

Q6-055 D (1-24)

Q6-056 A (14)

Q6-057 A (14)

Q6-058 E (14)

Q6-059 B (10-4) From EQ. 10-20, the value of the field strength is inversely proportional to the distance from the antenna. Therefore, if the distance is quadrupled, the field strength will be quartered so that its new value is (1/4) × 560 = 140 μV/m.

Q6-060 D (6-2) Total sideband power, $P_{SB} = 0.5 \times m^2 \times P_C$ (EQ. 6-10) $= 0.5 \times (0.8)^2 \times 500 = 160$ W.

Q6-061 B (3-6)

Q6-062 D (7-10) Refer to FIG. 7-12.

Q6-063 B (1-20) When the two capacitors are connected across the 120-Vdc source, the voltage across each capacitor is 60 V and its charge stored is 0.1 μF × 60 V = 6 μC. After the capacitors are disconnected and paralleled, the total charge stored is 2 × 6 = 12 μC. With all three capacitors in parallel, the total capacitance is 3 × 0.1 = 0.3 μF and the common voltage across each of the capacitors is 12 μC/0.3 μF = 40 V.

Q6-064 E (2-10) Voltage ratio, V_o/V_i = 1200 μV/120 mV = 0.01. Gain in decibels, $N = 20 \log 0.01 = 20 \times (-2) = -40$ dB. Amount of attenuation is equal to 40 dB.

Q6-065 E (14)

Q6-066 A (13-8) Refer to FIG. 13-13B.

Q6-067 A (14) Refer to (TAB. 14-3).

Q6-068 A (4-3) The circuit is a common emitter amplifier; therefore, there is a 180° phase change between the input and output signals.

Q6-069 E (14)

Q6-070 C (4-2)

Q6-071 A (6-7)

Q6-072 E (14)

Q6-073 B (7-6)

Q6-074 C (3-2) The input capacitor charges toward the peak voltage of the ac input. Therefore, the effective value is 0.707 × 9 = 6.4 V, rounded off.

Q6-075 C (14)

Q6-076 D (4-1)

Q6-077 A (1-12)

Q6-078 E (2-9) Because the components have no resistive losses, there is no true power dissipated and the power factor of the circuit is zero.

Q6-079 D (14)

Q6-080 A (4-11) The circuit is that of a voltage follower; therefore, the value of V_o is $+4$ V.

Q6-081 E (14)

Q6-082 C (7-4)

Q6-083 E (2-8) The circuit is capacitive. Because $R = X_C = 100\ \Omega$, the phase difference is $-45°$.

Q6-084 C (1-9) Question 6-084 refers to a circuit, such as shown in FIG. 1-25B. If the value of R_S is decreased, then by EQ. 1-38, the current, I, increases.

Q6-085 E (6-5)

Q6-086 E (14)

Q6-087 D (6-5) The designator 2K80H3E has a necessary bandwidth of 2.80 kHz, which is greater than that of any of the other choices.

Q6-088 E (2-7) Impedance, $Z = E_{RMS}/I_{RMS} = 100\text{ V}/0.2\text{ A} = 500\ \Omega$.

Q6-089 E (14)

Q6-090 D (1-6) Because the resistor is inversely proportional to the square of the diameter (EQ. 1-27), the resistance is multiplied by a factor of $\frac{1}{2^2}$ and is therefore quartered.

Q6-091 C (2-3) Angular velocity, $\omega = 2\pi f = 2 \times \pi \times 60 = 377$ rad/s, rounded off.

Q6-092 A (1-3) *Charge* $Q = I \times t = 5.5\text{ A} \times 1800\text{ s} = 6300\text{ C} = 6300/3600\text{ Ah} = 1.75\text{ Ah}$.

Q6-093 A (6-3)

Q6-094 B (App.) Standard Time and Universal Time Coordinated are independent of daylight savings time and therefore the answer is the same for either June or December. 3 PM EST = 1500 + 0500 = 2000 UTC (EQ. 10-35)

Q6-095 B (14)

Q6-096 E (10-6)

Q6-097 B (10-9)

Q6-098 B (14)

Q6-099 D (1-14) For a balanced bridge, $R_x = R_3 \times R_1/R_2 = 5.7 \times 10/1000 = 0.057\ \Omega$.

Q6-100 E (14)

Test 7

Q7-001 E (2-9) If the frequency is steadily increased, the reactance of the capacitor, C, falls. The impedance of R//C is reduced; therefore, there is less voltage drop across this parallel combination. It follows that the output voltage, V_o, must steadily increase.

Q7-002 D (14)

Q7-003 A (4-1)

Q7-004 B (14)

Q7-005 D (5-3)

Q7-006 E (14)

Q7-007 A (11-6)

Q7-008 E (8-3)

Q7-009 D (2-11) Because the inductors and capacitors are assumed to have no resistance losses, the series LC combination behaves as a short circuit, whereas the parallel combination is equivalent to an open circuit. Consequently, the source current equals 24 V/12 Ω = 2 A.

Q7-010 E (9-1)

Q7-011 D (14)

Q7-012 A (9-2)

Q7-013 E (13-11)

Q7-014 D (1-7) The circuit represents a voltage divider. By the VDR (Section 1-7), the voltage between the points B and D, $V_{BD} = E \times R_{BD}/R_T$ = 500 V × (40 kΩ + 10 kΩ)/(200 kΩ + 40 kΩ + 10 kΩ) = 100 V.

Q7-015 C (14)

Q7-016 E (2-7) *True power* = $E_{RMS} \times I_{RMS} \times$ *Power factor* = $E_{RMS} \times I_{RMS} \times \text{Cos. } \phi$ watts (EQ. 2-27). Both Choices A and C are required.

Q7-017 D (2-1) Angular frequency, $\omega = 2\pi f$ radians/second (EQ. 2-6). If $f = 1$ Hz, $\omega = 2\pi$ radians/second.

Q7-018 C (14)

Q7-019 D (4-11) The circuit is that of a modified noninverting comparator, which is driven into negative saturation so that the value of V_o is zero.

Q7-020 E (4-11) The circuit is that of a modified noninverting comparator, which is driven into positive saturation so that the value of V_o is +6 V.

Q7-021 A (14)

Q7-022 B (App.) Three land miles is equivalent to 3 × 0.87 = 2.61 nautical miles.

Q7-023 C (14)

Q7-024 E (5-3) The required product factor for the multiplier stages is 2208/184 = 12, which would require two doubler stages and a tripler stage (2 × 2 × 3 = 12).

Q7-025 A (3-6)

Q7-026 A (14)

Q7-027 A (8-1)

Q7-028 C (14)

Q7-029 E (7-1)

Q7-030 E (14)

Q7-031 A (10-7) Refer to FIG. 10-26.

Q7-032 E (14)

Q7-033 A (1-6) Because $R = \rho L/A$, the new resistance is $100\ \Omega \times 2/(10/5) = 100\ \Omega$.

Q7-034 D (14)

Q7-035 D (2-12) The bandwidth is equal to $\sqrt{2}\ kf_o$ Hz. If k is increased, the bandwidth is greater and the degree of selectivity is reduced.

Q7-036 A (14)

Q7-037 D (6-1) On the scale provided, $E_{max} = 1.5E$ and $E_{min} = 0.5E$. Since the modulation appears to be symmetrical, percentage modulation $= [(E_{max} - E_{min})/(E_{max} + E_{min})] \times 100\% = [(1.5E - 0.5E)/(1.5E + 0.5E)] \times 100 = 0.5 \times 100 = 50\%$.

Q7-038 B (14)

Q7-039 C (1-23)

Q7-040 D (13-13) The total memory capacity is $2^{12} = 4096$ words.

Q7-041 B (14)

Q7-042 A (2-11) When the resistor is added in parallel, the impedance of the circuit is decreased.

Q7-043 C (14)

Q7-044 B (10-10) The ELF band covers the frequency range of 300 Hz to 3 kHz or 300 to 3000 Hz.

Q7-045 A (14)

Q7-046 A (11-3)

Q7-047 A (5-5) A loss of 7 dB is equivalent to a power ratio of 1/5 (TAB. 2-3). The radiated power of the spurious emission is $5 \times 1/5 = 1$ W.

Q7-048 D (10-10) The higher the radio frequency, the less is the amount of static interference.

Q7-049 C (1-24)

Q7-050 A (14)

Q7-051 E (6-2) Total sideband power for 60% modulation, $P_{SB} = 0.5 \times (0.6)^2 \times 1000 = 180$ W. Total sideband power for 80% modulation, $P_{SB} = 0.5 \times (0.8)^2 \times 1000 = 320$ W. Percentage increase in the total sideband power is given by: $[(320 - 180)/180] \times 100 = 1400/18 = 78\%$.

Q7-052 B (13-4) By the repeated division method, $4376/16 = 273$, remainder 8; $273/16 = 17$, remainder 1; $17/16 = 1$, remainder 1; $1/16 = 0$, remainder 1. Therefore, $4376_{10} = 1118_{16}$.

Q7-053 C (4-10)

Q7-054 E (14) Refer to (TAB. 14-3).

Q7-055 D (7-12) The BFO output frequency is $455 \pm 1 = 454$ kHz or 456 kHz.

Q7-056 E (14)

Q7-057 A (1-21) The time constant of the circuit is $RC = 10 \times 10^6 \times 0.1 \times 10^{-6}$ s $= 1$ s. After 0.5 time constant, the capacitor is charged to $0.393 \times 10 = 3.93$ V (TAB. 1-7)

Q7-058 C (6-5) Refer to (TAB. 6-2).

Q7-059 E (14)

Q7-060 D (3-1) The diode D2 is reverse biased and does not conduct (to a first approximation). The diode D1 is forward biased and has a voltage drop of 0.7 V. Therefore, the voltage drop across R1 is $10 - 0.7 = 9.3$ V.

Q7-061 A (8-1) Modulation of 80% corresponds to a frequency swing of $\pm$ (80/100) $\times$ 5 $= \pm$ 4 kHz.

Q7-062 D (8-1) Modulation index, $m = f_d/f_m = 4\text{ kHz}/2\text{ kHz} = 2$.

Q7-063 B (8-1) Required bandwidth $= 2(m + 1) \times 2\text{ kHz} = 12$ kHz.

Q7-064 D (14)

Q7-065 A (6-5) Refer to (TAB. 6-1).

Q7-066 E (8-4)

Q7-067 D (4-7)

Q7-068 A (14)

Q7-069 C (10-10)

Q7-070 A (7-7)

Q7-071 E (1-13) Using Kirchhoff's Current Law at the junction Z, the current flowing through the 9-Ω resistor is $12.5 - 2.5 = 10$ A. The voltage drop across the 9-Ω resistor is 10 A $\times$ 9 Ω $= 90$ V. Therefore, the voltage at the point X, with respect to the point V_{XZ}, $=$ 90 V. Voltage drop across the 4-Ω resistor is 2.5 A $\times$ 4 Ω $= 10$ V. It follows that the voltage at the point Y, with respect to the point Z, is $100 - 10 = 90$ V. Because each of the points X and Y has the same voltage difference (90 V), with respect to the point Z, the reading of V is $90 - 90 = 0$ V.

Q7-072 E (14)

Q7-073 B (10-10) The operating frequency of the Omega navigation system is 10.2 kHz, which lies within the very low frequency (VLF) band of 3 to 30 kHz.

Q7-074 E (14)

Q7-075 D (1-19) Because the value of the self-inductance is directly proportional to the square of the number of turns, the self-inductance is increased.

Q7-076 C (14)

Q7-077 E (13-3) Binary number, $11011001_2 = \underbrace{011}_{3}\,\underbrace{011}_{3}\,\underbrace{001}_{1} = 331_8$.

Q7-078 A (6-5) Refer to (TAB. 6-3).

Q7-079 A (14)

Q7-080 B (2-14) If there are three anodes in the electron gun, the voltage difference between the middle anode and the other two results in the formation of an electrostatic lens. This voltage difference can then be varied until the lens brings the beam to a focus at the screen.

Q7-081 A (7-5)

Q7-082 B (14)

Q7-083 E (9-3)

Q7-084 E (14)

Q7-085 A (1-19) The three inductors are in parallel. Therefore, the total self-inductance, $L_T = 1/[(1/10) + (1/10) + (1/5)] = 1/(4/10) = 10/4 = 2.5$ H.

Q7-086 D (14)

Q7-087 E (4-6) The collector current waveform consists of narrow spikes that "flick" impulse the tank circuit into continuous oscillation. A circulating current then flows between the inductor and the capacitor and a sine-wave voltage output appears between the collector and ground.

Q7-088 E (14)

Q7-089 B (10-4) Refer to (TAB. 2-3). A gain of +3 dB is equivalent to a power ratio of 2 so that the effective radiated power is $2 \times 12.5 = 25$ kW.

Q7-090 E (10-7) The Marconi antenna has an omnidirectional radiation pattern in the horizontal plane (choice A). The radiated signal is vertically polarized and requires a vertical antenna for its reception (choice D). Choices A and D are true.

Q7-091 A (7-2) *Frequency of the image channel* $= 156.8 + 2 \times 10.7 = 178.2$ MHz.

Q7-092 E (10-5)

Q7-093 B (4-3) The transistor is of the pnp variety and both batteries are providing incorrect bias so that the emitter-base junction is cut off.

Q7-094 E (4-4)

Q7-095 B (4-2) By the voltage division rule, the base voltage, $V_B = +20 \text{ V} \times 5 \text{ k}\Omega /(5 \text{ k}\Omega + 15 \text{ k}\Omega) = +5$ V.

Q7-096 C (6-3)

Q7-097 D (9-1) The difference frequency between 98.9 MHz and 121.3 MHz is $121.3 - 98.9 = 21.4$ MHz, which is equal to 2×10.7 MHz or twice the value of the receiver's intermediate frequency. Consequently, the problem is caused by image- channel interference.

Q7-098 D (4-10)

Q7-099 D (10-3) The theoretically "best" value of the SWR with zero reflection is 1. In EQ. 10-15, if $P = 0$, $S = (1 + 0)/(1 - 0) = 1$.

Q7-100 E (1-11) Total resistance in the series circuit, $R_S = 10 + 5 = 15\ \Omega$. Power dissipated in the series circuit, $P_S = (10 \text{ V})^2/15\ \Omega = 6.67$ W. Total resistance of the parallel circuit, $R_P = 10 \times 5/(10 + 5) = 50/15 = 3.33\ \Omega$. Power dissipated in the parallel circuit, $P_P = (10 \text{ V})^2/3.33\ \Omega = 30$ W. Required ratio, $P_P/P_S = 30/6.67 = 4.5{:}1$.

Test 8

Q8-001 A (5-6) In the absence of the signal, R1 and R2 provide voltage divider bias so that the voltage across the resistor R2 is 15 V × 5 kΩ/(5 kΩ + 10 kΩ) = 5 V.

Q8-002 A (5-6)

Q8-003 D (5-6)

Q8-004 C (5-6) C11 is a bypass decoupling capacitor; if this component open-circuits, there might be some intercoupling between the stages, but this would not have a severe effect on the circuit's performance. All the other choices result in zero output to the transmission line.

Q8-005 E (5-6) If C3 open-circuits, a negative feedback voltage is developed across R3. This reduces the gain provided by Q1; therefore, the transmitter's power output decreases.

Q8-006 D (5-6) If R3 short-circuits, the transistor Q1 is no longer provided with voltage divider bias and the stability of the circuit is reduced.

Q8-007 D (5-6) Refer to SEC. 5-6.

Q8-008 C (5-6) Because of the presence of C11, the collector of Q3 will be virtually at RF ground, although its dc voltage is +15 V. Consequently, the transmitter's RF power output falls to a very low level.

Q8-009 A (5-6) It is important to carry out the tuning procedure in radio silence so that there is minimum interference with other stations.

Q8-010 C (5-6)

Q8-011 D (5-6) Adjust the value of C10 to reduce the amount of the input signal to the base of Q3. This will lower the amount of the signal bias and increase the angle of flow for the collector current. The harmonic amplitudes will then be reduced.

Q8-012 B (12-3) The range in nautical miles is 105/12.37 = 8.49.

Q8-013 D (2-10) *Voltage ratio* = $10^{-20/20}$ = 0.1. *Output signal voltage* = 250 × 0.1 = 25 mV.

Q8-014 C (12-3) The total distance in nautical miles is 2 × 87/12.37 = 14.07.

Q8-015 C (2-10) *Power* = $10^{-20/10}$ = 0.01 mw = 10 μW.

Q8-016 E (7-12)

Q8-017 E (14)

Q8-018 A (14)

Q8-019 D (8-3) Refer to FIG. 8-6B.

Q8-020 E (14) 15 ppm = 15 × 10^{-4}% = 0.0015%.

Q8-021 E (6-3)

Q8-022 E (14)

Q8-023 E (5-3)

Q8-024 A (4-10)

Q8-025 E (10-3)

Q8-026 A (6-6)

Q8-027 E (2-14) The period, T, covers four major divisions, which are equivalent to a time interval of $4 \times 50 = 200\ \mu s$. Frequency, $f = 1/T = 1/(200 \times 10^{-6}\ s) = 10^6/200\ Hz = 5\ kHz$.

Q8-028 D (2-14) The peak value covers two major divisions, which is equivalent to $2 \times 10\ mV = 20\ mV$. *The RMS value* = $0.707 \times$ *peak value* = $0.707 \times 20 = 14.1\ mV$, rounded off.

Q8-029 D (5-4) *Oscillator frequency* = $2182/(2 \times 2 \times 2) = 272.75\ kHz$.

Q8-030 E (14)

Q8-031 D (12-14)

Q8-032 C (5-5) Because the operating power is equal to $E \times I \times F$ watts, raising the value of the dc supply voltage will increase the operating power.

Q8-033 E (14)

Q8-034 C (4-11) The gain of the noninverting amplifier is $1 + R_f/R_i$ (EQ. 4-14) $= 1 + 150/10 = +16$.

Q8-035 E (14)

Q8-036 C (7-8)

Q8-037 A (11-2)

Q8-038 E (14)

Q8-039 B (12-3) The total time interval is $7.5 \times 12.37 = 93\ \mu$seconds.

Q8-040 E (9-1) The value of the intermediate frequency is $167.7 - 157.0 = 10.7\ MHz$. The image-channel frequency is $167.7 + 10.7$ (or $157 + 2 \times 10.7$) $= 178.4\ MHz$.

Q8-041 E (14)

Q8-042 A (2-1) *Generated frequency* = $np/60 = 1000 \times 6/(60 \times 2) = 50\ Hz$.

Q8-043 E (1-22) *Full-scale deflection current* = $\dfrac{120\ V}{3750\ \Omega} = 0.032\ A$. When 135 V is applied, the current is $0.032\ A \times 7.5/12 = 0.02\ A$. *Total resistance* = $1.35\ V/0.02\ A = 6750\ \Omega$. The value of the additional resistor is $6750 - 3750 = 3000\ \Omega$.

Q8-044 E (14)

Q8-045 D (7-7)

Q8-046 C (11-5)

Q8-047 D (14)

Q8-048 A (7-5)

Q8-049 D (14)

Q8-050 E (9-1)

Q8-051 B (4-12) Refer to FIG. 4-70.

Q8-052 E (4-12) Refer to FIG. 4-71.

Q8-053 D (4-7) The JFET has a low gate current and therefore a very high input impedance.

Q8-054 E (14)

Q8-055 C (1-24)

Q8-056 C (2-12) *Total secondary voltage* = 2 × 300 = 600 V. Turns ratio, $N_p/N_s = E_p/E_s$ = 100 V/600 V = 1:6.

Q8-057 E (1-23)

Q8-058 D (14)

Q8-059 E (4-2) The circuit shows a pnp transistor, which is using base bias. The polarity of the battery is correct.

Q8-060 E (6-5) In the order of choices, the necessary bandwidths are 2.80 kHz, 2.66 kHz, 300 Hz, and 6.00 kHz.

Q8-061 C (10-10) A transmitter in the MF band must radiate a vertically polarized radio wave.

Q8-062 D (2-11) Choices A and B will cause the resonant frequency to change. Choices C and E will raise the value of Q and therefore decrease the bandwidth. The Q factor must be lowered to increase the bandwidth.

Q8-063 E (14)

Q8-064 A (1-20)

Q8-065 B (14)

Q8-066 A (6-4) *Percentage increase in the antenna current* = $(\sqrt{1 + m^2/2} - 1) \times 100$ (EQ. 6-12) = $(\sqrt{1 + (0.8)^2/2} - 1) \times 100 = (\sqrt{1/32 - 1}) \times 100$ = 15%, rounded off.

Q8-067 C (14)

Q8-068 E (1-18)

Q8-069 E (4-3)

Q8-070 E (13-11) To produce a "high" output, both inputs to the right-hand AND gate must be "high" so that the elements A and B must not be changed. Changing either C or D will still result in a "low" input to the OR gate. However, if E is changed from "low" to "high," the output from the OR gate is "high" and the output is also "high."

Q8-071 E (6-3)

Q8-072 E (4-10) Frequency shift at the oscillator stage is +10 Hz/MHz/°C × 3 MHz × (−20°C) = −600 Hz. Output frequency shift = (−600 Hz) × 2 × 2 × 2 = −4800 Hz. *Transmitter's output frequency* = 3 MHz × 2 × 2 × 2 − 4800 Hz = 23.9952 MHz.

Q8-073 A (4-4) Collector current flows throughout the cycle of the input signal.

Q8-074 E (14)

Q8-075 B (14)

Q8-076 E (1-6)

Q8-077 D (14)

Q8-078 C (6-3) Total sideband power, $P_{SB} = 0.5\ m^2\ P_C$ (EQ. 6-10) $= 0.5 \times 1^2 \times 100 =$ 50 W. The modulator's output power is 50/0.8 = 62.5 W and the required ratio is 125 W/62.5 W = 2:1.

Q8-079 B (1-3) Current, $I = P/E = 60\ W/120\ V = 0.5\ A$.

Q8-080 A (4-1)

Q8-081 D (6-7)

Q8-082 B (14)

Q8-083 A (6-2) Because neither the second harmonic (30 MHz) nor the third harmonic (45 MHz) is present, the input signal cannot be a square wave, a triangular wave, or a sawtooth. The input must therefore be a 15-MHz sine wave.

Q8-084 A (14)

Q8-085 A (14)

Q8-086 E (13-8) Refer to FIG. 13-15B.

Q8-087 E (13-12)

Q8-088 E (14)

Q8-089 D (14)

Q8-090 B (6-5) Refer to (TAB. 6-2).

Q8-091 A (5-2) *Maximum permitted deviation* $= 156.4 \times 10^6 \times 10/10^6$ Hz = 1564 Hz = 1.564 kHz.

Q8-092 E (14)

Q8-093 E (14)

Q8-094 C (1-8) The power delivered by the source is the product of the source voltage and the source current. Because the ground points must be regarded as joined by a path of zero resistance, the source voltage, E, is the same as the voltage measured between the points W and Z. *The source current* =

$$\frac{V_{WX}}{150000} = \frac{V_{YZ}}{2000} = \frac{V_{WZ}}{150000 + 2000} = \frac{V_{WZ}}{152000}\ A$$

Therefore, the power is $V_{WZ} \times \dfrac{V_{WX}}{150000}$ watts.

Q8-095 E (12-8)

Q8-096 B (1-4)

Q8-097 B (8-3) The frequency deviation at the transmitter's output stage is $6 \times 50/100 =$ 3 kHz. The deviation at the oscillator is 3/12 kHz = 250 Hz.

Q8-098 C (9-1) The frequency of the oscillator is 121.5 − 10.7 = 110.8 MHz.

Q8-099 A (App.) The temperature in degrees Celsius is 5(86 − 32)/9 = 30° C.

Q8-100 B (8-1) Modulation index, $m = f_d/f_m$ (Equation 8-1). Therefore, m = 18 kHz/300 Hz = 60.

Test 9

Q9-001 A (14)

Q9-002 E (11-3)

Q9-003 A (8-3) Refer to FIG. 8-2.

Q9-004 C (13-5) Refer to FIG. 13-7.

Q9-005 D (1-13) Identify all corresponding electrical points and label the different points as A, B, C. The 10-kΩ and 5-kΩ resistors are mounted in parallel between the points A and B, and the two 1-kΩ resistors are in series (A to C to B) between the same two points. These conditions are illustrated in the schematic (d)

Q9-006 B (5-2) Frequency tolerance in ppm $= \pm 0.01\% \times 10^4$ (EQ. 5-2) $= \pm 100$ ppm.

Q9-007 B (14)

Q9-008 E (3-4)

Q9-009 B (14)

Q9-010 E (4-10)

Q9-011 D (4-10)

Q9-012 E (14)

Q9-013 E (9-2)

Q9-014 A (7-8)

Q9-015 E (14)

Q9-016 E (1-4) Maximum voltage, $E = \sqrt{P \times R} = \sqrt{2\text{ W} \times 15000\ \Omega} = \sqrt{30000}$ = 173 V, rounded off.

Q9-017 D (2-14) *Power factor* = 90 W/(12 V × 9 A) = 90 W/108 VA = 0.83.

Q9-018 E (7-4)

Q9-019 B (App.) A temperature of 0°C (pure melting ice) is equivalent to 32°F (Fahrenheit). Moreover, a temperature of 100°C (pure boiling water) is the same as 212°F. It follows that a temperature difference of 212 − 32 = 180°F must be equal to 100 − 0 = 100°C. Therefore, 100/20 = 5°C is the same as 180/20 = 9°F. The conversion equations between the two temperature scales are:

$$T^\circ F = 32 + \frac{9\,T^\circ C}{5}$$

and:

$$T^\circ C = \frac{5}{9}(T^\circ F - 32)$$

Consequently, if T = 40°C, the corresponding Fahrenheit temperature is 32 + 9 × 40/5 = 104°F.

Q9-020 D (2-12) The transformer is over-coupled; therefore, the coupling factor must be reduced to below its critical value.

Q9-021 D (11-5)

Q9-022 E (5-3)

Q9-023 B (8-1) The frequency deviation stays the same, but the value of the modulation index, *m* (= f_d/f_m) is increased. Consequently, the number [= 2(*m* + 1)] of significant sidebands is greater.

Q9-024 D (1-23)

Q9-025 E (1-6) The lower the gauge number, the thicker is the wire and the less is its resistance. The thickest #4 wire will therefore have the greatest current capability and the smallest power loss.

Q9-026 E (14)

Q9-027 A (9-3)

Q9-028 D (4-9) Because $E = 15$ V and the zener diode voltage is 6 V, the voltage drop across $R = 15 - 6 = 9$ V.

Q9-029 C (4-9) The emitter-base junction is forward biased such that $V_{BE} = 0.7$ V and the base is positive, with respect to the emitter. Because the zener diode voltage is 6 V, the output voltage, V_L, across the load, R_L, is $6 - 0.7 = 5.3$ V.

Q9-030 D (14)

Q9-031 C (14)

Q9-032 A (2-11) When the parallel LCR circuit is resonant at the input signal frequency, its impedance rises to its maximum value. Then, the voltage across the load will also be at its maximum level.

Q9-033 C (2-11) There are no legitimate calculations that will enable you to obtain the correct answer. However, the sheet of copper, with its large cross-sectional area, will not suffer appreciably from skin effect. The important word is "thin;" the question does not specify how thin. Therefore, you can reduce the sheet's thickness until the sheet vanishes and there is no impedance!

Q9-034 C (14)

Q9-035 A (7-1)

Q9-036 C (2-8) Voltage across the inductor, $V_L = I \times X_L = 0.1\ \text{A} \times 600\ \Omega = 60$ V. Voltage drop across the resistor, $V_R = \sqrt{E^2 - V_L^2} = \sqrt{110^2 - 60^2} = 92.2$ V. True power, *TP* $= I \times V_R = 0.1\ \text{A} \times 92.2\ \text{V} = 9.2$ W, rounded off.

Q9-037 A (9-2)

Q9-038 C (14)

Q9-039 E (8-1) For FM, the power remains the same during modulation. Consequently, the ratio is 1:1.

Q9-040 D (14)

Q9-041 D (5-5) A loss of 7 dB is equivalent to a power ratio of 1/5 (TAB. 2-3). *Harmonic radiated power* = 5 × 1/5 = 1 W.

Q9-042 E (10-2) For a matched line, the length is not critical.

Q9-043 E (14)

Q9-044 E (14)

Q9-045 B (14)

Q9-046 E (7-2) *Image-channel frequency* = 1 MHz + 2 × 455 kHz = 1.91 MHz = 1910 kHz. Choices A and C are both true.

Q9-047 D (4-6) If the capacitor, C, open-circuits, negative feedback is developed across the resistor, R; therefore, the RF power output decreases.

Q9-048 A (2-7) *True power* = $E_{RMS} \times I_{RMS} \times \text{Cos.}\phi$ watts.

Q9-049 D (10-3) The combination of the λ/4 line and its terminating short is equivalent to a tank circuit.

Q9-050 C (14)

Q9-051 D (4-6)

Q9-052 E (3-1) The diode is reverse biased and therefore behaves as an open circuit (to a first approximation). By the voltage division rule, the IR drop across the resistor R3 is: V_{R3} = 10 V × 300 Ω/(100 Ω + 200 Ω + 200 Ω) = 5 V.

Q9-053 D (6-5)

Q9-054 D (1-19)

Q9-055 A (13-3) From EQ. 13-1, $673_8 = (6 \times 8^2) + (7 \times 8^1) + (3 \times 8^0) = 443_{10}$.

Q9-056 D (14)

Q9-057 D (4-3)

Q9-058 D (14)

Q9-059 C (6-7)

Q9-060 E (10-4) Frequency of the third harmonic 3 × 2182 = 6546 kHz = 6.546 MHz, rounded off. Choices A and D are true.

Q9-061 E (14)

Q9-062 C (1-15) Resistance of each lamp, $R = (6\ \text{V})^2/3\ \text{W} = 12\ \Omega$. Total load, R_L = 12 Ω/2 = 6 Ω. Current, I_L = 6 V/(6 Ω + 1.2 Ω) = 6/7.2 = 0.83 A.

Q9-063 A (6-3) When modulation is applied, the carrier component is unchanged; therefore, the dc input power remains the same.

Q9-064 E (14)

Q9-065 C (2-6) Capacitive reactance, $X_C = 1/2\pi fC = 1/(1000 \times 0.001\ 10^{-6})$ Ω = 1 MΩ.

Q9-066 D (10-10)

Q9-067 B (14)

Q9-068 E (2-2) Refer to EQ. 2-2.

Q9-069 B (14) The tolerance is 10 ppm, which is equivalent to 10 × 156.8 = 1568 Hz.

Q9-070 A (1-15) Total power, P_T = 325 + 50 = 375 W. Total current, I_T = 375 W/12.6 V = 29.96 A. Period of time, t = 55 A.h/29.76 A = 1.8 A.h.

Q9-071 B (6-1) Because the percentage of modulation for a voice transmission changes from instant to instant, only unmodulated values are normally entered into the station's log.

Q9-072 E (14)

Q9-073 E (10-10) From EQ. 10-32, $UTC = PST + 8$ hrs $= 1500 + 0800 = 2300$ hrs.

Q9-074 E (14)

Q9-075 C (4-2) If both S1 and S2 are closed, the two emitter-base junctions will be provided with forward (base) bias. Therefore, both transistors conduct and the lamp L1 is lit. However, the V_{CE} voltage of Q2 will be too low to light L2 because the main flow of the current will occur through Q2, R_3, Q1, L1, and V_{cc}.

Q9-076 E (14)

Q9-077 E (1-11) The maximum voltage that can be safely applied across a 100-Ω resistor is $\sqrt{10 \text{ W} \times 100\ \Omega} = 31.6$ V. The maximum voltage that can be safely applied across the 10-Ω resistor is $\sqrt{10 \text{ W} \times 10\ \Omega} = 10$ V. Consequently, the applied voltage must not exceed 10 V. Power dissipated in the 100-Ω resistor equals $(10 \text{ V})^2/100\ \Omega = 1$ W; power dissipated in the 10-Ω resistor equals $(10 \text{ V})^2/10\ \Omega = 10$ W. Total maximum power dissipated is $1 + 10 = 11$ W.

Q9-078 D (14)

Q9-079 C (10-10)

Q9-080 B (6-5)

Q9-081 E (6-5)

Q9-082 E (10-7) The frequency of the seventh harmonic, $f = 7 \times 450 = 3150$ kHz $=$ 3.15 MHz. Choices A and B are both true.

Q9-083 A (14)

Q9-084 D (6-6) The receiver is only required to intercept the WWV signal and does not need to be calibrated.

Q9-085 A (10-7) *Effective power input* $= 100 - 1 = 99$ W. *Total attenuation of line* $= 6$ dB $\times$ 50 ft/100 ft $= 3$ dB. Refer to (TAB. 2-3). An attenuation of 3 dB corresponds to a power ratio of 0.5. *Output power to the antenna* $= 0.5 \times 99 = 49.5$ W.

Q9-086 A (14)

Q9-087 B (1-4) Maximum current, $I = \sqrt{P/R}$
$= \sqrt{1/2 \text{ W}/10000\ \Omega} = \sqrt{1/20000}$ A $= 7.1$ mA, rounded off.

Q9-088 B (4-10)

Q9-089 D (10-2) Because 1 statute or land mile $= 0.87$ nautical mile (EQ. 10-35) and 1 knot $= 1$ nautical mile per hour (EQ. 10-9), 10 statute miles per hour $= 10 \times 0.87$ nautical miles per hour $= 8.7$ knots.

Q9-090 C (10-7)

Q9-091 D (10-4) *Overall dB gain* $= (-3 \text{ dB} \times 200 \text{ ft}/100 \text{ ft}) + 9 \text{ dB} = 3$ dB. Because a gain of $+3$ dB is equivalent to a power ratio of 2, the effective radiated power is 2×500 W $=$ 1000 W.

Q9-092 A (14)

Q9-093 C (4-10)

Q9-094 A (2-6) Although the inductive reactance is directly proportional to the frequency, the inductance, L, is independent of any change in the frequency. Consequently, the value of the inductance remains at 5 H.

Q9-095 C (1-21) *Time constant* = $R \times C$ seconds.

Q9-096 C (1-15) For maximum power transfer, the value of R_L must be matched (made equal) to the sum of all the resistances that are not associated with the load. Therefore, the required value of R_L is $10 + 20 = 30\ \Omega$. Note: this result is also true for an ac circuit provided that the circuit contains resistance only.

Q9-097 A (3-3) Refer to FIG. 3-12A. Diode D1 must be reversed.

Q9-098 E (13-2) Refer to (TAB. 13-1). Hexadecimal number, D_{16}, is equivalent to decimal number, 13_{10}. Alternatively, from EQ. 13-1, $1101_2 = (1 \times 2^3) + (1 \times 2^2) + (0 \times 2^1) + (1 \times 2^0) = 8 + 4 + 0 + 1 = 13_{10}$.

Q9-099 E (3-6)

Q9-100 D (14)

Element 8 Practice Tests

Test 1

Note: All questions refer to material contained in chapters 11 and 12 of TAB Book #4055

Q1-01 D *The pulse repetition time* = 1/*pulse frequency* = 1/400 s = 2500 μs.

Q1-02 A *The duty cycle* = *pulse width/pulse repetition time* = 0.5/2500 = 1/5000. *The average power* = *peak power* × *duty cycle* = 500 kW × 1/5000 = 100 W.

Q1-03 E

Q1-04 A

Q1-05 B *The total time interval* = 7.5 × 12.37 = 93 μs.

Q1-06 E

Q1-07 E

Q1-08 A

Q1-09 D

Q1-10 D

Q1-11 A *The cut-off wavelength* = 2 × *the width dimension of the waveguide* = 2 × 3.0 = 6.0 inches.

Q1-12 C

Q1-13 D

Q1-14 C

Q1-15 D

Q1-16 D

Q1-17 C

Q1-18 B *The range in nautical miles* = 105/12.37 = 8.49.

Q1-19 E

Q1-20 E

Q1-21 C

Q1-22 A

Q1-23 C

Q1-24 E

Q1-25 C *The bandwidth required by the IF stages* = $2/t$ MHz where t is the pulse duration in microseconds. The bandwidth is therefore 2/0.5 = 4 MHz.

Q1-26 E

Q1-27 A

Q1-28 D The maximum range separation = $0.5 \times 328/2 = 82$ yards.

Q1-29 B

Q1-30 E

Q1-31 C

Q1-32 E

Q1-33 C

Q1-34 A The maximum range obtainable is proportional to the fourth root of the transmitter's peak power output. The maximum range is therefore multiplied by $\sqrt[4]{16} = 2$

Q1-35 E

Q1-36 C The total distance in nautical miles is: $2 \times 87/12.37 = 14.07$.

Q1-37 E

Q1-38 D *The pulse width* = *duty cycle/pulse frequency* = $2 \times 10^{-4}/400 = 0.5 \times 10^{-6}$ s = 0.5 μs.

Q1-39 A *The peak power* = *average power/duty cycle* = $200/(2 \times 10^{-4}) = 10^6$ W = 1 MW.

Q1-40 C

Q1-41 D

Q1-42 B

Q1-43 B

Q1-44 C

Q1-45 D

Q1-46 B The time interval that corresponds to a range of 0.5 nautical mile is 12.3678/2 = 6.1839 μs. *The frequency of the range-marker oscillator* = $10^6/6.2839$ Hz = 161.7 kHz.

Q1-47 B

Q1-48 C

Q1-49 C

Q1-50 E

Element 8 Test 2

Q2-01 D

Q2-02 E

Q2-03 A The wavelength in centimeters is: $3 \times 10^{10}/(9.35 \times 10^{-9}) = 3.21$.

Q2-04 C

Q2-05 D

Q2-06 C

Q2-07 C

Q2-08 A

Q2-09 D

Q2-10 C

Q2-11 B

Q2-12 D The range in nautical miles is: $49.5/12.37 \approx 4$.

Q2-13 D

Q2-14 E

Q2-15 E

Q2-16 B

Q2-17 B

Q2-18 D

Q2-19 E

Q2-20 B

Q2-21 E

Q2-22 E

Q2-23 D

Q2-24 C

Q2-25 A

Q2-26 E

Q2-27 C

Q2-28 E

Q2-29 C

Q2-30 E

Q2-31 D

Q2-32 E

Q2-33 C

Q2-34 B

Q2-35 E

Q2-36 E

Q2-37 C *The pulse frequency* = 1/*pulse repetition time* = 1/(*pulse width*/*duty cycle*) = *duty cycle*/*pulse width.*

Q2-38 E

Q2-39 C

Q2-40 A *The time interval between pulses* = 1/500 s = 2000 μs. *The maximum range in nautical miles* = (2000 − 750)/12.36774 = 1250/12.36774 = 101.

Q2-41 B

Q2-42 D

Q2-43 E

Q2-44 E

Q2-45 B

Q2-46 A *The duty cycle* = *pulse width*/*pulse repetition time* = *pulse width* × *pulse frequency* = $0.2 \times 10^{-6} \times 500 = 10^{-4} = 0.0001$.

Q2-47 A *The pulse frequency* = 1/*pulse repetition time* = $1/(2000 \times 10^{-6}) = 500$.

Q2-48 D *The duty cycle* = *average power*/*peak power* = 150 W/600 kW = 1/4000. *The pulse width* = *pulse repetition time* × *duty cycle* = 2000 × 1/4000 = 0.5 μs.

Q2-49 A

Q2-50 A

Glossary

Aeronautical mobile service A mobile service between aeronautical stations and aircraft stations, or between aircraft stations, that survival craft stations may participate in.

Aeronautical station A land station in the aeronautical mobile service. In certain cases, the station may be located on board ship or on a platform at sea.

Aircraft station A mobile station in the aeronautical mobile service, other than a survival craft station, located on board an aircraft.

Base station A land station in the land mobile service that is carrying on a service with land mobile stations.

Coast station A land station in the marine mobile service.

Coordinated universal time (UTC) UTC is equivalent to mean solar time at the prime meridian (0 degrees longitude), formerly called *GMT*.

Duplex operation A mode of two-way communications where both persons can talk at the same time, like on the telephone. This requires the use of two frequencies: one for receiving and one for transmitting. *See* simplex.

Effective radiated power Effective radiated power (ERP) in a given direction is the product of the power supplied to the antenna and its gain relative to a half-wave dipole.

Emergency position-indicating radiobeacon station A station in the mobile service, the emissions of which are intended to facilitate search and rescue operations.

Facsimile A form of telegraphy for the transmission of fixed images. The images are reproduced in permanent form at the receiver.

Fixed public service A radiocommunications service carried on between fixed stations open to public correspondence.

Fixed service A service of radiocommunications between specified fixed points.

Fixed station A station in the fixed service.

Frequency tolerance The maximum permissible departure by the center frequency of the frequency band occupied by an emission, from the assigned frequency.

International Fixed Public Radiocommunication Service A fixed service, the stations of which are open to public correspondence and which in general, is intended to provide radio communication between any one of the states or U.S. possessions or any foreign point, or between U.S. possessions and any other point. This service also involves the relaying of international traffic between stations that provide this service.

Land mobile service A mobile service between base stations and land mobile stations, or between land mobile stations.

Land mobile station A mobile station in the land mobile service who are capable of surface movement within the geographical limits of a country or continent.

Land station A station in the mobile service not intended to be used while in motion.

Maritime mobile service A mobile service between coast stations and ship stations, or between ship stations, or between assorted on-board communication stations. Survival craft and EPIRB stations also participate in this service.

Mobile station A station in the mobile service intended to be used while in motion or during halts at unspecified points.

Navigational communications Safety communications that pertain to the maneuvering of vessels or the directing of vessel movements. Such communications are primarily for the exchange of information between stations and, secondarily, between ship stations and coast stations.

Operational fixed station A station that provides control, repeater, or relay functions for its associated coast station.

Point of communication This means a specific location that is designated in the license that a station is authorized to communicate for the transmission of public correspondence.

RACON Radionavigation system.

Radionavigation A system of determining the position of a vessel by the use of radio waves.

Survival craft station A mobile station in the maritime or aeronautical mobile service that is intended solely for survival purposes.

Other Bestsellers of Related Interest

ELECTRONIC COMMUNICATIONS —John J. Dulin, Victor F. Veley, and John Gilbert

Use this broad study from three well-known electronics experts to prepare for your FCC General Radiotelephone Operator License or CET exam, then keep it on your desk as a handy working reference on communications questions. The book's readable, easy-to-follow format places the chapters in a logical sequence. Each topic discussed in a chapter contains a limited number of concepts, which the authors explore in depth. 688 pages, 566 illustrations. **Book No. 3365, $24.95 paperback only**

INDUSTRIAL ELECTRONICS CET EXAM STUDY GUIDE—Sam Wilson

This comprehensive review of all the information needed to pass the journeyman-level CET exam includes both basic theory and practical information on industrial electronic equipment and components and digital electronics. The practice questions and examples help you pinpoint your strengths and weaknesses so you'll know where to concentrate your study efforts. 330 pages, 155 illustrations. **Book No. 3311, $16.95 paperback only**

GENERAL RADIOTELEPHONE OPERATOR'S LICENSE STUDY GUIDE—3rd Edition —Thomas LeBlanc, NX7P

Increase your chances of passing the FCC's GROL exam when you refine your knowledge with this guide—it's been revised specifically to complement the test's newest version. Licensed radio operator Thomas LeBlanc stresses learning concepts rather than depending on rote memory of the test answers. That way, you're assured of having a thorough grasp of each subject on the test. Using this guide as a serious study tool is one of the best ways around to make sure you only have to take the test once! 344 pages, 214 illustrations. **Book No. 4075, $17.95 paperback only**